THE BE
YOU SHO
IS YOURSELF

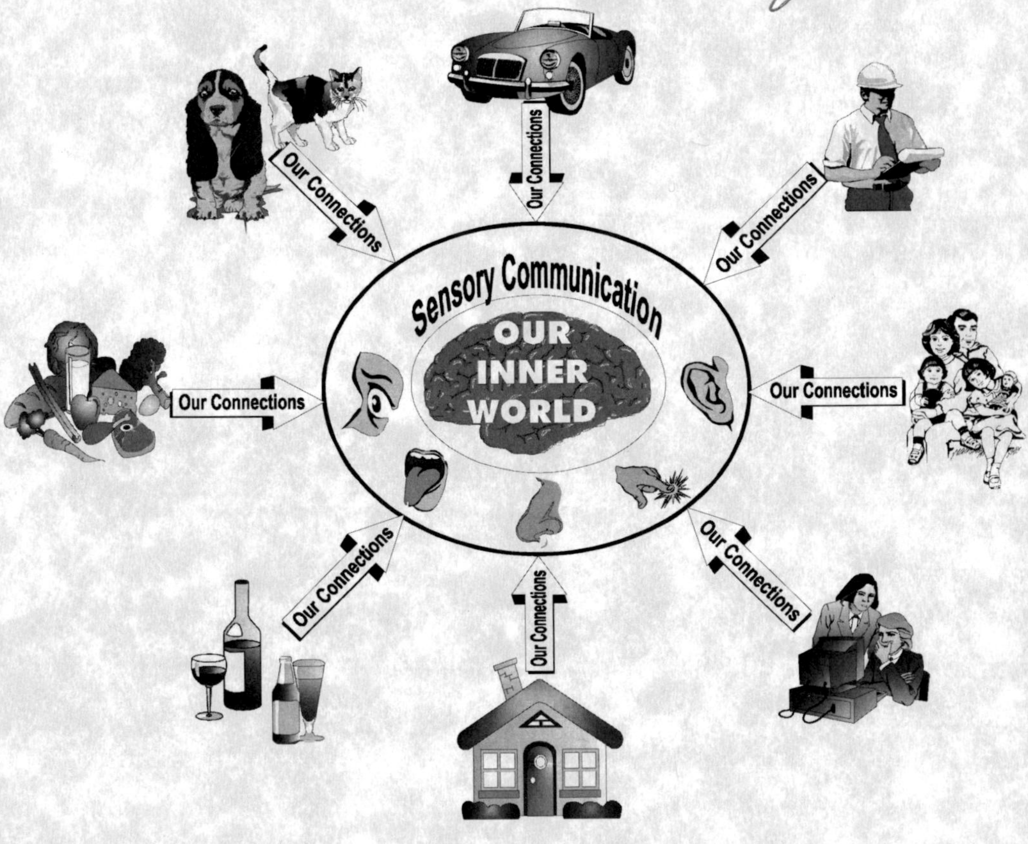
Sensory Communication
OUR
INNER
WORLD
Our Connections
Our Connections
Our Connections
Our Connections
Our Connections
Our Connections
Our Connections
Our Connections

Personality Finesse

How we nurture our nature

to balance EMOTIONALITY RATIONALITY our personality

by Dr. Dean C. Bellavia

Personality Finesse…how we nurture our nature

A publication of The Bio-Engineering Co.

Library of Congress Control Number:

2009906948

ISBN 978-0-692-00457-9

For my wife Cindy and my girls
Rachel, Rebecca, and Claire

The reasons why I have to better evolve.

Table of Contents

Preface
& Other Good Stuff

Preface stuff
Dealing with *Technical* stuff
The *Essence* of this book

A preface, "an author's preliminary statement or essay introducing a book that explains its scope, intention, or background," is supposed to give you confidence in the book and the author's many accomplishments and credentials. In this book, my decades of working with and analyzing thousand of people to quantify and qualify personality are not important. What are important are *your* background, your accomplishments and your understanding of yourself and others. Only your experiences, knowledge and beliefs matter for understanding human personality, which this book should help you to better organize and finesse.

It takes all kinds

Much research is overly detailed "not being able to see the forest for the trees." Much research is lacking detail "not being able to see the trees for the forest." What we want to do is "be able to see the forest (personality) and also be able to see the trees (its components)." Hopefully, this book achieves that goal.

We all exist in two worlds

Personality is our "evolutionary survival system," making us react to what we perceive in our two worlds: our *inner-world* (inside our body) that no one else has privy to; and, our *outer-world* (outside our body) that everyone has privy to.

Our inner-world (*our* personality) is sensorially connected to the outer-world and interprets it using our unique memories. As members of that outer-world, we also infer the inner-worlds of others (*their* personalities). Although our inner-world interpretations are unique, our outer-world inferences aren't. For example, we have our own inner-world interpretation of an orange (it's round, orange in color, it's sweet, has a name, etc.), but we share this "common perception" of that outer-world with others.

The common perception is the link between our inner-world and the inner-worlds of others. It is the basis for all understanding, all learning and the basis for all bonding (love) as described in Chapter 4—it is also the basis for human personality. Without this common perception, no one has a person-ality—no one has a common personality trait (shyness, aggressiveness, etc.) that we can use to understand his or her reactions.

Nevertheless, helpful as they are, personality traits are just gross perceptions of the outer-world; they are not a true inner-world understanding of what causes that gross perception. One purpose of this book is to help you under-stand your inner-world personality by understanding your inner-world's construct (sensory system, rational brain, and emotional brain) to help you to lead a better and more fulfilling life.

I think that I shall never see what makes a personality

The human brain and sensory system *are* human personality, and personal-ity's evolutionary purpose is physical and social survival. Personality is ever-evolving, instantly integrating sensory information that supports our transient understanding of survival and discarding the rest.

The physical structure of this self-nurturing entity dictates our personal na-ture and thus, we cannot simply defined personality in terms of outer-world traits. We must define it using our brain's functional structures and the manner in which they react to the sensed outer-world.

For example, someone new to an omelet might conclude that it is composed of white, pink and green things in some yellow stuff, instead of accurately concluding that it is a combination of onions, ham, chives, etc., cooked with eggs—the same holds true when defining personality. We could conclude that it is composed of aggressiveness, extroversion, timidity, agreeableness, conscientiousness, etc., instead if accurately concluding that it is a reflection of our evolving inner-world's genetics and learned memories.

This book shows that human personality is a reflection of our brain's genetic structure and learned memories that cause the reactions we present to the outer-world that are inferred by the inner-world memories of others. Chapters 1 and 2 describe the *physical* evolution of personality over millions of years and how we *socially* evolve each day with our sensory, emotional and rational memories. Frankly, you'll find that human personality is simple to understand and paraphrasing Einstein and others; "If it's not simple it's not right!"

What you want is what you get

We all need to know what to expect of *others,* and most of us are perfectly happy relying on inferred outer-world personality traits, that is, until others act out of character and make us feel uneasy. Even so, this is sufficient for most people when dealing with others—not so when dealing with them-selves.

When they apply those personality traits to themselves, they realize that their lives are missing something—the fact that you're interested in reading this book indicates your need to address your own personality excesses and deficiencies. There are certain aspects of life that you want *more* of, like being able to share love with others, being more outgoing, doing a better job at work, or having more control over your life. And there are certain aspects of your life you want *less* of, like being less fearful, being less angry, being less sad, or being less manic. On the other hand, if your life is not want-ing—give this book to someone whose life is.

If you want a better life you need to realize that just wishing for it will not get you there—you need to know what makes you tick and how to modify it. *Permanent* change cannot occur by simply avoiding unwanted or embracing wanted reactions (as discussed in Chapter 14); you must refurbish the ma-chinery that causes these reactions—your sensory, emotional and rational memories. Thus, this book will dwell on how these memories interact to produce the *you* that the outer-world perceives, giving many real life exam-ples of what these interactions produce. Of course, you can stay where you are, or you can go on a wonderful journey of enlightenment and growth that, until now, wasn't very easy to do nor lasting.

The course of true understanding does *not* include the abnormal

Most books about understanding ourselves are derived from studies of the abnormal (mentally traumatized) people—I based this book on the study of thousands of *normal* healthy people just like you. We are all as different from each other as we are similar, but most of us *are* normal—even those of us that seem abnormal because our personality is a little extreme. This book will help you to understand the basis of your normal personality and what you might do to better balance it, so that you can lead a more productive and happier life in your inner-world and project the kind of traits that make those in the outer-world want to stay connected to you.

The course of true understanding *does include you*

I provide many examples to "ground" you to the concepts discussed—many come from my inner-world, but apply to the outer-world we share. Hopefully they will suffice—if not, consider your own experiences—if so, consider your own experiences anyway.

Many of us suffer from "anger management" or "road rage" issues, erroneously sensing confrontation that doesn't exist. Many of us are too fearful, erroneously sensing danger that doesn't exist. Many of us are too sad, erroneously sensing disconnection from others that doesn't exist. And strange as it may seem, many of us experience erroneous joy that gets in the way of a productive life and can cause us harm. But, we can significantly lessen excessive emotion through its understanding and by proactively changing how we think about it. How we use our brain *is* our personality, but our brain is plastic and thus moldable; we can change our inner-world personality to one that will get us what we want in the outer-world of others.

It takes all kinds to make a book

This book contains two parts: Part-I contains the succinct bottom line, giving you an inward understanding of genetically evolved personality—what I call "Symbiotic Personality." Part-II contains *handy references* should you desire to know more about your inner workings and how you might best interact with others. One of these handy references is the synopsis.

The best things in life are *browser-friendly*

The structure of this book is allows you to quickly access the information you are interested in—tables of contents and indices are not always sufficient. Each chapter contains themes (as listed in the Table of Contents) and each theme contains a flow of topics starting with a descriptive bolded phrase (like "The best things in life are *browser-friendly*"), typically a droll version of a popular American saying. You can read the topics in order or skim through them to quickly find what you want.

For you "get it done directors" in the crowd, who only want to know what you want to know and don't have time to read the rest to get at it, there is a handy synopsis in the second part of the book. This synopsis is a succinct description of the flow of topics for all of the chapters, in order. Thus, one can get an understanding of the entire book by reading through the synopsis, or skim it to find something of interest and then quickly zero in on page and passage. I have also provided an index, even though I rarely find them useful when reading reference books—but this index is different.

Why have two when one will do—better

Most non-fiction books omit glossaries because they may not consider themselves a reference book. But glossaries are very helpful, especially when presenting new philosophies containing words with conflicting definitions. Most reference books have indices, but they only tell us where that word appears in the book, which may not be of much help. Actually, most people look up an indexed word to find its meaning or to find useful information related to it. In this book, I have combined the glossary and index to save you time and frustration, giving you the meaning of the word or concept and where you might best locate relevant information about it. In addition, to make it even easier for you to discriminate "the forest from the trees," check out the book's *essence* at the end of this preface.

It's your book...do with it, as you will.

It's your life...*deal with it* as you may.

Oh, and by the way, once you have successfully finessed your strong emotions and weak styles to some degree, go to the PersonalityFinesse.com website and tell us your success story—We'd love to hear about it!

More Good Stuff ⫸

You *can* have your π and know it too

We all have difficulty with new technical stuff, but with a little help, we can understand the *concepts*—the good stuff—if we can just get past the *words*—the difficult stuff. The fact is, unless you understand the concepts behind how your brain works, you will not, fully understand *why* your personality makes you who you are—you do not though, have to remember all the descriptive words. By persevering, you will understand how your unique personality (brain) works and how to make the best of it. You will also understand why others react as they do and how to best deal with them.

On the road to understanding, I have placed warning signs—π signs to be exact. Much of the time they refer to technical terms and how to deal with them. Other times they refer to variations on the "brain diagram" below and its five key parts: rational brain, pre-frontal cortex, emotional brain, sensory cortex, and thalamus. Take a moment to review this simple brain diagram (inside the box below) to better understand your personality's brains.

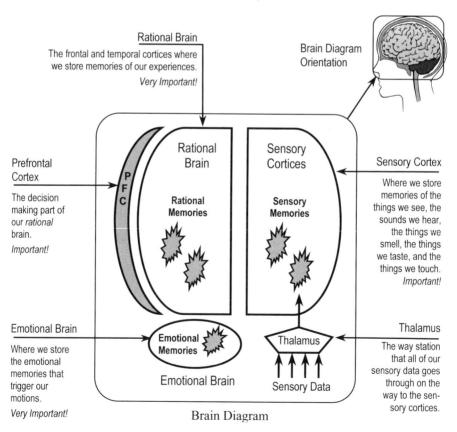

Rational Brain
The frontal and temporal cortices where we store memories of our experiences.
Very Important!

Brain Diagram Orientation

Prefrontal Cortex
The decision making part of our *rational* brain.
Important!

Rational Brain — Rational Memories

Sensory Cortices — Sensory Memories

Sensory Cortex
Where we store memories of the things we see, the sounds we hear, the things we smell, the things we taste, and the things we touch.
Important!

Emotional Brain
Where we store the emotional memories that trigger our motions.
Very Important!

Emotional Memories — Emotional Brain

Thalamus — Sensory Data

Thalamus
The way station that all of our sensory data goes through on the way to the sensory cortices.

Brain Diagram

The *ESSENCE* of this book

1. We live in two worlds: our inner-world (our brains) and the outer world (everything outside our brains). Our sensory system is the connection between these two worlds.

2. We have a fast acting emotional brain for physical survival—it contains the memories of the four basic emotions: anger, fear, joy, and sorrow— Ignore the other emotions for now!

3. We have a slower reacting rational brain for social survival—it contains the memories of the four rational styles: analyzer, director, relator, and socializer—Hold that thought!

4. The two brains compose "Symbiotic Personality," which has four parts: *emotional genetic* (anger, fear, joy and sorrow emotions), *emotional learned* (emotional memories), *rational genetic* (analyzer, director, relator, and socializer styles), and *rational learned* (rational memories).

5. Symbiotic Personality is defined as: "When our emotional brain alerts our rational brain to a possible threat and our rational brain decides how to deal with it."—It's quite simple in concept!

6. Our sensory memories identify what we sense (sights, sounds, etc.), which trigger emotional memories of possible threats, which trigger rational memories that deal with the possible threat and quell the emotional alert. The director style quells anger, the analyzer style quells fear, the relator style quells sorrow, and the socializer style quells joy. —The pairing off of emotion and style is the symbiotic part!

7. The rational brain uses the rational memories attached to the sensory memories that caused the emotional alert to quell it. Once the emotional alert's cause is identified, the rational brain turns off the emotion (like turning off a smoke alarm once the cause of the smoke is identified).

8. The rational brain's identification of an emotional alert's cause always quells the emotion, except when we rationalize (when we try to justify our negative emotional outbursts)—rationalization re-triggers and intensifies an emotion and strengthens its undesired trigger-memory.

9. Unfortunately, we cannot erase emotional memories, but we can finesse them if we avoid rationalization. By doing so, we give ourselves other options for rationally reacting to an undesired emotional outburst.

10. This finessing can reduce our anger, fear and sorrow significantly, providing us with the ability to share love with others and take control of many aspects of our lives.

11. We can more easily explain concepts such as "nature vs. nurture," "levels of consciousness," "knowledge/intelligence/wisdom," "love," "the self"" and "pure free will," with symbiotic personality than we can without it.

We can evolve beyond our genetics in our own lifetime!

Chapter 1
Nature's Gifts

Nature *and* Nurture
The Human Brain: *Personality*

π   This chapter has some technical information, *but it's fun information.*

Nature *and* Nurture

Have you hugged a sponge lately?

Evolution 101:3 our nature is written in our 3.5+ billion year old genome that started with bacteria, which changed water, carbon dioxide and sunlight into oxygen. It took bacteria about 3 billion years to evolve into multi-cellular organisms (prokaryotes and eukaryotes), arriving at the first animal, the sponge, about 565 million years ago.

Tens of millions of years later the Cnidarian (the C is not pronounced), which is commonly referred to in its myriad of forms as coral, evolved from the sponge and is a truly exemplary animal in today's terms. It was the first animal to use tentacles to reach out and grasp, swallow and digest food, the first animal to develop weapons (sharp, barbed, spear-like projections that snared its prey at the speed of a bullet), the first animal to engage in chemical warfare (using tiny sacks of toxic chemicals that it shot at its victims to paralyze them), the first animal to develop a working community of coral (the Great Barrier Reef), and the first animal to develop a neuro-muscular system to control its motion to move from place to place and eventually swim as a jellyfish—laying down a genome for higher species to evolve from; and it didn't even have a brain.

From Cnidarians, mollusks, fish and eventually land-dwelling animals evolved, with mammals appearing about 200 million-years ago and primates about 50 million years ago.

1

Running down the evolutionary ladder, "Hominids" (human-like primates) evolved from chimpanzees about 4 million years ago (remember Lucy?) and "early Homo sapiens" evolved from hominids about 700,000 years ago. "Pre-modern Homo sapiens" evolved about 150,000 years ago from "early Homo sapiens," eventually evolving into "modern man" about 50,000 years ago. "Neanderthals" also evolved from "early Homo sapiens" about 125,000 years ago and died off about 32,000 years ago, because their genome didn't provide them with the rational ability to survive. About 100,000 years ago it seems [4], modern man's brain began to evolve towards socialization—community— in order to survive.

It's survival of the fittest *community*

An evolving theme of nature is "community"—we need to work together to survive. Just for fun, let's see if we can create an evolutionary ladder for "community." Nature's first community would have been the atom, a *community of elements* (the electrons, protons and neurons that nature forged in the stars)—or for you purists, the first community would have been the proton or neutron, a *community of quarks*. The next rung in the ladder would be the molecule, a non-living *community of atoms* (the building blocks of nature). Climbing way up the ladder, we advance to the genome, a *community of molecules* that lead to living (reproductive) cells such as bacteria, which jumped a rung when it evolved to the eukaryote, a *community of cells* working together for the successful survival of the "organism." But we can't stop here; there are ladder extensions.

A big step was the first animal (the sponge), as a *community of organs* working together for the animal's successful survival, which evolved to the many species past and present. The greatest advancement on community ladder came with the rational brain of the mammals (no, not the mammalian/emotional brain—that was only for selfish physical survival). This rational brain created a *community of animals* working together for the society's survival, and the last rung was the *community of Homo sapiens*— now modern man. Who knows, the final rung on the community ladder might be *a community of minds*, held together by pure thought—but we already do that; refer to "bonding thoughts" on pages 42 to 47. So I guess we have completed the construction Nature's evolutionary communications ladder, but it came at a great cost.[1,3]

2

Opening a can of worms

The most significant evolutionary step occurred over 500 million years ago with the land flatworm. It evolved a brain consisting of a few hundred neurons at the top of its spinal cord that regulated body functions (breathing, metabolism and the like); it could also limitedly respond to light, heat, moisture and the odors of prey. Among other things, this primitive brain evolved into the "reptilian brain," similar to the human brainstem and cerebellum.

Next, the "mammalian brain" evolved, storing memories that it compared to sensory input to alert the mammal to possible threats; it also contained instinctive memory that made the mammal *react* to physically survive. Unfortunately, the emotional alerts weren't very accurate, requiring the evolution of more complex sensory cortices (sight, sound, etc.) to store sensory memories for more accurate alerts.

As mammals, primates and eventually humans developed complex brains in order to survive…here we go with all of that technical talk, but it is interesting…nature added other cortices (parietal, motor, frontal, temporal, etc.) for storing previous experiences and our reactions to them for later reference. Nature added the parietal and motor cortex for automatic physical reactions (small and large motor functions) and added the motor and pre-motor cortices, which contained instinctive memory to help the mammal socially survive. The addition of the temporal, frontal and pre-frontal cortices (the "rational brain") allowed us to accurately identify the cause of emotional alerts and to react more appropriately to them in increasingly more complex societies.

Nature's hardware and software

The first priority of evolution is to survive long enough to pass on our genes. The first priority of survival is to efficiently use limited food supplies to develop and maintain evolutionary *hardware* and *software*. Every species is a predator (a diner) to get food, and a pray (a dinner) to be food. As a predator, a species may develop offensive hardware such as tooth and claw, size, speed, toxins, etc.; it may also develop offensive software (a brain) that might include the ability to react to sensations to obtain food. As a pray, a species may develop defensive hardware including size, camouflage, speed, level of reproduction, etc.; it may also develop defensive software (a brain) to react to what is sensed to avoid being eaten.

You are probably asking yourself, "Why didn't all of the animals develop a more sophisticated brain?" The answer is *economics*. The amount of energy required to maintain an ounce of brain matter (neurons) is 20 times the amount of energy required to maintain an ounce of other organs. Stated another way, it takes 20 times the food supply to maintain evolutionary software than it does to maintain evolutionary hardware, and due to a limited food supply, most species invested more in hardware than in software. Of those species that invested heavily in software, some were successful like modern man and some were unsuccessful like Neanderthals (just ask one, oh yeah, you can't, they're extinct).

Nature's Survival System—for us

Due to the relatively limited nature of mammalians to reproduce and successfully evolve in a hardware-dominated world, our ancestors had to invest in software that could instantly react to predators and all threats to their physical survival. The current state of

Our Software Survival System IS **Human Personality**

the art in genetic software is the pre-frontal cortex of the rational brain. This software gives us the ability to reason, choose how to react, plan, and to develop spoken and written languages. So you may ask, what does evolution and survival have to do with human personality? Everything!

The Human Brain: Personality

No man is a disconnected island

To understand human personality we must understand how our brain helps us to survive. We only exist within our minds—within our inner-world (inside our body)—and only if we can sense it through physical pain or somatosensory awareness. Nothing exists outside of our body (the outer-world) unless we sense it. If we couldn't see, hear, smell, feel or taste, there would be no way to know that the outer-world exists, except maybe if it banged into us causing internal pain or dysfunction.

And just because it's there, it doesn't mean that we sense all of it. We only sense what *seems* important, ignoring all else. What is truly important becomes a "connection" between our inner-world and that outer-world—if unimportant it doesn't. To put it another way: if something from the outer-world is important it becomes a sensory memory (i.e., a connection); if unimportant, it does not become a memory.

I connect, therefore I am

Since the outer-world only exists for you—you can only infer how it exists for others. The fact that the outer-world does materially exist and that others can sense it too, allows us to share common connections (things that are important to both of us). The diagram below shows physical examples of sensory connections—they exist and are important to us. Our sensory system detects them and our sensory memories recognize them; we can also recall these sensory memories even when not presently sensing them.

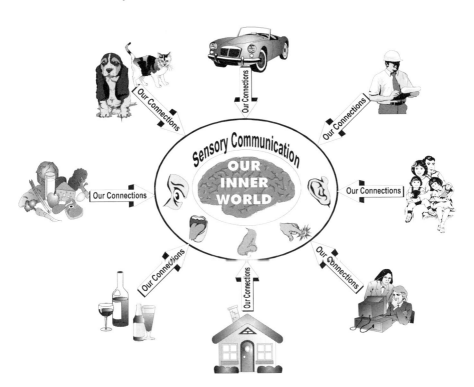

For example, as a child you probably had a toy that brought you great joy and although long-gone, memories of the fun you had with it will last your lifetime. And every time some sensation reminds you of that toy, you re-connect with it, just as if you had it in your hands again. These are rational and emotional memories triggered by the sensory memories of experiences with that toy.

Some connections are important—some not so

Since memories represent connections, all that we are exposed to *and* re-member is a connection, but some connections are more important than oth-ers. For example, an important physical connection may be our shiny new red sports car. But because of the way, our brain stores information, similar red sports car, any sports car, or any red car for that matter can get our atten-tion and seem important. But, they are not *our* red sports car and are thus, unimportant connections quickly dismissed from memory.

The key to identifying an *important* connection is the emotion that alerts us to it. As noted in Chapter 7, joy alerts us to important connections and as noted in Chapter 4 sorrow alerts us to disconnection from our important connections. If something evokes joy or sorrow, then they are important connections. For that matter, anything that evokes fear or anger is also an important connection, otherwise it wouldn't evoke those feelings. Bottom line: We all have important and unimportant connections that alert us to the outer-world to help us survive it.

And, not all connections are positive

The diagram above shows positive connections, but we also have negative connections. A negative connection might be a boss who fired us without cause, a vicious dog that must be avoided, a lover who jilted us, the pur-chase of an expensive item, car, home, etc., that we thought would be won-derful and ended up being a nightmare. These and many more connections that are negative evoke anger, fear or sorrow when we sense and identify them. And let's not forget the nothingness—sensed non-connections that mean nothing to us—that we dismiss as quickly as we sense them.

Thus, our connections represent what is important to us in the outer-world and with some connections being more important than others, whether posi-tive or negative. When we are important to others, we are a connection of

6

theirs to the outer-world, and they are one of ours. For example, a child is a very important connection for a parent, and a parent is a very important connection for a child.

Reactions speak louder than worms

All of our sensed connections are important to our survival, although sensing them is not enough. We must *react* to survive. We sense others through their reactions, and others sense us through our reactions—we call it communication. Communication, like community, has an evolutionary ladder with the land flat worm hanging off the lowest rung. The primitive brain of the land flat worm used olfactory (smell) and touch (heat) sensors to communicate to it the existence of its prey, which it reacted to by ensnaring it. As the outer-world became more complex, populated and dangerous, the reptilian brain evolved a step up the ladder from the land flat worm's brain since it contained better sensory systems (sight, sound, etc.). This allowed the reptilian brain to identify more accurately the communications from the outer-world to better react.

A giant step in communications on the evolutionary ladder came with the mammalian brain, which produced emotional alerts to scant outer-world stimuli and quick intense reactions. Unfortunately, mammals whose alerts were inaccurate became extinct and fell off the ladder while those who evolved more sensory cortices, to store more accurate sensory information, better survived. Finally, as the outer-world became more community-oriented, social survival became crucial, which eventually led to the evolution of "modern man's" rational brain, teetering at the top of the ladder, to accurately identify the cause of the emotional alerts and more appropriately react. For example, if confronted by another we can rationally react by discussing our point of view instead of emotionally reacting by hitting him over the head with a club, thereby avoiding the negative repercussions of that physical communication.

Our distinction as humans

Presently, the highest rung on the communication ladder is the language area of modern-man's rational brain that allows us to voice our opinions and thus, learn from each other. Using these language areas, the brain developed *written* sensory information (books, etc.), which has allowed us to communicate our pre-stated opinions to others without ever meeting them. Inventions such as phones, TV and the Internet have extended our *real-time* communications far beyond what is in front of us. We have evolved an inner-world level of communication that allows us to better understand the outer-world and socially react our intentions back to it. To accomplish this, our brains obviously needed more than just sensory memories.

We all have Alzheimer's without memories

As crucial as sensory data is to our survival it is fleeting and worthless unless stored as memory—without memory, whatever just happened, didn't. Likewise, sensory memories are of little value unless they help us to physically survive—this is the emotional brain's job. Emotional memories record sensory experiences that threaten or propagate our physical survival and later alert us when we experience similar sensory input. Although very helpful, emotional alerts may be erroneous, causing inappropriate reactions.

For example, a hunter may encounter what appears to be a threatening wolf and in a panic shoots it, only to discover that it was a farmer's pet. The hunter's inaccurate reaction may result in the hunter being attacked by the farmer—a definite threat to the hunter's physical survival. Should the hunter survive the farmer's retaliation he will now have rational memories that will help him to better identify what he senses when hunting—especially when near a farm.

Although important, physical survival is insufficient for humans who also require social survival—this is the rational brain's job. Sensory memories create and trigger emotional memories that create and trigger rational memories that give us choices about how to best react. For example, our upset boss may angrily confront us for something we may or may not have done. We can emotionally respond by yelling back, possibly losing our job or we can rationally respond by calmly finding a resolution to the problem—that is of course if we can calm down the boss.

In a nutshell

The purpose of our *sensory system* is to communicate the outer-world (physically outside of us) to us and to catalog those experiences as sensory memories for future reference. The purpose of our *emotional brain* is to record emotional memories of sensory experiences that physically threaten our survival and to alert us when we re-sense that threat. The purpose of our rational brain is to enhance our physical survival by accurately identifying a possible threat and reacting appropriately, using rational memories from similar experiences. In Chapter 2, we will discuss the four *primary emotions* of anger, fear, joy and sorrow, along with the four *rational styles* of director, analyzer, socializer and relator. Each primary emotion has a physical survival purpose, each rational style has a social survival purpose[2], and each style and emotion has its own *unique* set of memories to react with.

You *are* unique, but why?

Ok, let's get it over with. Every book that suggests a genetically based system to define personality runs the risk of offending the reader as being non-unique, no matter how accurate and useful the system is. We all want and need to feel unique, different, and not just some human clone—well help is on the way, and it isn't just some rationalization; it's a fact. Yes, our wired-in-genetic personality makes us similar, but our learned personality (memories) makes each of us truly unique, like no one that has come before you or will ever follow.

Most people define their uniqueness as a blend of their mental skills with regard to reading, writing, mathematics, philosophies, etc., and their physical skills such as artistic talents, manual skills, people skills, etc.—this is correct since our blend of skills resides in our learned memories. Here we go with the technical stuff again—our unique physical skill memories reside in our parietal and pre-motor cortices, our unique mental skill memories reside in our frontal and temporal cortices, and our unique emotional memories reside in our emotional brain.

But you may retort, many of us react similarly in similar situations, especially if we have a "similar personality." But don't forget, we interpret those situations with uniquely created and interacting sensory, rational and emotional memories. Digressing for a moment—that's why it is so difficult to teach others using *our* uniquely interacting memories when they are trying to learn with *their* uniquely interacting memories. Digressing even further—Hint: don't pooh-pooh their interpretation of what you are teaching if it is not based on the same memory interactions as yours, just be happy that they get the point when they express what they have learned back to you *in their own terms*.

Getting back to your uniqueness, we all react with our own special flair using our own unique verbal and physical expressions, most of which we learn from our parents and siblings (making us less unique), and some of which we create (making us more unique). In general, we don't feel unique when our reactions are similar to others, but we should since our reasoning is different. For example, some people go to work for a paycheck and others go to work because it is a wonderful way to express their creativity or to help others—but they all go to work. All this adds up to a cherished uniqueness we call *personality*—it is what I call "Symbiotic Personality."

Oh yes, I almost forgot—we all have an inner-world where only we exist—if that isn't unique I don't know what is. And of course, that inner-world houses our unique *inner-world personality*—but we do *react* to given situations in a consistent manner—which creates our *outer-world personality*—which others judge us by and which is what most people refer to when discussing human personality.

REFERENCES Interpreted as Support for My Conclusions:

1. Nature, PBS Home Video, *Triumph of Life*, (2000 Thirteen/WNET, NY)

2. Dean C. Bellavia, *The One-Second Personality*, (Buffalo, The Bio-Engineering Co., 1995)

3. Peter D. Ward & Donald Brownlee, *Rare Earth, why complex life is uncommon in the universe*, (Copernicus Books, 2000)

4. Rita Carter, *Mapping the Mind,* (U of CA Press, 1999)

Chapter 2
Symbiotic Personality

Human Personality
Symbiotic Personality
Nurturing Our *Free Will*—Personality *Finesse*

Human Personality

It's the only game in town

If this book provides you with just one insight, it should be that personality is our human survival system, nothing more and certainly nothing less! It was our survival "software" that allowed us to prevail in a world of predators with superior survival "hardware." Our personality contains human *nature*, our four wired-in *genetic* emotional alerts produced by our emotional brain and our four rational *reactions* produced by our rational brain. Our personality also contains human *nurture*, our learned emotional *memories* that trigger emotional alerts and our learned rational memories that trigger rational reactions. Together, our genetic nature and our learned nurture comprise our human personality, which is both unique (learned) and similar (genetic) to others.

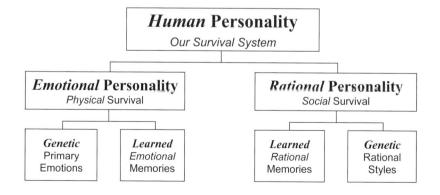

11

Faster than a speeding bullet—emotional survival

Our emotional personality is located in our 200-million-year-old emotional (mammalian) brain and is capable of expressing four primary emotions that is verifiable through similar physical reactions and facial expressions that all humans share.[2,3] Anger, fear, joy, and sorrow are the only emotions whose facial expressions cannot be faked by the rational brain; they are unique! The four primary emotions (triggered in 60 milliseconds by sensory input and emotional memories) do NOT involve rational thought (formed about 500 milliseconds later). The rest of our emotions (disgust, frustration, shame, surprise, etc.) are rational emotions because they require rational thought to trigger them.

π **The rest of this section contains technical information *crucial to understanding personality*—**but you can handle it.

Emotions produce hormones, peptides, and monoamine chemicals that create both physical preparedness and sensory acuity. This is why we physically *feel* emotions and do not physically feel rational thoughts, unless of course they trigger rational emotions. Primary emotions can range from mild to extreme, depending on the level and duration of emotional chemicals. A surge of emotional chemicals only lasts for milliseconds, but the emotion's "mood," as the chemicals ebb out of our system, lasts for seconds; much longer if the emotion is extreme or rationalized.

Emotional Alerts

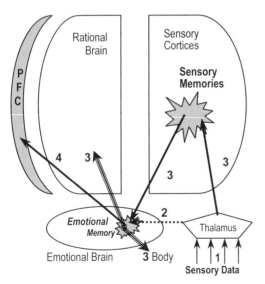

1. The thalamus (sensory crossroads) receives sensory data.
2. Scant sensory data *preconditions* an emotional memory in 20 milliseconds.
3. Within 60 milliseconds, this sensory data excites *sensory* memories that then excite the preconditioned emotional memory, creating an emotional alert that sends pulses of emotional chemicals into the brain and body.
4. The Pre-Frontal Cortex (PFC) is alerted to the emotional alert, which holds its attention until the cause of the alert is identified by rational memories and the emotion is quelled.

12

And that bullet needs a trigger or two

Emotional *alerts,* triggered by a combination of sensory input and emotional memories, require the fulfillment of the emotion's survival purpose. The amygdala (an important part of the emotional brain) contains emotional memories that can trigger emotions when it receives specific sensory data. The diagram on the previous page shows that sensory data goes directly from the thalamus (the crossroads of sensory data) to the amygdala in about 20 milliseconds[7] preconditioning an emotional memory for a *possible* emotional alert. The sensory data also goes indirectly from the thalamus, via the sensory cortices back to the amygdala in about 60 milliseconds[6] to trigger that pre-conditioned emotional memory and thus, an emotional alert. An emotional alert can be mild or strong as explained in Chapters 4 through 7, but they can also be extreme as detailed in Chapter 8.

There's an *emotion* and a time for every purpose under heaven

Emotional alerts triggered by sensory input along with emotional memories achieve a "physical survival purpose" that can be categorized as either people-oriented or task-oriented (not involving others). Joy and sorrow are people-oriented since joy "alerts us to *our connections*" and sorrow "alerts us to *our disconnections.*" Fear and anger are task-oriented since fear "alerts us to *danger*" and anger "alerts us to *confrontation.*" Bottom line, our *physical* emotions alert us to threats to our *physical* survival.

200 million years in the making—Rational survival

Our rational personality, located in our million year old rational brain, is capable of *reason* (the capacity for logical, rational, and analytic thought). Every *thought* (the excitation of attached sensory and rational memories) precedes a rational *reaction*, which is the physical and mental manifestation of that thought. It is a mental manifestation because it results in new memories to record the experience for future reference. It is a physical manifestation when it results in a physical act, which when outwardly viewed projects the *rational survival purpose*[4] of the style.

Like the four primary emotions, two of the rational styles are people-oriented and two are task-oriented. The socializer and relator styles are people-oriented since the socializer style records rational memories and physically acts "to *address* our connections" and the relator style records memories and physically acts "to *maintain* our connections." The director and analyzer styles are task-oriented since the director style records memories and physically acts "to *get resolution*" and the analyzer style records memories and physically acts "to *unerringly proceed*" towards resolution.

Slow but more sure—rational reactions

Unlike emotional alerts taking tens of milliseconds, rational reactions take hundreds of milliseconds as shown in the diagram below.

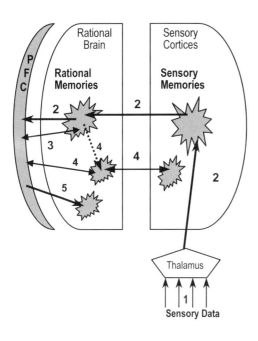

Rational Reactions

1. The thalamus (sensory crossroads) receives sensory data.

2. Within 60 milliseconds, sensory data excites sensory memories that excite attached rational memories attaching them to the Pre-Frontal Cortex (PFC).

3. Within 500 milliseconds, the PFC uses those rational and sensory memories to decide how to rationally react.

4. The PFC may also involve attached *related* rational memories, along with attached sensory memories to decide how to rationally react.

5. A new memory is created in the frontal cortex to record that experience for future reference, similar to the memories in **4** in this example.

If the *style* fits, wear it

Each rational style exhibits many *outwardly viewed* attributes, as detailed in Chapter 9; this defines our "Rational Personality Pattern" as detailed in Appendix-B. One strongest style dominates this pattern since we react with it much of the time and always when distressed. This pattern also contains weak styles that are rarely used and moderate styles that are use as needed, when not distressed. Thus when *outwardly viewed*, **style strength** is defined as: *strong*—we use that style much of the day, *weak*—we use that style little of the day, and *moderate*—we use that style as needed. Refer to

Appendix A to determine your strong, moderate and weak styles. In Chapter 12, we will show that when *inwardly viewed*, style strength is a direct consequence of the excitability or inhibition of our primary emotions. In summary, our human personality, our "software-survival-system," *is* our emotional alerts plus rational reactions, which I call "Symbiotic Personality."

Symbiotic Personality

Am I the Diner or the Dinner?

To survive in an ever-evolving universe, mammals, not yet being the dominant species, needed a brain that could successfully deal with the age-old question—"Am I the diner or the dinner?" And nature being what it is didn't discard a perfectly good mammalian brain, but instead expanded upon that emotional brain with a rational brain[1] to validate the emotional brain's reactions in a less physical, more social environment. This outgrowth resulted in a symbiotic relationship between the emotional brain's alerts and the rational brain's reactions. The following three principles define this relationship and are the essence of Symbiotic Personality:

1. The four rational styles evolved from the four primary emotions—a fact of nature:
   - The analyzer style evolved from fear.
   - The director style evolved from anger.
   - The relator style evolved from sorrow.
   - The socializer style evolved from joy.

2. When we trigger a primary emotion, its symbiotic rational style must *identify* what triggered it in order to quell it—a fact of nature:
   - Analyzer memories identify the *danger* and quell the fear.
   - Director memories identify the *confrontation* and quell the anger.
   - Relator memories identify the *disconnection* and quell the sorrow.
   - Socializer memories identify the *connection* and quell the joy.

3. When a rational style's purpose must be attained we're compelled to express its symbiotic emotion—an observation of nature:
   - *Fear* compels us to *unerringly proceed* with the analyzer style.
   - *Anger* compels us to *get resolution* with the director style.

15

- *Sorrow* compels us to *reconnect* with the relator style.
- *Joy* compels us to *address our connections* with the socializer style.

In Principle 3, a rational thought (not sensory input) triggers a *primary* emotion (called a *rational* emotion since rationally triggered) that turns on the symbiotic rational style, compelling us to attain its purpose. For example, if we are a strong director efficient and experienced at wiring 120-volt systems, the fear from realizing the danger that we were working with a 240-volt system would turn on our analyzer style and make us unerringly proceed to avoid being electrocuted.

The following diagram illustrates the symbiotic relationship between the four primary emotions and the four rational styles.

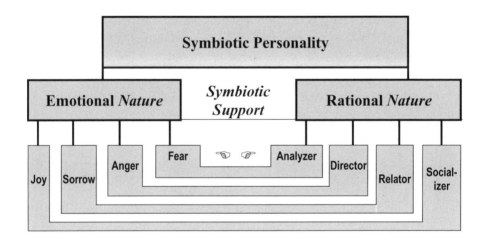

Not unproven principles

Symbiotic personality is supported by neural research, which has shown[5,7] that there is a cyclic relationship between the expression of emotion by the emotional brain, its triggering of rational thought in the rational brain, and that rational thought's feedback to the emotional brain that quells the emotion. This fact arose when people who had suffered a stroke that severed the axons going from the emotional brain to the rational brain *could* express emotion, but couldn't rationally validate expressing it—the rational brain wasn't aware of the expressed emotion. It was also shown[6] that certain people suffering from depression couldn't quell the emotion because of severed axons going from the rational to emotional brain, causing repetitive re-expression of the emotion. This well-accepted concept of rational thoughts turning off emotions *is* symbiotic personality, which is this cyclic process.

Too much of a good thing

Symbiotic cycles (Principle #2) represent how we react much of the day and are, in fact, how we emotionally think. Sensory input triggers an emotion that's cause is identified with its symbiotic rational style's rational memories that are attached to those sensory memories, followed by a quelling of that emotion, allowing its "emotional chemicals"—hormones, monoamines and peptides (ignore the technical words)—to ebb as we rationally react in thought word or deed. The process of expressing, identifying the source of and thus quelling an emotion, and then rationally reacting is a "symbiotic cycle."

π   This diagram is technical, but *crucial to understanding Symbiotic Personality.*

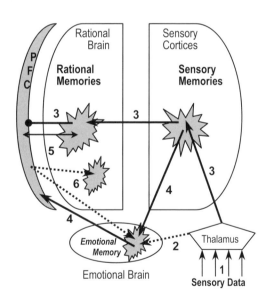

One *Symbiotic Cycle*

1. Sensory data is received at the thalamus.
2. Scant sensory data *preconditions* an emotional memory in 20 milliseconds (ms).
3. Sensory data excites sensory memories that excite attached rational memories that are made available to the Pre-Frontal Cortex (PFC).
4. Sensory memories excite the emotional memory in 60 ms, creating an emotion that alerts the PFC to a possible threat.
5. The PFC takes about 500 ms to identify what triggered the emotion using attached rational and sensory memories.
6. Once sorted out, the PFC quells the emotion and rationally reacts, recording the entire experience as a new memory for future reference.

17

The symbiotic cycle in the diagram on the previous page is the combination of the previous "emotional alert" and "rational reaction" diagrams. It shows sensory data going directly from the thalamus to the amygdala in about 20 milliseconds [7] preconditioning an emotional memory for a *possible* emotional alert. The sensory data also goes indirectly from the thalamus via the sensory cortices and back to the amygdala in about 60 milliseconds [6] to trigger that pre-conditioned emotional memory and create an emotional alert. At the same time, those sensory memories excite attached rational memories that excite the Pre-Frontal Cortex (PFC). The PFC identifies the *cause* of the emotional alert with rational memories attached to sensory memories that triggered the emotional alert.

For example, it identifies the cause of the *confrontation* triggering the anger, or the cause of the *danger* triggering the fear, or the cause of the *disconnection* triggering the sorrow, or it identifies the *connection* triggering the joy. Once we identify the cause, the neural loop from the sensory to emotional to rational memories is complete, and the PFC sends an inhibitory signal to that emotional memory to quell it. The PFC then decides how to rationally react using those attached sensory and rational memories along with other attached rational memories from similar past situations. The final step is for the PFC to record in the frontal cortices a *new* rational memory of the entire experience for future reference. Wow, that's a mouthful!

Many are recalled, but few are chosen

When we cannot identify the cause of the emotional alert with one symbiotic cycle, there is a second cycle using refreshed sensory data and attached rational memories to try again to identify the cause of the alert.

For example, if we hear a threateningly loud noise, we express fear followed by the analyzer style to identify the possible danger causing that noise—*1ˢᵗ symbiotic cycle*. The fear is re-expressed if analyzer and sensory memories of that sound do not identify the danger, possibly considering visual sensory input in that sound's direction along with attached analyzer memories to identify that sighting—*2ⁿᵈ symbiotic cycle*. Once the fearful sound is identified, the fear memory is inhibited, and the symbiotic cycles cease as we unerringly proceed with the analyzer style if a danger exists or we react with other style's rational memories if the danger is erroneous.

Its beauty is its simplicity—but it's a nag

Nature's symbiotic cycle is simple and reliable—it has to be to work so many times a day. It's a closed system: The rational memories attached to the sensory memories that triggered the emotion contain the information to identify its cause. For emphasis—sensory memories excite emotional memories that excite rational memories that identify and quell the emotion and determine how we rationally react.

This sense, alert, identify and quell of a single symbiotic cycle, or sense, alert, try to identify, alert, try to identify, etc., of multiple symbiotic cycles *always* happens. The identification of the cause of the alert, whether in one or many symbiotic cycles, *always* quells the emotion! When we cannot rationally identify the cause of the alert, the cycle is incomplete and will nag at us with more cycles until identified or until we are distracted (it can't go on forever). For example, if we express fear and can't identify its cause, it will nag at us until we identify the danger or we are distracted from it—the same holds true for anger, sorrow, and joy.

It's a stock deal with a nice dividend

A symbiotic cycle identifies the cause of an emotional alert using the rational memories of that symbiotic style. For example, when we express fear we use the analyzer style's rational memories to identify the danger—we cannot use another style's rational memories for reasons explained in Chapter 12. In summary: We only use analyzer memories to identify the danger, we only use director memories to identify the confrontation, we only use relator memories to identify the disconnection and we only use socializer memories to identify the joy. It is obvious when we correctly identify the cause of the emotion since the emotion disappears—if not, we didn't correctly identify it. And once identified, we do not have to only use that style's memories to react, we can use other style's memories instead.

Save us from our rationalizations

The major problem we have with emotions is that we don't properly identify their cause, allowing them to hijack our PFC and rationalize—that is, come up with bogus reasons why we expressed that emotion, thus re-expressing it until distracted by something else. You will hear a lot about "rationalization" (a series of erroneous identifications of what triggered the emotion) in this book. It keeps us from finessing our erroneously triggered strong emo-

19

tions and elevates our fear, anger, or sorrow, and yes even our *joy*—see page 113 to find out why this is not good—making us react inappropriately much of the time.

They all have their survival purpose

To understand Symbiotic Personality, we need to understand the symbiosis between an emotion's purpose and its rational style's purpose. As mentioned previously, the outer-world only exists because we can sense and catalog it with sensory memories. Emotions evolved to instantly alert us, to improve our survival rate—once alerted its done it job. The rational brain evolved to better manage (identify and quell) emotions, since emotions can be erroneous and because we must shut them off once, they have alerted us. This is analogous to a smoke alarm whose purpose is to alert us to smoke and possibly fire, but once alerted and we identify the cause of the smoke we must turn the alarm off or the intense sound will drive us crazy.

Rational memories also evolved to give us a *choice* of how to deal with the cause of the emotion, for example the "fight or flight" reaction to a danger that triggered fear. Once we identify the fear, we may flee if we continue to use analyzer memories if we are a strong analyzer. If we are a strong director, we might fight if we feel confronted and become angered. Bottom line, we identify and initially react with the rational memories symbiotic with the emotion, but will probably switch to our strongest style to react once we quell the emotion.

Each style's social survival purpose should coincide with its symbiotic emotion's physical survival purpose—which is logical since the rational brain evolved from the emotional brain. The purpose of fear is to *alert us to danger,* and the analyzer style must provide an *unerring procedure* to flee from that danger—should we decide to fight we may not prevail. The purpose of anger is to *alert us to confrontation,* and the purpose of the director style is *to get resolution*—by quickly deciding what to do about that confrontation before it overpowers us. The purpose of sorrow is *to alert us to our disconnections,* and the purpose of the relator style is *to maintain our connections*—so we do what is necessary to reconnect. The purpose of joy is *to alert us to our connections,* and the purpose of the socializer style is *to address our connections*—once we identify that connection's importance.

In summary, the purpose of an emotion is physical survival; its symbiotic rational style's purpose is social survival through appropriate reactions. You will hear a lot about appropriateness in this book; it refers to acting in an acceptable manner—to belong. Everybody wants to belong to something whether they admit it or not—it's a genetic imperative, and a choice.

We all have a choice

Most emotions are valid and healthy, but some are erroneous when triggered by deep-seated emotional memories, causing pain for all involved. We rationally react to an emotional alert in three ways:

1. The emotion is valid and quelled:
   a. The anger is valid and quelled; we identify the confrontation and the situation is quickly resolved.
   b. The fear is valid and quelled; there is danger and the analyzer style helps us to unerringly proceed to avoid harm.
   c. The sorrow is valid and quelled; there was a disconnection and the relator style helps us identify the disconnection and reconnect.
   d. The joy is valid and quelled; we identify an important connection and our socializer style helps us to address that connection.

2. The emotion is erroneous and quelled:
   a. The anger is erroneous and quelled, hopefully allowing the sorrow emotion to trigger the relator style to apologize and reconnect.
   b. The fear was erroneous and quelled, allowing a more appropriate emotion and rational style to take over if needed.
   c. The sorrow was erroneous and quelled, allowing a more appropriate emotion and rational style to take over if needed.
   d. The joy emotion was erroneous and quelled, allowing a more appropriate emotion and rational style to take over if needed.

3. The emotion is erroneous and **not** quelled:
   a. The anger is erroneous and rationalization causes futile attempts to identify non-existent confrontation.
   b. The fear is erroneous and rationalization causes futile attempts to identify non-existent danger.
   c. The sorrow is erroneous and rationalization causes futile attempts to identify non-existent disconnection.
   d. The joy is erroneous and rationalization causes futile attempts to identify unimportant connections.

Of the three possible outcomes of a symbiotic cycle above, only outcomes #1 and #2 are appropriate; outcome #3 isn't, and *choosing* outcome #2 over outcome #3 defines the degree to which we finesse our nature.

In a word—survival

To ensure human survival in a *physical* world, nature has gifted an ever-vigilant emotional brain to alert us to possible physical threats. To better identify those possible threats and to ensure human survival in a more *social* world, nature has gifted us a rational brain containing nature's greatest gift, the ability to choose how to appropriately react. Together they form Symbiotic Personality, which allows us to react appropriately for our physical and social survival.

Nurturing Our *Free Will*—Personality *Finesse*

A half-billion years in the making

Personality finesse is an inevitable part of evolution that started about half a billion years ago with the brain of the land flat worm. Natures finessed that tiny brain into the reptilian brain, then into the mammalian brain, and then into the rational brain to help us better react to our environment to survive. Nature's last finesse was the addition of the prefrontal cortex and language centers in the human brain, which allows us to finesse our own brains to react more appropriately. We have the individual choice to use this gift to finesse our genetic personality and react more appropriately now, or we can wait a few hundred thousand years (if humans survive that long) for nature to evolve us into it. The better choice is not to wait!

The greatest tool ever invented

Ok, here we go again, another controversy; this time between definitions of the conscious and unconscious mind (brains)—I choose the following because it makes sense. Nature's tool for finessing our personality is our *conscious* prefrontal cortex (PFC), which allows us to *choose* how to react. The rest of the *rational* brain is *unconscious,* since it automatically reacts in the same manner to the same sensory stimuli with the same unconscious memories, never making a decision to do otherwise. The conscious brain (PFC) is responsible for creating unconscious memories, and a perfect example of this is learning how to drive a car.

You're never too old to learn

I taught my old daughters how to ride a two-wheel-bike, which is mostly physical training; when it came time to teach them to drive a car, their training needed to be more cerebral. Learning to ride a 20-pound bike involves conscious avoidance of falling, which doesn't exist when driving two tons of a protected environment that gives us a false sense of security, allowing for dangerous distractions. Thus, our number one training rule was no music, no discussion—no distractions of any kind, not even a response to my remarks, which would distract her from what she needed to concentrate on—driving.

Since driving is mostly unconscious and learning is conscious, this rule allowed her conscious PFC to lay down unconscious driving memories (experiences). For example, the simple act of stopping at a stop sign takes conscious effort to learn. Memories are required to stop *at* the sign, not way before it, not rolling through it without fully stopping, and certainly not stopping in the middle of the intersection. Once the unconscious learns how to respond to a stop sign the conscious mind is no longer necessary, except to make sure that there is no cross-traffic before proceeding. As this example illustrates, we use our rational conscious brain to create or modify unconscious *rational* memories to react on their own. Unfortunately, we cannot change *emotional* memories; we can only avoid or finesse them.

Between a choice and a hard place

Our emotional brain (especially the amygdala) represents our *sub-unconscious* (usually referred to as the *subconscious*) brain containing emotional memories. We create new and modify existing unconscious analyzer, director, relator, and socializer memories with every experience. We create new subconscious emotional memories as needed, but once created we cannot change them. We can, though, attach rational memories that unconsciously quell those subconscious emotional memories, as discuss in Chapters 13 through 15.

We trigger most of our emotions with emotional memories that are rationally understandable and easily identified and quelled, but some are difficult to identify, causing severe pain and years of therapy. Thus, if our subconscious (emotional) brain is rationally inaccessible, if our unconscious brain works on autopilot, and if our conscious brain (PFC) allows us to choose how to react, which one might involve free will?

Correct! Now for a BIG can of worms

Everybody has an opinion of what free will is, but we are going to develop our own (or my own if you disagree). So, starting with the dictionary we have—*FREE:* {not controlled by anybody or anything}…*WILL* {the mental faculty by which one deliberately chooses or decides upon a course of action}…*FREE WILL* {1) The ability or discretion to choose, or 2) the power attributed to human beings of making free choices that are unconstrained by external circumstances or by an agency such as fate or divine will}—as usual, the dictionary falls short of a satisfying definition of *pure* free will. It seems that we can only express pure free will if our decisions are devoid of learned or genetic influences.

Where there's a will, there's a choice

Since only conscious reactions of *choice* can involve pure free will, should we assume that *all* conscious reactions involve pure free will? Some people think that it is impossible to express free will since all of our choices are a product of what others teach us, making it their will. Others think that it's impossible to express free will since our genetic styles and emotions dictate our choices. Conversely, many others think that humans naturally express free will simply because they can make choices, whether influenced or not. But since the purpose of the rational brain is to socially survive, our choices must also be socially appropriate. Thus, the question is not whether we possess an uninfluenced free will; the question is whether we can choose to appropriately react.

This leaves us with a possible definition of pure free will: "the ability to consciously, appropriately react." On the surface, this definition seems no different than the rest, with the proviso that our conscious choice be appropriate, but we must look deeper to see its true meaning, which is based on the only free choice we have; to control our conscious, unconscious, and subconscious reactions. Put another way, free will must involve a choice to appropriately react, when it's *contrary* to our personality.

We all think we're appropriate

Since propriety is at the core of our definition, we need a satisfying definition of appropriateness. As mentioned on page 2, humans need to be part of a community; by acting appropriately, we become accepted by that community. But, does reacting appropriately mean acting in a manner that *we* feel is appropriate, just because we're use to acting that way?

For example, if unaware that our emotional outbursts negatively affect others, are we still appropriate having them? Are our actions acceptable to our community? Probably not, so who decides what reactions are inappropriate? We do, but there's a catch. If we decide that the outbursts are inappropriate simply because society says so, then it is not *our* free will since society is dictating our choice. But, if we decide that our outbursts are inappropriate because they are going against what we desire from that community, then we are exerting pure free will by reacting contrary to our personality. Of course, that community may dictate our lifestyle, but we chose to live there so it's still an expression of our pure free will.

With this in mind, we can now define *pure* free will as "the ability to react appropriately, contrary to our personality" since our entire personality (learned and genetic, emotional and rational) affects our decisions. But, how can we react contrary to our uncontrollable emotional outbursts? We can't! But we can use pure free will to decide to attach unconscious rational memories to identify and quell emotions *as* the outbursts occur.

Our strongest style is our own worse enemy

Using pure free will to control emotional outbursts involves the *conscious* use of an appropriate rational style instead of the unconscious use of our strongest style. This might involve the use of our weak relator or socializer style in *people-oriented* situations or the use of our weak director or analyzer style in *task-oriented* situations. It is inappropriate to work on tasks and get results when others are relying on us to simply listen to or interact with them. It is also inappropriate to socialize with others when we are supposed to be working on or completing our necessary tasks. Through practice, we can express our free will and finesse our natural personality; except when distressed, which strips away whatever free will we have.

Where there's a will, there's a finesse

Pure free will *is* personality finesse, which gives us "the ability to react appropriately, contrary to our personality." Personality finesse cannot eliminate inappropriate emotional alerts, but it can reduce their occurrence. Personality finesse can help us go against our natural personality and choose the most appropriate emotion and rational style to get the most out of life.

Willingly moving on

Now that we have Symbiotic Personality under our belts, Chapters 4 through 7 will help you to better understand the essence of the four rational styles and their symbiotic emotions. But before discussing them, we need to know more about memory, *the other half of personality*.

REFERENCES Interpreted as Support for My Conclusions:

1. Daniel Goleman, *Emotional Intelligence,* (NY, Bantam, 1995)
2. Paul Ekman, "An Argument for the Basic Emotions", *Cognition & Emotion*, 6, 1992, 169-200
3. Paul Ekman, "Facial Expression and Emotion", *American Psychologist, 48*, 1993, 384-392
4. Dean C. Bellavia, *The One-Second Personality*, (Buffalo, The Bio-Engineering Co., 1995)
5. PBS DVD Video, *The Secret Life of the Brain*, (2001 Thirteen/WNET New York)
6. Joseph LeDoux, *Synaptic Self,* (Viking, 2002)
7. Rita Carter, *Mapping the Mind,* (U of CA Press, 1999)

Chapter 3
Memory
...The Other Half of Personality

Nurturing Our Personality
Types of Memory

Nurturing Our Personality

There's more in heaven and earth than can be seen by your eyes

Ask five people what they remember about an automobile accident and they'll give you five different accounts. Memory is not an exact perception of what is, nor is it an exact duplication of what we perceive, it's just an adequate representation of the outer-world. There is much more visual, auditory, olfactory, touch, taste and somatosensory information in any one experience than can ever be perceived, much less remembered. Nonetheless, the brain has a high capacity for recording our experiences by deconstructing and scattering what we perceive throughout the sensory cortex.

For example, a single *vision* is decomposed and stored in eight areas of the visual cortex (for size, color, shape, distance, etc.) and are later reassembled when recalling that vision. This is an efficient storage system since most sensory experiences are similar to others, for example, there are many visions containing the color green. This system of deconstruction and reassembly is similar to language where one word may be used in many sentences and thus, all we need to do is remember the words and the grammatical rules for reassembling them to create an indefinite number of sentences—the same holds true for all visual, auditory, etc., sensory memories.

Beauty is in the eye of the beholder

Memory is a representation of what we sense in our inner-world, which may be different from what others sense in their inner-world, but that doesn't matter as long as we concur on what we perceive. For example, one eve-

27

ning my wife and I were enjoying a radiant sunset and she pointed out the beautiful red and gray hues. But, I didn't see red and gray hues; I saw red and blue hues and corrected her, upsetting her. I then realized that I was wearing my tinted eyeglasses and that she wasn't even wearing her glasses, distorting both of our perceptions. The point is, we both agreed that it was a beautiful sunset no matter what we thought we sensed. Bottom line, just because two people share the same experience, it doesn't mean that they share the same interpretation of that experience, even when it seems obvious; but it doesn't matter as long as they concur.

Once bitten twice shy—we only have what we remember

Getting back to memories—an experience only represents pertinent sensory information in enough detail to adequately record the outer-world. But sensory memory is worthless unless it creates a reaction to appropriately survive that sensory experience. To best understand this, let's consider a new experience and how we create memories to deal with it, for example, consider an experience involving a multi-colored snake we've never seen before (see diagram below). Sensory stimuli (the sight of the snake) create a visual sensory memory whose axons extend to the emotional and rational brains.

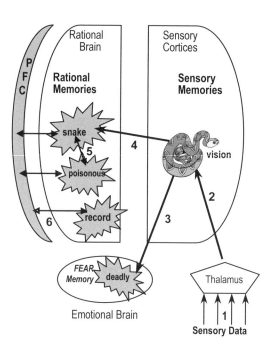

Creation of *New Memories*

1. Sensory data passes through the thalamus to the sensory cortices.

2. The perceived snake vision is compared to sensory memories.

3. That vision memory creates a fear (danger of being bitten) emotional memory.

4. Sensory memory axons are attached to rational (analyzer) memories of snakes.

5. The "snake" rational memories are connected to the "poisonous" rational memory.

6. The entire experience is *recorded* as a set of sensory (vision), emotional (deadly), and rational (snake & poisonous) memories attached to rational memories of that experience for future survival reference.

Since we know that a snake can be poisonous (deadly), the sensory axons excite emotional brain neurons, creating an emotional memory triggered by that sensory input (that vision of the snake). Simultaneously, those same sensory axons excite rational brain neurons, attached to identifying "snake" memories. Together, the new sensory, emotional, and rational memories create an overall record (new rational memories) of that initial experience.

But, the main value of this initial experience is to survive it both now and in the future. Thus, we need to know whether that colorful snake is poisonous. Sooo, we whip out our handy-dandy pocket snake-guide and look for its picture, only to find that it is highly poisonous. The snake's picture in the guidebook excites the same sensory (vision), emotional (fear) and rational (snake) memories, which are now being attached to the rational memory of the word "poisonous," creating a powerful fear memory attached to rational memories that identify that colorful snake as a deadly danger. Should we survive this experience (not get bit) and see that kind of snake on another hike, the vision of it will trigger strong fear exciting rational memories that identify that snake as poisonous, urging us to quickly avoid it. And, each time we re-experience it, we attach that new experience's rational memories to the memories of the last experience, which are attached to the memories of the experience before that, etc., providing us with a chronology of those experiences, with this newest experience being foremost.

All good things come in threes

Memories are simple, they record: (1) our sensory experiences, (2) our emotional alerts, and (3) our rational reactions to them, for our survival.

> **THE BIG PICTURE—sensory memories take a snapshot, sound bite, etc., of the outer-world. Emotional memories scan the snapshot, etc., decide whether it is a threat or not—if so, it *alerts* us. Attached rational memories identify the validity of the sensory input that caused the alert so that we can appropriately *react* to it and survive.**

We physically form a memory when interconnected neurons structurally and chemically change as they hook up with other neurons in a neural pattern—that memory can be permanent or fleeting.

Types of Memory

It helps to read this

The various kinds of memory help us to identify and react to the outer-world and each kind has a different function, although, they can all be categorized by "type" and "duration." Memory type refers to its location and function in the brain; memory duration refers to how long the memory lasts. Another wormy subject—classification—there are many systems of memory classification, mostly based on author preference. I chose one with you in mind to make it easiest for you to remember; we'll get to it after the technical classifications listed below.

Type-wise—technically, there are six types of memory:

1. *Sensory* Memory—is stored in the sensory cortices for identification of our perception of outer-world connections.

2. *Emotional* Memory (also called *implicit* memory)—is mostly stored in the amygdala; it triggers a primary emotion for a specific sensory input. The emotion expressed can be intense like terror or alerting like fear.

3. *Conscious* Memory (also called *working* memory) is attached to the prefrontal cortex (PFC) of our rational brain; we use it to make decisions.

4. *Episodic* Memory—the hippocampus encodes it as a sequential recording of our experiences; it is stored in our frontal cortices.

5. *Semantic* Memory—is stored in our rational brain's temporal cortices and contains facts such as names, numbers, places, poems, melodies, formulas, etc.; we process these facts with the PFC and frontal cortices.

6. *Procedural* Memory—is stored in the putamen of our emotional brain for unconscious physical procedures such as walking, driving, riding a bike, typing, eating, etc. There is also procedural memory stored in the caudate nucleus for automatic daily procedures such as locking the door, washing, putting things away, etc.

Now forget about it

Forget about procedural memory (it has no effect on learned personality). Remember emotional memory (the uncontrollable aspect of personality). Combine conscious, episodic, and semantic memory and call it rational memory (the controllable aspect of personality), which takes conscious effort and days or years to form—rational memories come in three flavors.

Duration-based; three types of rational memory

1. *Short-term* memory—lasts for about three seconds (for phone numbers, etc.); we processed it using the pre-frontal cortex (PFC). The PFC also uses *working* memory that can last up to 30 seconds to process a task, before the working memory is lost to distraction.

2. *Mid-term* memory—lasts from 30 minutes to two years;[1] we processed it in the hippocampus and stored it in the frontal and temporal cortices.

3. *Long-term* memory—lasts a lifetime although, its *access* lessens with non-use; we processed it in the frontal and temporal cortices.

Short-term rational memory is fleeting, and long-term memory is permanent, but mid-term memory is an ongoing process that dwindles with time. For example, consider the creation of mid-term memories involving the memorization of a list of 10 words. After a period of memorization, we forget 40% of them after 20 minutes, 55% after an hour, and 70% by the next day.[3]

It's never too late to survive

If you ask someone what the purpose of memory is, he or she will say something like "it's so that you can remember something." A brilliant retort, but useless since the *purpose* of rational memory is to socially survive, which affects the *process* of rational memory—which is its creation. The process starts out with an important short-term memory that we turn into mid-term memory, eventually ending up with long-term memory. We can never forget long-term memory—unless destroyed by disease—although, some memories may be more difficult to access than others, especially when not accessed for many months or years. We can convert short-term memory into mid-term memory if we rehash it enough. For example, if the PFC is holding a phone number in short-term memory, we will forget it after three seconds unless we repeatedly voice that number in our mind or aloud within that 3-second window until dialed within 30 seconds. This conscious PFC repetition of that phone number creates a 30-second short-term memory of that experience—we turn most 30-second PFC short-term memory into mid term memory, which may or may not be turned into long-term memory.

It's déjà vu, all over again

The rest of this chapter is a bit technical, but it's worth it! Research shows[1] that, while experiencing important sensory input within a 30-second-short term memory window, the PFC triggers the hippocampus to replay that encoded sensory input through the sensory cortices, thereby re-exciting the rational memories in the frontal cortex that are attached to the PFC, which then re-triggers the hippocampus—a cyclic process. This looping process strengthens the frontal cortex short-term memory with each loop, creating mid-term memory. When the sensory experience is not of consequence—it is not a survival issue—the looping never occurs.

Another mechanism that comes into play is *focus*. When using the PFC to sort out sensory input, our reptilian brain's "reticular system" focuses our attention on pertinent sensory information, ignoring all other. For example, it will direct and hold our head and focus our eyes on an object until we identify it. This focus causes a similar sensory pattern to repeat in tens of milliseconds, strengthening the memories recording that experience. For example, if we are on a jaunt through the woods and surprised by a stick that looks like a snake we focus on it. Since our visual system presents us with about 20 separate visions of that snake/stick every second, it fortifies that sensory image, re-triggers, and strengthens that frontal cortex memory for as long as we focus on identifying that stick/snake. This focused sensory experience along with hippocampal looping establishes mid-term memories.

To sleep, perchance to dream, perchance to remember

The hippocampus *replays* mid-term memories during sleep, reinforcing that frontal cortex memory and mixing it with permanent memories of similar experiences, thereby strengthening old and adding new memories. It is my belief that as we sleep the hippocampus replays its efficiently encoded sensory information *through* its intimately close thalamus, exciting the sensory and thus, the mid-term memories attached to them. We do not need hippocampal encoding of all sensory data of an experience; we only need enough coding to excite the sensory memories that excite the most important aspects of that experience's mid-term memories—those important to our survival. This sparse (imprecise) hippocampal encoding also excites other rational memories with similar encoding, thus relating and making all involved memories more interactive and long term. This sparse hippocampal encoding to excite memories is similar to the sparse sensory data required to pre-conditions an emotional alert in 20 milliseconds (see the page 12 diagram).

The hippocampal replay that turns mid-term memories into long-term memories is not possible when awake, since the hippocampus is too busy creating mid-term memories from the constant barrage of sensory input. The hippocampus probably has a hierarchy of memory processing: 1) it processes immediate sensory input that excites emotions and creates an emotional memory of a threat with attached rational memories that sort it out; 2) it processes important input from the PFC to turn 30-second short-term memory into mid-term memory through focus and looping; and, 3) it processes that mid-term memory into long-term memory as we sleep.

All good things come to those who work at it

Even though the hippocampus replays the mid-term memories as we sleep, it doesn't guarantee long-term memory, since we only retain about 30% of a mid-term memory by the next day. But, when we sufficiently fortify those memories while awake, we can turn that experience into long-term memory while asleep. For example, if we recite the Gettysburg address every day for seven days, we fortify that mid-term rational memory until it becomes permanent memory. Each time we repeat it, we retain 30% *of what was forgotten* the previous day, retaining about: 30% on day one, then 51% by day two, then 66%, then 88%, then 92%, then 94%, and finally 96% by day seven, making it available for future reference. When not sufficiently fortified, some of the mid-term memories will fade away, which is why we can only partially remember. For example, we may only remember, "Four score and seven years ago…uh…conceived in liberty and dedicated to the proposition…uh…all men are created equal…uh…" Should we recite the Gettysburg Address piecemeal every month or so it will take much longer to create long-term memories of the entire address.

All good things must come to an end

π The rest of this section has much technical information, *but you can handle it.*

Hippocampal strengthening of mid-term memories into long-term memories during sleep can last for up to two years,[1] after that, the hippocampus gives up—why—we don't exactly know. The answer may lie in research done over the past decade [2] on neurogenesis (the creation of new neuron stem cells) and neuromaturation (turning new neuron stem cells into functioning neurons). In the following discussion, the neurogenesis and neuromaturation only refers to hippocampal neurons and not to the neurons of sensory, emotional or rational memories.

A rat's hippocampus produces 5,000 to 10,000 new neuron stem cells every day (a human's hippocampus produces less). Alcohol and nicotine reduces that number—exercise and eating blueberries increases it. The new stem cells require about seven days to fully mature into functioning neurons with dendrites, axons, terminals and neurotransmitters. Once matured, they have another seven days to attach to other neurons in the hippocampus or die off. Unfortunately, they only attach to other hippocampal neurons if there is something new to learn. If an experience is not new, we already know it and there is no reason to learn it.

I feel that the purpose of this seven-day use-it-or-lose-it window is to first build a hippocampal code composed of newly matured neurons and then use that code overnight to change mid-term memory into long-term memory. But how is this hippocampal code created? It's simple—the hippocampus simultaneously creates the code out of newly matured neurons as it and the PFC loop a 30-second short-term memory into a mid-term memory during the day. This newly created hippocampal code is then available that night to change that mid-term memory into long-term memory as we sleep.

But you may ask, "What triggers the hippocampus to loop at night?" And the answer is again simple: long-term memory is worthless unless it promotes survival. And almost everything important to our survival involves emotions. For example, if a conscientious student must learn and then recite the Gettysburg Address in front of her class the next day, fear of humiliation urges her to learn it or look foolish in front of her peers—her social survival is at stake (in her mind anyway).

You might have also noticed that when a mid-term memory is very important to our survival almost any sensory input reminds us of it during the day, rehashing and fortifying that mid-term memory throughout the day. The same thing happens overnight when any brain activity—dreams, sensory input, etc.—triggers that emotional memory, which triggers that hippocampal code, which replays that mid-term rational memory. This fortification may involve one excitation of that hippocampal code and the triggering of that mid-term memory, or it may involve many excitations. For many excitations, producing many fortifying hippocampal loops, the process is probably the same looping process that occurs while awake. That is, the hippocampus plays its code through the intimately close thalamus, exciting the sensory memories that excite attached mid-term memories that excite the

PFC, which re-triggers the hippocampus to loop again until distracted by similar memories that make it go off on another train of thought.

Human evolution—more social than physical survival

Before human communities learned to rely on each other, physical survival preempted social survival. At the present stage of human evolution, physical survival, other than food, shelter, and being attacked—then again, how often are we physically attacked—is not as high a priority as social survival. We probably trigger most of our emotions by repetitious experiences with those close to us and thus, emotional triggers are more rational (social survival) than primary (physical survival). In other words, more emotions are *rational emotions* (rationally triggered) than primary emotions (sensorially triggered). This causes us to create more mid-term and long-term memories with rational emotional triggers. It also gives us the ability to have control that is more rational. That being said, we will now digress into the purpose of this book—personality finesse and memory.

Every time we have an emotional outburst (for example, after our spouse makes "that remark" or gives us "that look" confronting and angering us, or frightening us), that experience's emotional, sensory and rational memories become more permanent through daily and nighttime hippocampal looping. This is great for positive emotional experiences we want to relive, but can be very destructive for negative emotional experiences we'd rather forget. We can though, exert rational control over our negative emotional outbursts by consciously attaching rational memories that quell and weaken the negative emotional memory while awake, and strengthening that newly attached mid-term memory overnight—this is the basis of personality finesse.

Wired in survival memory

A final topic on memory types is the mammalian brain's wired-in instinctive emotional memory for physical survival. For example, ducking within milliseconds when an object is hurling towards our head, turning away from noxious fumes, cupping our ears for loud noises, etc., which are automatically triggered by quick visual changes, intense smells, loud sounds, etc., for physical survival. There are also genetically wired-in instinctive memories that automatically trigger reactions for social survival (see page 226).

Well, that's it for the learned (memories) aspect of our symbiotic personality, but before moving on to each emotion and its symbiotic style, it might be fun to know how smart we really are.

How smart are we?—knowledge, intelligence and wisdom

The dictionary defines *knowledge* as "the sum or range of what has been perceived, discovered, or learned," Thus, our knowledge is the sum of our memories—and the more memories we have (and the more detailed those memories are) the more knowledge we have, making every one of us knowledgeable to some extent—we all have memories.

The dictionary defines *intelligence* as "the capacity to acquire and apply knowledge." Thus, we have the capacity to act more intelligently, the more knowledge (detailed memories) we acquire, but only if we *apply* that knowledge. But apply it to what? Apply it to our survival, what else! Thus intelligence, as nature intended, is our capacity to survive physically and socially. We're all intelligent, but the better we react with our knowledge to survive physically and socially the more intelligent we are. Of course, we all have our own acquired definition of survival and thus, we're all intelligent if we react to attain *that* level of survival—as long as we have accurate knowledge—this brings us to "wisdom."

The dictionary defines *wisdom* as "an understanding of what is true, right, or lasting; insight"—with the definition of *insight* being "the capacity to discern the true nature of a situation." Thus, wisdom requires that our knowledge be an accurate (true, right, lasting) representation of what is, assuring that our appropriate, intelligent reactions guarantee our survival.

So, how smart are we? That's a trick question since the definition of *smart* is "characterized by sharp, quick thought." It is the reaction *speed* at which we apply our knowledge more than the wisdom or propriety that we react with. It means that we give relevant snappy comebacks—this must be why we call someone a "smart-aleck" or words to that affect.

REFERENCES Interpreted as Support for My Conclusions:
1. Rita Carter, *Mapping the Memory,* (Ulysses Press, 2006)
2. Tracy J. Shores, "Saving New Brain Cells," *Scientific American*. March 2009. 47-54

Chapter 4
Sorrow and its Symbiotic Relator Style

Sorrow and the Relator Style
Inner-World of the Relator Style—*Maintaining Connections*
Outer-World's View of the Relator Style

If *YOU* are a Strong Relator

F I N E S S I N G   S O R R O W

When you express *sorrow*...
Identify the real disconnection...

Your sorrow will disappear and...
You will know whether the disconnection is
real or erroneous!
You will be free to think and act otherwise!
You will react more appropriately!

Eventually...

Your erroneous disconnections will lessen!
Your sorrows will no longer control you!
You will annoy others less!
You will enjoy a better life!

There is less happiness in a sorrowful life!

Sorrow and the Relator Style:

Survival of the disconnected

Our connections represent every person, thing, concept, etc., that is important to us—every permanent memory that we have. They are how we identify and prioritize the outer-world, storing our note-worthy (maybe that should be memory-worthy) experiences and ignoring all else—nothing else exists for our inner-world. Thus, we must maintain our connections for our survival, especially our connections to family, food, shelter, home, livelihood, etc., (which is where Maslow's hierarchy of needs kicks in). When disconnected from them our physical and social survival is at peril.

The prefix "dis" refers to "being deprived of" or "the absence of," and thus, *dis*connection is when we're deprived of our connections and deprived of our lifeline to the outer-world that sustains us. For example, if as a child we lose our parents they are no longer available to help us to physically and socially survive—if our home burns down that physical connection is gone.

We must maintain this tether to the outer-world to physically and socially survive. To maintain our present connections we need to know when we disconnect from them—the purpose of sorrow is to use our sensory and emotional memories "to alert us to these disconnections." Once alerted we need to rationally identify and repair it—the purpose of the relator style is "to maintain our connections" by repairing our disconnections with rational reactions that are dictated by our relator memories.

Together, sorrow and the relator style have a symbiotic relationship that helps us to stay connected for our survival—the *sorrow-relator symbiotic cycle*. When we sense disconnection, emotional memories trigger sorrow and relator memories that identify the disconnection's cause—one symbiotic cycle. If not identified, sorrow is re-expressed, exciting new sensory data and other relator memories to try to identify the disconnection, causing another sorrow-relator symbiotic cycle—many symbiotic cycles may be required to identify the disconnection. Once the alert's cause is identified, the PFC (pre-frontal cortex) turns off the sorrow and instantly records the experience as a new relator memory made up of sensory, sorrow, and other rational memories chronologically attached to past memories of similar situations. See the diagram on the next page.

π   This technical "symbiotic cycle" diagram should be familiar to you by now.

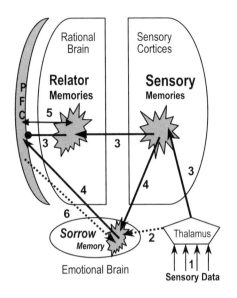

Sorrow/Relator **Symbiotic Cycle**

1. The thalamus receives sensory data.

2. Scant sensory data *preconditions* a sorrow memory in 20 milliseconds (ms).

3. The sensory memories excite attached relator memories that are made available to the PFC (Pre-Frontal Cortex).

4. Sensory memories then excite the sorrow memory in 60 ms, creating a sorrow alert that focuses the attention of the PFC on the excited relator memories.

5. The PFC uses attached sensory and relator memories to identify the disconnection.

6. If identified, the PFC quells the fear; but if not, the symbiotic cycle repeats until the danger is identified (sorted out).

For example, when we say or do something that upsets someone close to us, we can sense it from their facial expression or whatever; those sensory memories excite emotional memories that trigger our sorrow. Those sensory memories also excite relator memories that the PFC uses to identify the cause of the disconnection (what we said or did). If there is no disconnection, all is well, but if disconnected the PFC uses the attached relator memories and others to reconnect. Those relator memories may include apologizing, supporting the other person's needs, or saying or doing whatever is necessary to reconnect as in the diagram above.

Disconnection is such sweet sorrow

Throughout life, strong relators build a substantial number of sorrow memories in the emotional brain and relator memories in the rational brain. The frontal cortex stores these relator memories by recording each new sorrow-triggered experience and how the relator style dealt with it; it may also reference relator memories of previous similar experiences. Once we create this newly recorded relator memory, we can later reference it with or without triggering sorrow.

When we are naturally weak in sorrow, we have few sorrow memories to detect disconnection and few relator memories to identify the disconnection and reconnect with—but that doesn't mean that we're devoid of sorrow and relator memories. We all have repetitive home and work situations and we all have sorrow and relator memories that deal with them. For example, at work we use our sorrow and relator memories to maintain connections with co-workers. We may also have customer, client or patient connections, depending on our profession, and maintain connections with them. Most importantly, we have our family connections to maintain, probably using an even greater store of sorrow and relator memories than we have for work connections.

Thus, weak relators have sorrow and relator memories to maintain necessary relationships, but probably not at the level that they would prefer. Also, many weak relators, especially strong directors, would probably feel foolish expressing a lot of sorrow, although, sorrow doesn't always herald disconnection.

Disconnection is such erroneous sorrow

Just because we express sorrow, it doesn't mean that we're disconnected—the disconnection can be erroneous. A strong relator's sorrow alert has a hair-trigger that senses disconnection when none exists. This can be embarrassing to the strong relator and annoying to others. For example, a strong relator may sense erroneous disconnection from a co-worker who is upset about personal problems not related to their present situation. The strong relator would feel disconnected from the co-worker and try to reconnect by asking inappropriate personal questions, only to confuse or frustrate the co-worker and distract all from the present task.

When expressing sorrow from erroneous disconnection we need to consciously identify it as erroneous to quell the sorrow and move on. And the more erroneous similar disconnections we *consciously* identify to quell the sorrow, the quicker we will be able to identify them in the future. Eventually these erroneous disconnections will be *unconsciously* identified and quelled, allowing us to better interact with others or work on and complete our tasks, instead of trying to reconnect with someone that we're not disconnected from.

Indifference is no such sorrow

Not all disconnections are clearly real or erroneous with either strong or no sorrow, there are gray areas when we express mild sorrow. Strong sorrow alerts us to erroneous or obvious disconnection from someone or something important to us, but *indifference* can produce *mild* sorrow to alert us to *possible* disconnection.

Once alerted, the relator memories try to identify the indifference (one symbiotic cycle); if not identified mild sorrow is re-expressed and other sensory and relator memories try to identify the indifference in another symbiotic cycle. Once we identify the indifference the relator style may reconnect if disconnected or move on if not disconnected.

For example, if we are a strong relator and meet an old colleague that we haven't seen in many years and he acts indifferently towards us, we express mild sorrow. We then access relator memories about him to see if there was a previous disconnection. When we find none, we express mild sorrow, triggering relator memories that remind us that we now look very different since we lost all that weight and cut our hair—this identifies the reason for the indifference and quells the sorrow. We then react by saying hello and mentioning our name and previous employer, receiving a smile of recognition from the old colleague; from then on, we maintain that connection as we catch up on each other's lives.

And no sorrow is the sweetest of all

Whether our sorrow is strong and indicates real or erroneous disconnection or whether it is mild and indicates indifference and possible disconnection, it is identified by our relator memories, which record the experience for future reference along with its wealth of attached sensory, sorrow and relator memories of that experience. Strong relators have many sorrow memories, but sorrow is not necessary for them to *think* with their relator memories. For example, strong relators unemotionally use their relator memories to acknowledge their connections and to interact with them in a non-disconnecting manner.

In summary, *obvious* (or erroneous) disconnection causes sorrow and triggers the PFC to use attached relator memories to identify that disconnection and quell that sorrow. *Possible* disconnection (indifference) causes mild sorrow and triggers the PFC to use attached relator memories to identify the disconnection or not; then, it quells the sorrow before moving on. When we sense neither disconnection nor indifference, the PFC can access relator memories emotion-free to maintain connections—allowing us to feel love.

"All you need is love, love, love"

Or so *The Beatles* sang—but what is love? Love is very difficult to define in the outer-world since it is felt in our inner-world, and thus, we must define love from within and not from without.

To define what causes love we need to *inwardly view* our genetic and learned, rational and emotional personality. The genetic aspect of love is embodied in our emotions and relator style—the stronger our sorrow and relator style the higher our *genetic* potential to feel love. Some learned aspect of love are embodied in emotional memories that trigger it and the attached relator memories that identify it; thus, the more emotional and relator memories we have the greater our *learned* potential to feel love.

Two sides of the same coin—sorrow/love

It's a fact that when disconnected from someone important to us that we express sorrow. It's also been shown[2] that when apart (physically disconnected) from a loved one that our level of brain oxytocin drops. Both males and females have varying brain levels of oxytocin (and vasopressin) with females having much higher levels of oxytocin than vasopressin and males having much higher levels of vasopressin than oxytocin—similar to estrogen and testosterone levels. When referred to in the rest of this book we will only use the term "oxytocin"—π an important technical term to remember—and ignore the term "vasopressin."

We have known for a long time that oxytocin stimulates lactation and produces various physical reactions related to giving birth—we have only recently studied it as a component of emotion.

Getting back to disconnection, not only does the level of oxytocin drop in the brain when physically disconnected from loved ones, it significantly increases when physically reconnected—and when reconnected, that high level of oxytocin makes us physically *feel* love.

It is not important that sorrow decreases oxytocin brain levels with disconnection or that love increases it with reconnection. What's important is the *variance* from normal oxytocin levels that creates feelings of emptiness (disconnection) or fullness (love). It's a relief to quell the painful mood of sorrow and exhilarating to extend the mood of love, but the relator style must quell both—that's the way symbiotic cycles work. The body cannot function properly with excessive levels of emotional chemicals (hormones, peptides and monoamines) circulating around the brain, whether it causes the debilitating feelings of sorrow or wonderful feelings of love, it must moderate them all.

Love is blind

To experience love we need is to experience a *bonding* with someone, which we do every day with both established and new connections. When we meet someone new, the situation can cause us to instantaneously connect (bond) with him or her and experience love. I am not referring to the feeling of joy that we receive when returning a natural smile or identifying a possible connection (see Chapter 7). I'm referring to a bond of two entities into one, becoming of one mind and instantaneously having the same beliefs and concerns as another. Now this is scary, especially for strong directors who are self-concerned and self-directed, which is opposite to how we act when bonding and expressing love. But scary or not, strong directors have no control over it and must give in to the high oxytocin levels to become one with another when feeling love.

Stepping back for a moment—if increased brain oxytocin levels cause bonding, then what causes increased oxytocin levels? And the answer is...it is usually something we instantaneously have in common with another, a connecting thought about a shared connection. For example, long ago my toddler daughter and I were walking down a path next to a road. She was running about 20 feet in front of me, halfway between an approaching man and me. The man and I saw an approaching car, had the same bonding thought and an oxytocin rush as we simultaneously moved toward the street and my daughter. When we reached her the man expressed amazement over having had the same exact reaction at the same exact moment I did (our common connection was that he had a daughter the same age as mine).

Think about the last time you and someone shared the same exact thought at the same exact moment about a common connection—this is common among family members who share many common connections. Once the simultaneous thought occurs, your shared connection triggers increased brain oxytocin levels, making you feel as if you were one entity, followed by your relator style, which identifies that connection and quells the increased production of oxytocin.

Love you love my dog

We can expand "being of one mind" to our loving and lovable pets. Our pets are an important connection of ours, and we are an important connection of theirs. When we hold them and look into their eyes, a mutual connection bonds us and makes us feel love for them and they for us. This is probably why we feel such a strong love for our family members; they are an important connection of ours and we are an important connection of theirs—when sharing a thought we are bonded and feel love.

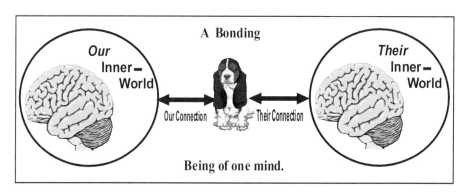

A Bonding

Our Inner—World   Our Connection   Their Connection   *Their* Inner—World

Being of one mind.

Love is conquered by all

When this shared connection is with someone close to us, we stay connected using our attached relator memories, possibly rationalizing those thoughts to extend the mood of love. But when that connecting thought happens with a stranger, our strongest style may disconnect us if our relator style is weak. If our analyzer style is strongest, we may fear this feeling as being dangerous, possibly expressing fear and disconnecting. If our director style is strongest, we may distrust this feeling and dismiss it, possibly expressing anger and disconnecting. If our socializer style is strongest, we might disconnect by ignoring their concerns/opinions while discussing our own.

To each his own—rational love

Whether disconnected or not, as wonderful as emotional love is, an *emotional* definition leaves us wanting for a more rational definition involving thoughts about our most important connections, our family or our loved ones. We have no control over emotional love (a shared connecting thought), but we do have control over rational love, which involves the rational acknowledgement of another's thoughts, making them our own. The rational aspect of love is probably what most people define as love. But, whether emotional or rational, love is described in many ways, although, it is a oneness, a shared connection making two entities one for whatever reason the two minds concur.

Loving minds think alike

Some of us rationally define love in terms of "romantic things" such as presents, shows of affection, love poems and letters, etc. Actually, this shows an appreciation of a loved one, but more importantly, it represents "mutual connections" as in the pet diagram on the previous page. Our connections to the world outside of us are the only things that exist for us. And when someone else has that same exact connection in his or her life, it creates an automatic bond between us; it makes us of one mind. "Mutual connections" create loving moments that increase brain oxytocin levels, which is probably a survival reaction that allows us to trust others like ourselves.

Not out of sight or mind—family love

Some people define love in terms of family, indicating that the love of a family member (parents, spouse, children, siblings, etc.) is special like no other, which is true, but only in intensity and frequency of sharing many mutual connections. The more time we spend experiencing life with another the more mutual connections we have, creating a greater opportunity to share loving thoughts; this is why love grows (and is experienced more often) in a lasting relationship or commitment and why a successful marriage takes years to perfect.

Some people attach to love the need for "commitment," indicating that we cannot love someone unless we are rationally committed to the relationship and avoid all that may destroy it. But our commitment is only as good as our ability to stay connected. If we do not have enough relator memories to help us rationally avoid disconnecting actions and situations, then we will probably do something that will disconnect us, sometimes permanently. Also, if we don't have enough sorrow memories to detect disconnection, then we won't know that we disconnected, negating all that follows.

Maybe it's all smoke and mirrors

Many of us would rather *not* have a reasonably accurate definition of love based on chemical variations (oxytocin) in the body that make us of one mind with a loved one. They would rather think of it in less concrete terms, which are fine, especially for those strong in the relator style. But for those of us weak in the relator style that find it difficult to express love, having an understanding of love can lead to a more loving life. We can accomplish this by finessing our relator style as detailed in Chapters 13 to 15.

It is better to have loved and lost than never to have lost at all

Those of us inclined to define love in terms that are more romantic would probably site a soul mate as proof that love is more spiritual than physical. For example, Romeo and Juliet, the most famous of all star-crossed lovers, were torn apart by their warring families. Unfortunately, things today are not that much different; family religion, race and economics continue to tear apart the union of many soul mates. But then again, many soul mates do experience a life together, although some eventually grow apart (create new but different connections), which lessens the opportunity to share mutual connections, and thus, they go their separate ways. Thus soul mates, should they exist, can share a oneness that lasts for hours, years or forever—but on the other hand maybe love is more spiritual.

Spiritual love—not out of this world

Many think that love is not physical but spiritual. As discussed on pages 4 and 5, neither the outer-world nor our inner-world exists except through the physical sensing of our connections and through our perceptible rational reactions. But things are more than just physical, there are ethereal *senses* such as telepathy, and there are ethereal *reactions* such as telekinesis.

Most of us have the ability to read the minds of others to some degree (especially family members), but feel uneasy discussing it. Very few of us have developed the ability to move objects with our minds, but some of us can. If we consider a spiritual love devoid of the physical world, we must consider telepathy as the sensation and communication link between two people sharing a mutual connection. Of course, we can believe that love is neither physical nor ethereal, but that might make it impossible to share with others, having no physical or ethereal sensation to link us.

But then again, maybe spiritual love has to do with the spirit world (mediums), which confounds the physical world altogether. Maybe love is a strong spiritual connection confounded by our natured and nurtured personality that just gets in the way, although, the *feeling* of love is more physical than not and can still be physically enjoyed. Whatever love's true definition, I feel that we can enhance it with a better understanding of its cause.

Inner-World of the Relator Style
Maintaining Our Connections

The *break up* to *make up* syndrome

Now we're getting into what most people feel comfortable with—our outer-world interpretation of the inner-world of others (refer to page 122 for terms that are even more familiar). Our relationships are cyclic: First we are connected; then we disconnect (*break up*); we then reconnect (*make up*)—only to repeat this cycle again and again. We start out connected to others, having no issues, only to experience rejection, invalidation or whatever, causing disconnection. When disconnected, sensory input excites sorrow memories that trigger mild to intense sorrow followed by relator memories that identify the cause of the disconnection. Once identified, we quell the sorrow and the involved sensory, sorrow and relator memories, along with related memories to decide how to proceed to reconnect. This "break up to make up cycle," results in the recording of a new relator memory containing all of the memories used in that experience.

Imitation is the sincerest form of flattery

We can also trigger sorrow by experiencing the disconnection of others, due to our natural tendency to *mimic* another's facial expression—especially the unique expression of the four primary emotions[1]. Physically, we mimic the emotions of others using instinctive emotional memories in the caudate nucleus (see page 227). The next time you strongly sense sorrow in another, think about your own facial expression, it's probably mimicking theirs.

Disconnection happens

The more important another person is to us the more intense our sorrow when disconnected from them. For example, a rude clerk in a store might evoke mild sorrow with their *indifference*, while our spouse shouting "I want a divorce!" will cause intense sorrow. The more intense the sorrow the lower the oxytocin brain levels and the more we are compelled to identify the cause of the disconnection and reconnect. By the way, have you ever wondered what you *feel* when you express sorrow? Sorrow makes us feel alone and abandoned in the universe, cut off from our connections (sort of like having no senses)—this is devastating to a species that requires connection to the outer-world for survival. And that's why sorrow exists—"to alert us to our disconnections"—making it painful to be disconnected from them and extremely painful to lose our most important connections.

Disconnection can occur for many reasons, but the vast majority of the time it is caused by: (1) negative emotional outbursts, (2) invalidation: rejection (abandonment or the death of another), (3) demeaning our integrity.

	Easily *Invalidates* Others	Is easily *Invalidated by* Others
Analyzer	YES	YES
Director	YES	NO
Relator	NO	YES
Socializer	NO	NO

Negative emotional outburst happens

For example, a strong director might feel confronted, display anger, and make an invalidating remark before that strong director even knows what happened. The target of the anger, possibly a strong relator, will feel sorrow and sense disconnection, compelling them to reconnect with us. But reconnection cannot occur unless *we* also stop the anger, express sorrow, identify the disconnection and reconnect with our compelling relator style.

Unfortunately, our sorrow won't occur if rationalization extends our erroneous anger, blocking our sorrow. Sorrow is rarely expressed if we are very weak in the sorrow emotion since we have few sorrow memories to detect disconnection and trigger sorrow; we would also have few relator memories to identify the cause of the disconnection and allow us to reconnect.

If I'm not validating—I'm invalidating

Invalidation is a form of rejection, a common cause of disconnection. It can be as subtle as an upward roll of the eyes, or it can be as devastating as being told in no uncertain terms how badly we messed up. Most of the time, we're unaware of how invalidating we are until confronted with it.

We all have a genetic potential to invalidate or be invalidated, depending on our naturally strongest style. The chart on the previous page shows that people strongest in the director or analyzer style easily invalidate, while people strongest in the analyzer and relator styles are easily invalidated. Fortunately, our strongest styles only give us the *potential* to invalidate or to be invalidated and we can avoid much of it if we are aware and not distressed.

If we are naturally strongest in the director or analyzer style, we must be aware of our potential to invalidate others, especially others strongest in the relator or analyzer style. Strong directors invalidate others through indifference and derogatory remarks. Strong analyzers invalidate others by imposing their opinions on them about how to proceed instead of accepting how others may proceed. There is an axiom that directors and analyzers (and probably all of us) can benefit from: "If I am not *validating* the people I am with, then I am probably invalidating them." To validate another we must acknowledge them by placing value on what they say and do.

For example, if we have people working for us who could do better, we can invalidate them by telling them what they do wrong and how to do it right. Or we can acknowledge them for what they do well and ask them how they might transfer those skills over to what they can improve. When using our people-oriented relator style we naturally acknowledge others—not so when using the people-oriented socializer style. We can be insensitive or make thoughtless remarks when using our socializer style, invalidating and disconnecting others from us—bottom line, only the relator style validates.

A major form of invalidation is self-invalidation when we unconsciously trigger and rationalize our anger, fear, joy or sorrow for absurd reasons, never quelling the emotion since we cannot identify its non-existent cause. Pages 58 through 61 give many anger examples, but strong analyzers, relators and socializers are equally self-invalidating with their absurd, rationalized reasons for expressing their symbiotic emotions.

Invalidation begets itself

Invalidation is difficult for strong directors and analyzers to avoid. Books and seminars on invalidation may help naturally strong invalidators to invalidate less, but they would be of little help when interacting with strong analyzers who are overly sensitive to invalidation or when interacting with strong relators who are overly sensitive to disconnection. Thus, the best way to deal with invalidation is to be aware of our potential to invalidate, try to avoid the rationalization that extends the invalidation, which inhibits our sorrow, clean up any actual or assumed invalidation and try to reconnect.

Consciously acknowledging the concerns, opinions and needs of others is also a big help and can create a loving moment. A periodic maintenance program can also help to reconnect and feel love—"The Relationship Game"—as discussed in Appendix D.

Do not go gentle into that good night

We all have a unique set of ethical principles dictated by on our experiences; they uniquely define our integrity. When we make decisions that conflict with these ethical principles, we demean our integrity. This disconnects us from ourselves, resulting in an expression of sorrow and a need to reconnect with our integrity.

Self-disconnection can also occur when we are dishonest with ourselves and/or don't keep our promises. Self-disconnection can occur when we don't take responsibility for our own lives and accept, or even expect, what we haven't earned (there's no free lunch). A subtle yet prime disconnection from ourselves occurs when we don't acknowledge ourselves for what we do well, belittling our efforts for not doing better. This is particularly evident in strong analyzers who have that nagging feeling that something in their process erred. Integrity is a choice, and we all choose to lead a life of integrity; it is built into our beliefs, but beliefs vary with experiences, upbringing and style strengths.

For example, if we were brought up where stealing from others was condoned we would not feel the sorrow of disconnection from our integrity should we take what is not ours. But if our beliefs condemned stealing we would feel the sorrow of disconnection from our integrity should we take anything not belonging to us, no matter how insignificant.

Conscience, thy name is disconnection

Our integrity is that sorrowful inner voice that alerts us to a potential violation of our ethical principles. When we make the right choices, for us, we *stay* connected with ourselves, and when we don't, we disconnect from ourselves. If dishonest, we must tell the truth or, better yet, learn to become more sensitive to the sorrow of personal disconnection due to *potential* dishonesty. For example, if we needed to bend the truth by omitting something that would be a gain for us at another's expense, we must be truthful. (It is all right, though, to bend the truth if it is in another's best interest.)

We also demean our integrity when we accept something for nothing (even a lottery winner has to buy a ticket); we should only accept what is due to us. For example, if a cashier gives us an extra $20 bill with our change, we should feel sorrow, realize why, and return the $20 to quell that sorrow—and probably feel love (a cheap price to pay for the experience).

The sorrow of disconnection also occurs when we renege on promises. We must keep those promises once made, even when it is to our disadvantage to do so. Most importantly, if we acknowledge ourselves for what we have accomplished and avoid self-put-downs for not doing better—are you listening you strong analyzers?—we can revel in the joy of accomplishment; there is no joy in a disconnected life.

To thy own self be true—then change

Strong directors and analyzers must suppress their potential to invalidate others, be aware of their disconnection from others or themselves, and clean up their act and reconnect. We all need to be less sensitive to invalidation, especially strong analyzers, and lead a life of integrity by avoiding disconnection from ourselves, making better choices, and giving ourselves kudos instead of put downs.

It's not whether you win or lose, but *that* you play the game

Avoiding disconnection is a major goal while maintaining our connections is a process. There are essentially two types of disconnection: ongoing and spontaneous. *Long-standing* unresolved issues that repeatedly disconnect us cause ongoing disconnection with parents, siblings, spouses, children and close friends. *Spontaneous* disconnection occurs when an issue arises that can be resolved almost instantly.

Ideally, we shouldn't have ongoing issues, only spontaneous issues that can be quickly resolved, but life isn't ideal. We all have emotional memories that trigger negative emotional outbursts, and we all have a potential to invalidate or be invalidated by others, causing spontaneous disconnection. Many of us have long-standing issues with family, friends, and ourselves that we need to resolve if we want to resolve our ongoing disconnection.

Playing "The Relationship Game" is the first step in reconnection for long-standing issues. It helps to play the game weekly for three or four weeks and then play it monthly or as needed. It is easy to play at a mutually convenient time and place when all are neither distressed nor distracted. Once together, each person needs to bring forth his or her issues with the others. When we bring forth an issue the person we have the issue with *must* listen, quelling any mental or verbal rationalization that would negate listening. Once everyone voices all of their issues, the game concludes with each person acknowledging every other person in the game by telling them what they admire about them. Refer to Appendix-D for game rules, aids and procedures.

Spontaneously heal spontaneous disconnection

To stay connected we must be ever vigilant of spontaneous disconnection and reconnect immediately. Unfortunately, reconnection may not always occur, for three reasons. One, we may not feel the sorrow of disconnection because of the rationalization that blocks the sorrow. Two, we may not express sorrow, even if we don't rationalize, because we have few sorrow memories to detect the disconnection. And three, we may express sorrow, but don't have enough relator memories to identify the cause of the disconnection, before being bumped out by our strongest style's memories.

For example, assume that our weak sorrow memories detect the upset in a loved one's face after we make an invalidating "director" remark about their not completing a task we asked them to. We instantly express sorrow and identify the disconnection of our remark, but are distracted by the incomplete task, branching over to director memories to complete the task ourselves, never reconnecting. Much of the time others are not aware that they have invalidated us; just as we are not aware that, we invalidated them. When this occurs we need the Relationship Game to reconnect.

Outer-World's View of the Relator Style

One hand washes the other

Our inner-world reacts to the outer-world we sense—those in the outer-world interpret these reactions as our personality. The following descriptions, along with the outwardly observed attributes detailed in Chapter 9 and Appendix B, should help you to better identify strong relators and to better understand how others interpret you when using your relator style. If you are a weak relator, this should match memories of your experiences with strong relators. If you are a strong relator, these descriptions should confirm what you already know about yourself.

Hear no evil

Strong relators listen intently and remember many details about us, for example, our names and the names of those associated with us, making us feel important and acknowledged. As they listen, they seem to consider our opinions very important, readily validating them by making our opinions their own. But, this doesn't mean that they're mindless, agreeing with everybody about anything; it just means that they try to understand the situation from our point of view and feel a compelling need to actively support it. Sometimes their support seems patronizing, especially to strong directors, for example, think of the last time you were with a strong relator who agreed with you when you knew that he/she knew nothing about that subject. I'm sure you appreciated the sincere acknowledgment, but still patronizing.

Speak no evil

You might have noticed that strong relators speak in an inflective and indirect manner, probably to avoid offending us and causing disconnection. Relators use up and down inflection to show emotion when speaking; you have probably heard them use such phrases as "Aw, poor baby!" or "You poor thing" and the like. Although inflective, indirectness is the hallmark of relator speech. Relators tend to ask a series of indirect questions leading up to a direct question to "feel us out." Once they are sure that we won't be upset they ask the direct question, otherwise they don't ask it, leaving us in a quandary with their "never mind, it wasn't important" parting comment.

For example, I was reading a magazine in my living room when my wife walked in and said, "Honey, what do you think of last year's summer purse?" as she waved it in front of me. Not being into her purse fetish and annoyed by the interruption, I abruptly replied, "It's OK." She then asked, "It's cloth and a little dirty, do you think I could put it in the washing machine?" Starting to become annoyed by this useless conversation I barked, "I don't really care where you put it! Why are you asking *me* anyway?" Seeing my frustration building, she finally asked the direct question, "Oh, all I want to know is, does it look good enough to take on our Florida vacation next month?" Relieved at her finally getting to the point I examined the purse and said, "If it's cleaned up it will probably be okay," after which she looked at the purse, smiled and said "Well, I think I'll get a new one anyway. I saw a purse that I liked at Bon-Ton's for only $39.95." Hearing this, I threw down the magazine, mumbled some obscenity under my breath and left the room shaking my head. Strong directors don't deal well with the indirectness of strong relators.

I never met a relator I didn't like

In summary, strong relators are "nice people" that support our experiences and opinions, but more importantly, there are survival purposes behind their reactions. Sorrow memories "alert them to disconnection" for physical survival and relator memories identify disconnection to rationally react if necessary "to maintain connections." By knowing a strong relator's inner purposes, we know that they have no choice but to act the way they do, especially when distressed; it is all part of our inner survival system.

A needed correction

You hear a lot about empathy being the basic human quality for peaceful coexistence. However, it is the relator style that motivates us to become one with others that the outer-world views as empathy. We can't learn to be more empathetic, but we can learn to use our relator style more.

REFERENCES Interpreted as Support for My Conclusions:

1. Rita Carter, *Mapping the Mind,* (U of CA Press, 1999)

2. Eric E. Nelson and Jaak Panksepp, "Brain Substrates of Mother Attachment: Contributions of Opioids, Oxytocin, and Norepinephrine," *Neuroscience & Biobehavioral Reviews. 22* (3). 1998. 437-452

Chapter 5
Anger and its Symbiotic Director Style

Anger and the Director Style
Inner-World of the Director Style—*Getting Resolution*
Outer-World's View of the Director Style

If *YOU* are a Strong Director

**F
I
N
E
S
S
I
N
G

A
N
G
E
R**

When you express anger...
Identify the real confrontation...

Your anger will disappear and...
You will know whether the confrontation is *real* or erroneous.
You will be free to think and act otherwise!
You will react more appropriately!

Eventually...

Your erroneous confrontations will lessen!
Your anger will no longer control you!
You will think better of others!
You will think better of yourself!

There is little happiness in an angry life!

Anger and the Director Style

Surviving our confrontations

The purpose of anger is "to alert us to confrontation" to physically survive, and the purpose of the director style is "to get resolution" as we socially survive by monitoring our anger. Together they form the anger-director symbiotic cycle that helps us to identify confrontation and resolve situations that are important to our survival, as in the diagram below.

When we sense anything that may herald confrontation, emotional memories trigger anger, which triggers the director style to use attached memories to identify that confrontation—one symbiotic cycle. If not identified, anger is re-expressed and new sensory data and attached director memories try to identify the confrontation—it may take many symbiotic cycles to identify the confrontation. Once identified, the PFC (pre-frontal cortex) turns off the anger and instantly records the experience as a new director memory made up of that experience's sensory, anger, and other rational memories chronologically attached to past memories of similar situations.

π   This technical "symbiotic cycle" diagram should be familiar to you by now.

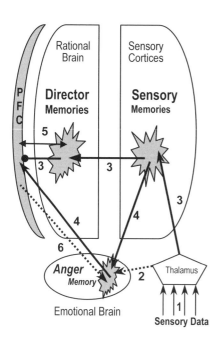

***Anger/Director* Symbiotic Cycle**

1. The thalamus receives sensory data.
2. Scant sensory data *preconditions* an anger memory in 20 milliseconds (ms).
3. The sensory memories excite attached director memories that are made available to the PFC (Pre-Frontal Cortex).
4. Sensory memories then excite the anger memory in 60 ms, creating an anger reaction that focuses the attention of the PFC on the excited director memories.
5. The PFC uses attached sensory and director memories to identify the confrontation.
6. If identified, the PFC quells the anger; but if not, the symbiotic cycle repeats until the confrontation is identified and the anger quelled.

56

A working example

Many times, we are distressed about completing an important task that requires information from someone remiss in providing it; this confronts us and provokes our anger. If we *rationalize* that anger, using director memories of that person letting us down in the past, we waste time provoking even stronger anger instead of identifying what's confronting us. Eventually, after another rationalization or two of erroneous elevated anger, director memories are accessed that identify the confrontation as this person's fear of providing us with inaccurate information. This frees up our PFC to quell the anger and record a new director memory containing the sensory, emotional and rational memories of that experience, including the rational reaction that resolved it. The resolution might be accessing that person's computer file containing the desired information and determining its accuracy for us. This group of sensory, emotional and director memories of this entire experience is now available for future reference to identify similar confrontation and resolve similar situations. And the more experiences we have the more resolutions we have to reference, making future occurrences more effectively resolved, which for the above example might be going directly to that person's files for the information desired.

Anger is an alert—not a reaction

It's weird that the purpose of anger is "to alert us to confrontation"; most people think that the purpose of anger *is* confrontation. True, when angered the *rational* choice may well be to physically assail, but that is rationally determined—unfortunately at times by rationalization. The purpose of anger (the released of brain chemicals, with its telltale facial expression) is to *alert* our rational brain and physically prepare us to decisively react. Anger is *not* the reaction that others judge us by; anger isn't a reaction at all—it's an alert. The *reaction* that the outer-world observes is rational and requires director memories to determine how to react. These director memories are our experiences, mostly about how we reacted the last few times that that situation occurred. And the more experiences we've had with a situation the more rational choices we have to decide how to react.

Bottom line, the purpose of anger is "to *alert* us to confrontation" so that our rational brain can decide how to deal with it and react—but what is confrontation?

Confrontation is ubiquitous

Other than a verbal or physical attack, confrontation comes in many forms, especially to strong directors who have a hair-trigger anger response and many anger memories to detect every conceivable type of confrontation, whether real or erroneous. An example of real confrontation is stepping into a crosswalk as a truck bears down on us with no sign of stopping, provoking our anger and rationally identifying the source of confrontation as being hit; we resolve the situation by quickly stepping back and cursing the driver as he speeds by. A less hazardous example is the confrontation of a noisy leaky faucet that we've ignored for weeks, confronting us to identify the leak and fix it. Things that keep falling over confront us, for example, books that keep falling off the shelf—have I made my point yet? No? Strong directors that are very organized have a place for everything and keep everything in its place, making it readily available when needed. When that needed object is not in its proper place, it confronts us, triggering our anger and rationalization by blaming others until we find it.

When playing games, strong directors are confronted by other players who also want to win, making them mildly to strongly angry when they lose, but this is just self-confrontation. Although ubiquitous, self-invalidation causes most of the confrontation perceived by the inner-world of strong directors.

Self-invalidation—a Hydra

Self-invalidation, like the Hydra, has many heads to lop off, and it will take a Herculean effort to eradicate them. Thus, it is important for strong directors to identify their many self-invalidations if they expect to rid themselves of their erroneous confrontation and anger. The following examples of self-invalidation should help to identify and eliminate yours.

Self-invalidation—self-confrontation

Self-invalidation causes other people's opinions to confront us. For example, a spouse's off-hand comment about where to go on vacation confronts us if we've already decided where *we* want to go. And should we allow our anger to elevate through rationalization, by remembering how he/she supposedly spoiled it for us in the past, we'll become enraged. By avoiding rationalization we can realize that the anger is due to the self-invalidation of our *self-directed* "don't tell me what to do" or *self-concerned* "only my concerns count" *attributes* (see page 117) and not a vindictive spouse.

58

Self-invalidation—second guessing ourselves

Other than off-hand comments that conflict with our needs, obvious confrontation for a strong director is another person's opinion on how that director might resolve a situation. Yes, strong directors are willing to listen to others when they have no solution and are not distressed, but directors rarely lack resolution. So, when they have already worked out a solution, they feel confronted when someone offers another, especially when the strong director has to do all the work. For example, if I'm going to do all the driving to another city and have chosen a specific route, I feel confronted when my wife suggests another route, whether I agree with her or not—again, the confrontation stems from "self-directed" self-invalidation.

Self-invalidation—less is more

If you are a strong director, have you ever wondered why you get angry when someone brings to your attention that someone makes more money than you or drives a car or has a house or job, etc., that is "better" than yours? The inference is that society might consider them more successful than you might. Luckily, constantly saying and believing, "Someone always has more than me—I like what I have," can rationally resolve this type of self-invalidation and the anger it produces.

Self-invalidation—upstaged again

Another type of self-invalidation is when we speak of our accomplishments and the listener tries to top us with something of their own, dismissing our accomplishments and thus, invalidating us—but they aren't, we are. We can deal with this all to common self-invalidation by telling ourselves, "They're not trying to belittle my experience they're just relating an experience of their own." Of course, if they're obviously trying to upstage us, they *are* invalidating us, but we should pity them instead of becoming angry.

Self-invalidation—don't look a gift horse in the mouth

Having problems accepting birthday, Christmas, etc., gifts? The reason is probably self-invalidation. Instead of graciously accepting a heartfelt gift from another, we think, "Where do they come off thinking that they're better than me, telling me what I need?" Again, the confrontation stems from the self-directed "don't tell me what to do" self-invalidation. What are your self-invalidating thoughts when receiving gifts—absurd and hurtful aren't they?

Self-invalidation—the green-eyed monster

My wife works with a strong director that resents another co-worker who has been there twice as long and makes more per hour. When compelled to interact on patient treatment the strong director spends more time rationalizing her anger about the higher-paid co-worker than she does getting their team tasks accomplished. But the strong director shouldn't feel confronted as being of lesser value because she makes less, since she does excellent work and knows it. To resolve this strong director's anger problem with her co-worker she needs to identify the confrontation as erroneous self-invalidation, accept that the pay scales are union-controlled and that longevity plays an important roll, and realize that she is just as important as her more highly paid co-workers. And when she consciously realizes this, instead of rationalizing her anger every time she interacts with a higher-paid co-worker, the anger will be consciously quelled, become less and less with each non-rationalized experience, eventually being unconsciously quelled.

Self-invalidation—self-deluding

Another example of self-invalidation involves my anger. One day I explained to my wife how self-invalidation causes the majority of a strong director's anger. Moments later, annoyed by my seemingly angry mood she asked me why I was angry. As I realized that I *was* slightly angry, she asked me "Well then, what self-invalidation is causing it since you seem to think that it causes most of your anger?" Caught unaware, I rationalized—I said that I was confronted by other published writers who I felt had little to say yet got published again and again. Noticing that my subtle anger elevated, she asked me again, "What self-invalidation is *really* causing it?" After a moment I responded with the fact that I had been researching and writing this book for 12 years, that it is about 98% complete, and that it still may not be good enough to publish because I might have missed something important—invalidating my work and thus myself. Once I identified that self-invalidation (I may not be a good enough researcher/writer), the anger noticeably disappeared. I then made a commitment to go with what I had, not be afraid that I may have missed something, and complete this book.

Self-invalidation—a driving force

On a positive note, self-invalidation is probably the major element in a strong director's drive to succeed. When a strong director feels outdone at something he or she is proficient at, he or she is driven to do even better—

whether he or she succeeds or not is another story. Think about the times you thought you were doing well at something, only to be obviously outdone by another—didn't that make you angry and motivated to try and outdo them?

Self-invalidation—it's erroneous

If you are a strong director the one thing you should carry away with you from this book is that "most of my anger probably stems from self-invalidation"—another is "Self-invalidation is erroneous." Yes, someone may belittle, degrade or even humiliate us, confronting us and justifiably triggering our anger, but that is rare in comparison to how much *we* invalidate (nullify, dismiss as unimportant, vitiate, etc.) ourselves, causing mild to strong anger. Erroneous director self-invalidation is as real as it is unnecessary, confronting us when no confrontation exists.

I came, I saw, I confronted

Other than erroneous inner-world confrontation caused by self-invalidation, strong directors are probably the greatest source of confrontation detected by others. Directors by nature invalidate others causing confrontation in other directors. But, invalidated relators, socializers and analyzers don't usually feel as confronted. Relators usually feel disconnected, analyzers usually feel they've erred, and socializers usually ignore it.

If you are a strong director, think about how many times you invalidate others throughout the day. This is difficult to do since you probably don't consider your typical interactions as confronting. To help you to better understand, identify every time *you* feel confronted (become angry) and identify how that person confronted you. Once identified, you'll know what you do to confront others—exactly what they do to you.

For example, if you ask someone for directions and they are rude, think about how you react when someone asks you a question when you were in a hurry or distressed. The more you identify how others confront you the more you'll identify how you confront others. In doing so, your confrontation of others will lessen as you see it from their point of view, eventually making your rational reactions more considerate of others. The "fly on the wall" technique might also help you to see how confronting people can be.

61

For example, if you see someone cutting in front of another you can understand that the rude person was confronting and that the person cut off was confronted. I find that it helps me to be less confronting if I think of how I am confronting others *before* I react. For example, if I'm in a hurry and feel a need to cut off another driver, I now think of how confronting it would be to the other driver, thus suppressing my cut off urges.

Identifying erroneous confrontation is half the battle

There are many other examples of what confronts us, and you might find it helpful to make your own mental list as you feel confronted daily. This will allow you to identify your confrontation as real (the confrontation exists) or as erroneous (there is no confrontation) to quell your anger. And once you put your anger into prospective, you'll realize that much of your confrontation is erroneous, except for mild anger—when hindered.

Hindrance—the lesser confrontation

Strong anger—as opposed to extreme anger on page 109—alerts us to confrontation, while mild anger alerts us to *hindrance*. For example, a tangled fishing line or electrical cord that needs to be unraveled before continuing is a hindrance. Things that catch on other things hinder us; for example, when we hook our clothing on something it's a hindrance. Other hindrances include approaching a cabinet or refrigerator, or heading for the bathroom, and having someone get there a split second before us, making us wait. Need more examples? Stop signs and stoplights hinder us, as do slow drivers and large trucks or buses blocking our view, not to mention icy roads. Poor whether conditions such as blinding snow and rain can hinder our completion of outside projects or delay an outdoor activity—in general, most of our anger is mild and caused by hindrances.

Most of the time, we can identify the hindrance and quell the mild anger realizing that we can do nothing about it, but sometimes rationalization elevates that hindrance to confrontation, elevating our anger from mild to strong, maybe even rationalizing it to rage. For example, a stopped truck may hinder us when we can't see what's going on; after too long that hindrance becomes confronting, elevating our anger and making us blast the horn or do something stupid like cutting somebody off to get around the truck, only to embarrassingly screech to a halt for a stopped school bus unloading a child in a wheelchair.

A tempest in a teapot

Hindrances that cause mild anger can elevate to strong confrontation and rage. For example (oh boy, another car example!), if stuck in the left lane behind a slow-moving car whose driver is afraid to pass a truck in the right lane going up a hill, we become annoyed since it hinders our progress. But after sufficient time the car still doesn't pass the truck or pull in behind it, we feel confronted, express anger and blast our horn. That may cause the fearful driver to feel confronted and "give us the bird" and a dirty look, enraging us. We thus, go around them on the shoulder, cut them off and break in front of them, causing them to swerve as we speed off—such is road rage.

Many things hinder strong directors, but they typically deal with them in an acceptable manner unless rationalization elevates hindrance to confrontation, provoking stronger anger and maybe even elevating to rage.

Time wounds all heels

Have you ever wondered why deadlines evoke your anger? It's because you have a goal and a short period of time to attain it and thus, anything that gets in the way of attaining that goal—which is *everything*—hinders you, causing mild anger. If there is no deadline you can work at your leisure and distractions can be absorbed in the extra time allotted, not making them hindrances. But, for example, when late for an airline flight everything that eats up that precious transit time becomes a hindrance and provokes our anger—and the less time we have the stronger our anger, making us feel like a heel when we arrive at the terminal with a carload of upset passengers.

Past confrontations hijack our brain

Throughout life, strong directors build a significant store of memories that detect confrontation or hindrance and attach newly created director resolution memories to them. The slightest sensory input can trigger this large, ever-present store of anger and director memories that typically have nothing to do with the present situation.

For example, someone wearing unusual cologne may have rudely belittled us; years later the smell (sense) of that cologne can trigger the anger memory of that invalidating experience. The anger is real, but the confrontation causing it is erroneous, which is nice, but we still have to identify the real experience as the cause of the confrontation to quell that anger. Unfortunately, we project that anger on the present situation, rationalizing whatever might seem confronting at the time, frustrating ourselves and increasing the anger (likely) until distracted or until we identify the real confrontation from years ago (unlikely). Erroneous confrontation from forgotten experiences can hijack our rational brain and threaten our physical and social survival— we must identify the real confrontation to regain rational control.

The distress before the storm

As a strong director, we have many situations that hinder us and many other situations that confront us. Hindrances and mild anger are easy to identify and quell for appropriate resolution, unlike strong anger due to confrontation. One key for maintaining control is to not allow hindrance to elevate to confrontation, which occurs when we are distressed. Being distressed primes our anger, making what hinderers us quickly confront us, producing stronger anger and possibly rage. For example, it is hindering when we can't find our car keys, but if we're distressed because we're late and need to catch a plane; that hindrance elevates to confrontation and strong anger, possibly yelling at or blaming others for the keys that we misplaced.

Making mountains out of mole hills

There are also insidious stressors that automatically elevate hindrances to confrontation, such as nagging physical pain (hindering us from doing certain tasks). For example, I had a pinched vertebral nerve causing pain and numbness in my left shoulder and arm, which lasted through months of physical therapy. During that time, the simplest hindrance would cause strong anger, even rage at times. Instead of consciously finding its cause I would unconsciously rationalize the anger—I needed to take my own advice and find out what was confronting me.

One day my wife made an annoying remark (all couples annoy each other from time to time), which I would normally identify as "the usual" to quell my mild anger—instead I rationalized and thus, elevated the anger. Fortunately, I caught myself, gained rational control and tried to identify the cause; the anger was erroneous because her remark couldn't have been that confronting. I thought about it and realized that my chronic pain was triggering the strong anger—that identification instantly quelled my anger. Days later I noticed the absence of that nagging anger and also noticed having more loving moments with her, which had been missing those many weeks. I was amazed that by simply identifying the cause of my anger that it disappeared, even though the nagging pain persisted.

Consciously identifying the cause of our confrontations is a very powerful tool, for it instantly quells our anger. It is also a powerful tool for helping to consciously quell future anger. For example, for weeks after realizing that my chronic pain caused distress, I would question whether any new anger was due to that distress or to real confrontation. Bottom line, the physically hindering chronic pain caused mild anger that I had to consciously control to keep it from elevating to strong anger or rage.

Identify hindrance to help others

Identifying a hindrance can also help others, for example, one day my wife notified me that our daughter had to leave immediately to meet her friends, hindering me from completing something I had planned to finish before taking her, expressing mild anger. As I was leaving, my wife asked me why I was angry and I said, "Because I'm being hindered!" which she instantly understood, quelling her sorrow of erroneous disconnection from me. Had I not said that, she would have thought that she disconnected from me. In saying it, I also helped my daughter. Identifying the cause of my anger instantly quelled it, allowing me to focus on my daughter and getting her and her friends to the movies instead of focusing on the hindrance of not completing my project.

It's better to have one bright thought than to curse the darkness

As angry as strong directors *can* be, most are just distant, determined, result-oriented people sometimes too sensitive to confrontation and hindrance. Contrary to popular belief, strong directors are perfectly happy resolving situations without anger, especially since it isn't necessary to get results. Director memories that identify the cause and react to anger are attached to, and easily referenced by, sensory memories of similar experiences. Thus, sensory input triggers sensory memories attached to the director memories that we use to unemotionally, rationally resolve the situation.

A simple example might be if you asked a strong director to change a light bulb. [No, this isn't a joke "How many directors does it takes to change a light bulb?" everybody knows directors work alone.] Anyway, the director uses that verbal sensory input ("dead light bulb") along with visual input (a view of the unlit lamp) to trigger interactive director memories that include visions of unscrewing the bulb and determining its wattage, obtaining a new bulb and screwing it into the lamp—before the task is even started—involving no emotion at all.

Don't get mad, get results

Confrontation combined with rationalization causes extreme anger or rage that hijacks our rational brain. Confrontation triggers strong anger, causing the PFC to use attached director memories to identify the confrontation and quell the anger to get resolution. Hindrances trigger mild anger, causing the PFC to use attached director memories to identify the hindrance and quell the anger to get resolution. When neither confronted nor hindered, the PFC unemotionally resolves the situation using director memories attached to sensory memories of similar experiences that require that type of resolution.

Sometimes, anger happens, and we can't stop it

One final comment on confrontation and strong anger: Sometimes we can't quell the anger from an experience, even when we identify the source of confrontation and momentarily quell the anger; we obsess about it for days! It may take much identification of the many possible sources to repeatedly quell the anger, until resolved. And, some seemingly resolved experiences haunt us for weeks, triggered by practically any sensory input—we just have to get through them in time and quickly quell the anger they cause.

The weak shall inherit the resolution

Those of us who are naturally weak in anger and the director style have fewer anger and director memories available to resolve situations. But we all have them since we all have repetitive home and work experiences attached to anger and director memories that we use to get resolution. For example, at work we make many decisions to get the required results using our director memories. We also have numerous repetitive tasks to complete at home with our director memories, which are more numerous than at work, making us more decisive (and angered) at home. How many times have you heard a meek co-worker describe how she "rules the roost" at home with her husband and kids? Thus, weak directors have many director memories to get repetitive results, but probably not at the level that they would prefer, and certainly not at the level required for resolving *new* tasks. One problem is that weak directors feel uncomfortable or guilty expressing anger to get results, although, anger isn't always necessary to make difficult decisions to attain results. Refer to Chapter 15 to learn how you can build your director memories and become more decisive.

Inner-World of the Director Style
Getting Resolution

Decisiveness—a survival necessity

Our decisions give us a sense of control over our lives—when unable to make crucial decisions we feel helpless, at the mercy of the world outside. When the situation is life threatening, not being able to decide and take control can scar us for life, as in the case of Post-Traumatic Stress Disorder. [1] Thus, the ability to make decisions and act upon them is not only helpful in daily situations it is vital to our physical and social survival. But making a decision is not easy when we have a weak director style, especially when we naturally renege on it should that decision have negative repercussions.

Strong analyzers renege on decisions if they feel that it caused them to err. Strong socializers renege on decisions when distracted from following up on them. Strong relators make decisions with their director style and renege on them with their relator style if they sense disconnection. Even decisive directors renege on their decisions, by replacing them with "revised decisions" should their results prove inadequate. Notwithstanding, we need to make decisions even if we might renege on them, to maintain some semblance of control over our lives in an imposing outer-world.

Decisiveness—propriety helps

Our life is a series of chronological events that we perceive, identify, and decide how to react to. We perceive these events with our five senses although; the director style uses visual-action sensory input. We make our decisions with or without anger. A decision provoked by confrontation and anger is typically inappropriate because it ignores sufficient facts and invalidates or intimidates others involved. A decision prompted by hindrances and mild anger is probably more appropriate as long as the anger doesn't elevate. An emotionless decision is the most appropriate when we need to get results without negative repercussions.

For example, we may need to complete a project at work and have sufficient time to unemotionally decide with our team how to best proceed with that project. When there is sufficient time to complete a project (if started *now*), mild anger alerts us to hindrances along the way that need to be identified, allowing us to complete the project in a timely manner. When the pressure to complete the project is too short a timeframe, strong anger from a confronting deadline makes us demand that everybody involved complete their part now, or else.

Decisiveness—requires director memories

Weak directors, especially strong relators, must use their director style to make crucial decisions, but they may not have a lot to work with. Unemotional decisions that get results are desirable, but weak directors have few director memories to decide with.

For example, if a weak director has a *new* type of project to complete immediately, they cannot access director memories of similar past experiences to quickly decide with. Instead, they have to work through their analyzer, etc., rational memories of similar previous experiences, which may take too much time, missing the deadline. Their lack of director memories won't allow them to deal with hindrances along the way or deal with the deadline confrontation, which would naturally evoke their anger. Had the weak director developed enough director memories of that situation, their anger would have more resolutions to consider and more ways of getting around the hindrances to complete the project on time. The ideal solution for a weak director is to create a new store of result-attaining director memories (see Chapter 15) that are directly attached to sensory memories or attached to emotional memories that trigger mild anger—these director memories can then be use to identify any hindrances along the way.

Outer-World's View of the Director Style

One hand slaps the other

Our inner-world reacts to the outer-world we sense—those in the outer-world interpret these reactions as our personality. The following descriptions, along with the outwardly observed attributes detailed in Chapter 9 and Appendix B, should help you to better identify strong directors and to better understand how others interpret you when using your director style. If you are a weak director, this should match memories of your experiences with strong directors. If you are a strong director, these descriptions should confirm what you already know about yourself. This understanding comes from personal research[3] and the research of others throughout the millennia.

I think, therefore I visualize

Strong directors think in a manner that gets results in using task-oriented interactive right-brain memories attached to visual sensory memories. They think that every situation requires resolution, and when seeking results their visualized thinking actually starts at the result. To do this they project themselves into the future and visualize the result. They then work backward from that result to the present and typically attain that result immediately. If the result is more cerebral than physical, they resolve it mentally and dismiss it from their mind as resolved, which can get them into trouble, as the following example illustrates.

One day I was in the kitchen with my wife discussing a complicated situation that needed resolution. During our discussion, my wife was called to the phone in another room, and while she was gone, I visualized the result we sought. I also visualized myself explaining it to her in the kitchen and her agreeing with me. Unfortunately, her call was long and I left to work on something else. A few days later, when the situation arose again I was surprised that she hadn't handled it in the manner that we had agreed upon. I asked her why, and she said that we had never decided on how to handle it. I, having a vivid recollection of the conversation, said that we had reached a decision and went on to explain our previous discussion in the kitchen. She disagreed, noting that she was on the phone and that we had never resolved it. I then realized that I had only visualized what I told her, storing that memory as the result and dismissing it from my mind as done. Just because strong directors create memories, it doesn't mean that they reflect reality.

I can't think when I concentrate

Directors think in an interactive manner, using director memories mostly attached to visual sensory memories. Unlike strong relators who store detail and procedures about people or strong analyzers who store details and procedures about tasks, directors store the *interaction* between tasks or things.

For example, if a strong analyzer has to drive to a nearby store, he/she will probably "read the procedure" of how to get there. He/she would think of the name of their street-1, then the name of street-2 to turn right onto, then the name of street-3 to turn left onto, and then the store's name-4 on its sign. If a strong director has to drive to that store, he/she would visualize the location of store-4, as if physically approaching its location on street-3 with its visual landmarks, which is attached to a visualization of the landmarks on street-2 and its approaching left turn onto street-3. Street-1 is ignored since directors ignore obvious steps to getting there. Once the entire route to the store is known, the director stores that series of memories as the route to the store (the result), as shown in the diagram on the following page. In the extreme, if very familiar with how to get somewhere, all a director needs to do is visualize destination-4. The other extreme is when a director doesn't know how to get there, he visualizes each step in the directions as given him, and once there, visualizes the entire process back to the starting point and stores that memory for future reference.

I have not yet begun to think

When directors observe something new, their interactive thinking automatically attaches new memory *interactions* to established memories.

For example, if we see a new breed of cat (a seal-point Siamese) we may think of it in terms of a familiar cat (a blue-point Siamese) and store memories about obvious differences (the seal-point is mostly brown instead of mostly white). We attach new memories (details) to our interactive cat memories to identify the newly discovered breed. We don't need a lot of details about that new breed; one or two will do to discriminate it from known breeds when we see it again. Memorizing a lot of details about something new is too much for sparse clusters of right-brain director memories.

If a director is interested in more than simply identifying something, he/she would study and store detailed left-brain memories about it, which would take time, as does the establishment of all long-term memories as discussed in Chapter 3. We all use right-brain processing for identifying (being aware of) things, whether a strong or weak director or socializer. But strong directors rely on these many interactive memories to quickly resolve situations, whereas weak directors strong in the relator or analyzer style prefer to use left-brain beliefs to *eventually* get resolution.

π   This technical diagram is a variation on the "thinking" diagrams on pages 82 and 100.

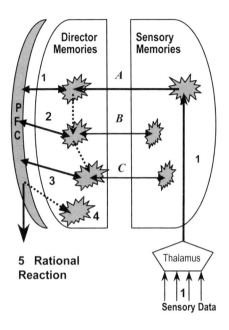

5 **Rational Reaction**

Director Thinking

1. When the director has to remember how to drive to a familiar store, it excites visual sensory memories attached to director memories (*A*) of the store's location.

2. Director memory (*A*) is also attached to interactive director/sensory memories (*B*), which the PFC (Pre-Frontal Cortex) then focuses on, which is the street that leads to the store.

3. Director memory (*B*) is attached to interactive director/sensory memories (*C*), which the PFC then focuses on, which is the street that leads to the street that leads to the store. This continues until the entire route to the store is determined.

4. The entire process is then stored as a new director memory (the result).

5. The reaction may be to drive to the store or explain the directions to another.

I never had a thought I couldn't change

The director style's right-brain interactive thinking is dynamic, as opposed to the analyzer style's *static* left-brain thinking. For example, when driving, an analyzer will see his/her car and the other cars in their present positions. When those positions change, he/she will view them in their new positions, anxiously dealing with the intervening position changes. Conversely, directors interactively view the motions and positions of all of the cars, anticipating (extrapolating) position changes from their motion and reacting to those changes as they occur, with little or no anxiety of their own, but probably causing much anxiety for the analyzers and relators in the other cars.

Extrapolation is the mother of invention

Interactive right-brain director thinking also allows for extrapolation: "to infer or estimate by extending or projecting known information." If we have past memories that A = B and acquire new memories that B = C, then we can infer that A = C. A simple example is, (A) we know of a highly contagious virus, and (B) a friend has been infected with it, then (C) we can extrapolate that should we visit that friend we will become infected.

Extrapolation can also be very creative when we have numerous "A" and "B" memories that generate creative "C" memories. For example, over decades I established many memories (A) about the attributes of the four rational styles as described in Chapter 9. After reading the work of Paul Ekman[2] and others, and drawing from my own research, I established memories about the four primary emotions (B). After a time, I extrapolated a one-to-one relationship between the four primary emotions and the four rational styles, leading me to symbiotic personality (C). Extrapolated right-brain thinking also creates music, math and art—it's the basis for everything new.

Right-brain socializers also extrapolate like directors, but about people, not tasks or things, unless it is their job to do so. Left-brain analyzers and relators can't extrapolate something totally new using old and new memories; they remember the past in detail, compare it to the present and assume that it will continue in the future. They have to go over to their right brain to extrapolate something totally new.

Do as I say and not as you say

Strong directors speak in a concise, definitive and rhetorical manner. They are concise because they ignore details, assuming that others already know them. They also assume that others share their visualizations, making it difficult for others to "read their minds," which frustrates them and others and strains what little patience directors have.

Strong directors also speak definitively, as if to say, "That's it! There's no need to consider your opinion!" Once said, they dismiss the issue from their minds as resolved. When responding to a statement they are rarely at a loss for offering a result, whether requested or not. For example, if we tell them that we have a headache, they say, "Take an aspirin!" with little thought as to whether we have a mild headache, a migraine or a brain tumor. They do not offer their definitive solutions for consideration; they expect them to be adopted as suggested. When their judgment call is proven inadequate, they replace it with another with as much finality of expression as the first.

For example, if we tell them that we suffer from migraines after they suggested an aspirin, they might say, "Then why don't you call a doctor and get a prescription for it!" Strong directors think that we're seeking their opinion to resolve a problem, not realizing that we just want them to listen. For example, if we tell them that we are unhappy with our job, they might dismiss our remark with, "Well then, quit, and get another one!" negating our need to discuss our concerns about the job. Socializers are never at a loss for words; directors are never at a loss for solutions, whether solicited or not.

Manners do not a director make

Strong directors also speak in rhetorical questions and expect immediate results. For example, if they want a glass of water they politely demand, "Why don't you get me a glass of water." This is in contrast to how an analyzer might ask, "May I please have a glass of water?" or to how a socializer might ask "Hey honey, can you get me some water?" or to how a relator might ask "If it isn't too much bother, when you get a chance, would you please bring me a glass of water? Oh, don't bother."

Asking for something and then waiting for an answer is too indirect for strong directors; rhetorically demanding and getting it over and done with is much more direct. The "Why don't you..." prefix is one hallmark of director speech. When listening to their "Why don't you..." phrases or the like, we shouldn't be irritated by the demand; we should realize that this is just the direct way they request things. Of course, proper manners are always more pleasant, but manners get in the way of directness.

If I told you once, I've told you a thousand times

When strong directors have something that they want to share, they are relentless when making their point. For example, if the discussion is about lazy co-workers and the strong director has an appropriate story of one of his/her co-workers, he/she will bring it up as if it were an epiphany. When strong directors make a point, they usually do it with such conviction that listeners believe them, but don't necessarily say so. If the strong director doesn't feel that we acknowledged the epiphany, he or she will incessantly repeat it, with numerous add-ons, until acknowledged, befuddling others who got the point the first time. The next time a strong director is making a point that you don't want repeated, acknowledge it with a statement such as "that's a good point" to quell their never-ending story before it starts.

I couldn't agree with me more

Strong directors listen to confirm what they already believe and have little use for anything that conflicts with it. The fact is they don't actually *listen* to words; they use words to *visualize* what they hear, but only hear what they can visualize with established memories, missing everything else, which makes us think that they aren't listening. To the contrary, when asking a question about something that is important to them (i.e., they seek knowledge) they will listen and attach the new insights (as new visual memories) to their established memories.

Strong directors use "selective hearing" that creates misunderstandings with others, for example, if a relator tells a director the merits of a person that the director doesn't like, those merits are not heard since they are blocked out by negative visualizations of the person referred to. And when the subject is discussed again, the director is sure that he/she never heard of those merits since he or she never stored a visual memory of what was said.

I never met a director I didn't dislike—initially

It isn't easy dealing with strong directors, but if we better understand them we can learn to better communicate with them, lessening the stress that provokes most of the problems we have with them. It is fun to know how strong directors visually think, speak and listen, but it is more important to realize the survival purposes behind those reactions. Anger memories "alert them to confrontation or hindrances" for physical survival and director memories identify real and erroneous confrontation and hindrances to rationally react if necessary "to get resolution." By knowing a strong director's inner purposes, we know that they have no choice but to act that way, especially when distressed; it is part of their inner survival system.

To know why the strong directors in our lives (important connections of ours) feel confronted and how they deal with it is much more fruitful than just ignoring or disliking them, for it gives us more insight into them and may even help prevent their future outbursts. Lets face it, if strong directors get angry with us, *we are confronting them*—we are typically the cause of their non-erroneous anger, not them! And by also knowing that most of a strong director's anger is erroneous, having nothing to do with us, we are in a position to help them calm down and appropriately deal with the situation, assuring them and us that our connection is still strong.

Chapter 6
Fear and its Symbiotic Analyzer Style

Fear and the Analyzer Style
Inner-World of the Analyzer Style—*Proceeding Unerringly*
Outer-World's View of the Analyzer Style

If *YOU* are a Strong Analyzer

**F
I
N
E
S
S
I
N
G

F
E
A
R**

When you express *fear*...
Identify the real danger...

Your fear will disappear and...
You will know whether it is *real* or erroneous danger.
You will be free to think and act otherwise!
You will react more appropriately!

Eventually...

Your erroneous dangers will lessen!
Your fears will no longer control you!
You will annoy others less!
You will have a better life!

There is little happiness in a fearful life!

Fear and the Analyzer Style

Survival of the dangers

The purpose of fear is "to alert us to danger" to physically survive; the purpose of the analyzer style is "to unerringly proceed" to socially survive by monitoring our fears. Together they form the fear-analyzer symbiotic cycle that helps us to identify danger and unerringly proceed when it is important to our survival. When we sense danger, emotional memories trigger fear followed by its symbiotic analyzer style to identify that danger—one symbiotic cycle. If not identified, the emotional brain expresses fear again, triggering another symbiotic cycle with new sensory data to identify the danger—it may take many symbiotic cycles to identify the danger. Once identified, the PFC quells the fear and instantly records that experience as a new analyzer memory composed of sensory, fear and other rational memories chronologically attached to past memories of similar situations.

π   This technical "symbiotic cycle" diagram should be familiar to you by now.

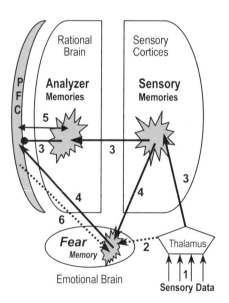

One Fear/Analyzer Symbiotic Cycle

1. The thalamus receives sensory data.

2. Scant sensory data *preconditions* a fear memory in 20 milliseconds (ms).

3. The sensory memories excite attached analyzer memories that are made available to the PFC (Pre-Frontal Cortex).

4. Sensory memories then excite the fear memory in 60 ms, creating a fear alert that focuses the attention of the PFC on the excited analyzer memories.

5. The PFC uses attached sensory, fear and analyzer memories to identify the danger.

6. If identified, the PFC quells the fear, but if not, the symbiotic cycle repeats until the danger is identified and the fear quelled, or until distracted.

In essence, sensory input triggers sensory memories attached to fear memories that trigger fear, while simultaneously exciting attached analyzer memories, which the PFC uses to identify the danger. If no danger then all is well,

76

but if danger exists the PFC uses those attached analyzer memories and other related memories to dictate how to proceed to avoid that danger. For example, if we hear a very loud noise while stepping into the street we express fear, which triggers the PFC to use attached sensory (auditory) and analyzer memories to identify that fearful noise (the possible danger). If not identified, fear is re-expressed, forcing us to look in the direction of the loud noise to see what made it, triggering the PFC to use attached sensory (visual) and analyzer memories to identify a truck riding over a loose manhole cover. The identification of the possible danger allows the PFC to quell the fear and to use all of the sensory, analyzer and other rational memories involved to react to the situation to safely cross the street. This example only required two symbiotic cycles, although it usually takes many before the analyzer memories can determine how to react unerringly.

Danger, danger everywhere—but not a risk to take

Strong analyzers seem to be afraid of everything, fearing situations that most of us would consider harmless, but this isn't true. Even the strongest analyzers can't deal with constant fear flooding their brain with powerful chemicals—their strong fear is however, overly expressed. Strong fear, when necessary, alerts us to imminent danger, but *mild* fear alerts us to *risky* situations. The fact is that strong analyzers are alerted more often to risk than to danger, storing many more risk memories than danger memories— they also store many non-emotionally-related analyzer memories.

When we express *strong* fear (high levels of emotional chemicals) "to alert us to danger," one or many symbiotic cycles use analyzer memories to identify that danger, quell the strong fear, store the entire experience as a new analyzer memory, and use these sensory, emotional and analyzer memories to rationally react to the situation. When we express *mild* fear (lower levels of emotional chemicals) "to alert us to possible risk", we go through the same symbiotic cycle as we do for danger. Analyzer memories identify the risk, quell the mild fear, and store the entire experience as a new analyzer memory. It then uses these sensory, emotional and analyzer memories, along with other rational memories to rationally react to avoid or deal with the risky situation. When we express *no* fear, sensory memories trigger analyzer memories to unerringly proceed in that situation, storing the entire experience as a new set of analyzer memories for future use. The analyzer memories recording the experience go through the usual mid-term to long-term memory process although, if not re-experienced soon, the non-emotional experience will probably fade faster than the risky experience, which will probably fade faster than the dangerous experience.

In summary, *dangerous* situations trigger strong fear, alerting the PFC to use analyzer memories to identify the danger, quell the fear, and rationally react. *Risky* situations trigger mild fear that alerts the PFC to use analyzer memories to identify the risk, quell the fear, and rationally react. If the situation is neither dangerous nor risky, the PFC uses the analyzer memories attached to the sensory memories to unemotionally react and unerringly proceed.

Discretion is the better part of valor

Strong analyzers build a significant store of sensory, fear and analyzer memories to regulate their lives. They store their analyzer memories in the frontal cortex (experiences) and temporal cortex (words). When we are naturally weak in fear and the analyzer style, we have few fear memories stored in the amygdala and few analyzer experiences stored in the frontal cortex—this reduces our ability to detect and appropriately react to danger or risk. The fact is we all have analyzer memories because we need to precisely perform numerous procedures to make it through the day. For example, at work, we perform many repetitive tasks using our analyzer style's detailed memory sequences to unerringly proceed without fear; we also unemotionally perform many tasks at home using detailed analyzer memories.

Another fact is that we all have analyzer memories because we all have fear memories—without them, we would take too many chances reducing our probability of survival. For example, walking into a racially populated bar and confronting its strong director patrons with irreverent racial epithets is a definite way to become extinct.

When in doubt do nothing—erroneous danger

Unfortunately, much of a strong analyzer's fear is erroneous, based on experiences imposed on the present. For example, we may have lived through a car crash, with its shattering glass and whining steel being ripped apart as we slam into other objects and come to a screeching stop. Later, should we hear a car harmlessly screeching to a stop on wet asphalt, the accident's fear memory triggers intense fear that hijacks our rational brain, which is trying to identify the erroneous danger. We rationalize that erroneous fear using analyzer memories until we identify it as being from the accident or until noticing, the screeching car, which distracts us. Most strong analyzers erroneously trigger fear, which they can reduce by avoiding rationalization and identifying the true danger, which has nothing to do with the present, thereby desensitizing those fear memories and leading a less fearful less anxious life.

The only thing we have to fear is anxiety itself

Anxiety (a *fear* of future events) occurs when things are not going well and will probably get worse—it can plague strong analyzers and affects us all. Anxiety can escalate to dread (a *terror* of future events), but most of the time it's just mild anxiety that haunts strong analyzers—they feel that something that they are responsible for will go wrong and that they can do little about it. In general, they feel that no matter what they do that they might have missed something that will cause them to err—but this anxiety is neither necessary nor helpful for survival, quite the contrary.

To avoid anxiety, strong analyzers need to *consciously* identify the danger that is triggering the fear, since the fear will be re-expressed until identified, no matter how long it takes, or until the time has passed and nothing has happened (the danger was erroneous). Once we identify the cause of the danger (whether real or erroneous) we quell the fear and rationally deal with it, consciously creating an analyzer memory to record that entire experience, hopefully reducing its reoccurrence.

For example, if we have completed a task for our boss and feel anxious about erring, we can attach an analyzer memory to that erroneous fear by saying "If there is a mistake, then I'll fix it; nothing's perfect." Other attached analyzer memories might include consciously saying, "My result is as good as anyone could have done. I fully understand the parameters of the task and how to get it done." Strong analyzers, being visual-word oriented, might find it more fruitful to write this down instead of saying it. If nothing else, writing or saying this will trigger memories of possible errors to check out, and if you don't find any all is well.

An ounce of identification is worth a pound of fear

Strong analyzers with overly excitable fear emotions can do little to stop fear and anxiety triggered by erroneous danger or risk. They can, however, identify the danger as erroneous and attach analyzer memories to that experience that *consciously* quells the fear in the present, creating a new analyzer memory to record that experience for future use. And when we similarly deal with that anxiety in the future, new analyzer memories recording those experiences will strengthen our ability to *unconsciously* quell the anxiety in the future. For example, we should say to ourselves every time we get anxious about a newly completed task, "My result is as good as anyone could have done and if there's a mistake I'll fix it—nothing's perfect," thereby quelling the fear. Eventually, we won't have to say it because we'll have so many experiences of saying it that we'll unconsciously identify and quell the fear before fully expressing it.

Inner-World of the Analyzer Style
Proceeding Unerringly

One step at a time

The task-oriented analyzer style's memories dwell on unerringly proceeding when performing new or repetitive tasks. When completing new tasks, strong analyzers have an idea of what the result might be and go about gathering as many details as possible to attain that result. Because the analyzer style uses detailed left-brain sequential memories it proceeds one step at a time, creating and refining each step in the process until all of the steps are accurately completed. Should the strong analyzer find something missing from the process, he or she expresses mild to strong fear, compelling him or her to identify that danger—the missing detail and its repercussions. Thus, it takes a much more time to complete a task with our detailed analyzer style than it does with our "let's try this result and see how it works" director style.

Practice makes perfect

Repetition helps strong analyzers to attain results in a shorter time frame than it took them the first time they did it. We all have repetitive tasks that we complete at home or at work. The sensory input and analyzer memories that identify the task lay out the sequential completion of that task. Thus, strong analyzers don't need to waste time figuring out how to unerringly proceed, they already know how—this, of course, applies to any repetitive task no matter what our strongest style since we all use our analyzer style to unerringly complete these tasks. Sometimes a repetitive task is the same as before and sometimes it varies, requiring the attachment of new analyzer memories to the ones used to previously complete that task. Thus, repetitive tasks are not only easier and faster to complete, their variations make them more interesting, stimulate our creativity, and reduce boredom—as long as they don't vary too much!

The devil is in the details

The key to an unerring process is in details and the checks and balances system that uses them. Known details are considered and unknown details are discovered along the way. The checks and balances system is a step-wise process of completing a step and making sure that it is correct, then completing the next step and making sure that it compliments all of the previous steps. This continues for every step on the journey to the result— refer to page 192 (Checks and Balances System) for this analyzer process. Fear is the guide for the unerring journey, compelling strong analyzers to fully understand what they are doing before proceeding on to the next step. Fear of dangerous repercussions is expressed when they are at a loss and are not sure how to proceed, although, fear is rarely required for repetitive tasks.

The devil is in our strongest style

When strong in the analyzer style, we use careful forethought and sometimes fear to proceed without error. When weak in the analyzer style we still proceed in the same unerring manner, guided by mild to strong fear— unfortunately, our strongest style easily distracts us. But, when attaining unerring results in situations that are life- or livelihood-threatening, fear is strongly expressed compelling the use of our weak analyzer style, which keeps our stronger styles from taking over.

For example, using the preceding "frightening manhole-cover noise" example, to survive we must stay with our analyzer style until we identify the danger. Once the danger is identified (the threatening manhole cover noise), our strongest style can displace the analyzer style (for example, our overriding strong director style might find the truck confronting and express anger, identifying the confrontation as the truck not having the right of way, stepping into the street and getting run over). It is fortunate for those of us who are weak in fear that it is available to protect us should we heed its warning—that's its job! Unfortunately, strong analyzers reacting erroneously are less fortunate.

Outer-World's View of the Analyzer Style

One hand wringing the other

Our inner-world reacts to the outer-world we sense—those in the outer-world interpret these reactions as our personality. The descriptions below, along with the outwardly observed attributes detailed in Chapter 9 and Appendix B, should help you to better identify strong analyzers and to better understand how others interpret you when using your analyzer style. If you are a weak analyzer, this should match memories of your experiences with strong analyzers. If you are a strong analyzer, these descriptions should confirm what you already know about yourself.

To think, perchance to analyze

Analyzers think in such a manner as to proceed unerringly. They think in the present, concentrating on what they already know about the subject and find it difficult to see the broader view. The old saying, "You can't see the forest for the trees" refers to analyzers even though very strong analyzers "can't see the forest for the *bark*."

π   This technical diagram is a variation on the "thinking" diagrams on pages 71 and 100.

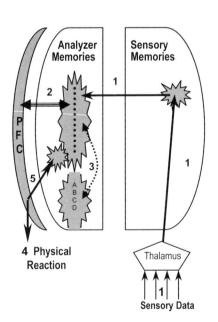

4 Physical Reaction

Thalamus

1
Sensory Data

Analyzer Thinking

1. When the analyzer has to remember how to drive to a familiar store, it excites sensory memories attached to detailed, sequential analyzer memories of the store's location.

2. The PFC then literally reads the sequential memory of the route to the store without skipping a detail.

3. The description includes attachments to language center memories for the street (A,B,C) names and for the store (D).

4. The analyzer physical reaction might be the telling of the route to the store.

5. A record (analyzer memory) of that experience is created and attached to all involved sensory, emotional and rational memories for future reference.

Analyzers think in a sequential manner, considering one detailed memory at a time. Thus, when remembering, they access one subject at a time and work their way through it before moving on to another. For example, if they think about how to drive to a familiar nearby store, they first think of their street, then the name of street to turn right on, then the name of street to turn left on, and then the store's name on its sign. This is in contrast to interactive director thinking that considers similar aspects of many associated memories simultaneously (refer to page 71).

Nobody's perfect

Strong analyzers by nature assume that simply because they believe something that it must be correct, creating most of their problems with the rest of the world who may believe otherwise. We all believe our detailed analyzer memories to be facts—strong analyzers believe this ever more so. This closed-minded thinking inevitably leads strong analyzers to view the world in terms of black and white, right and wrong. If what they experience matches their beliefs, all is right; if not, all is wrong. The many memories supporting their beliefs, even if erroneous, compel them to think this way. For example, strong analyzers who believe that Sir Isaac Newton's equations accurately described motion can't accept that he might be wrong and that Albert Einstein's equations might be correct (at least at high speeds and gravity), even when provided with incontrovertible proof.

Analyzers can't accept that their beliefs are incorrect for if they did they would doubt all of their related beliefs, which is intolerable in their black and white inner-world. Remember, we all live in our own inner-world of perception and reaction, relying on it for our survival. When a strong analyzers becomes aware of a belief that conflicts with theirs, they express fear, compelling them to rationalize why their belief is correct. And God forbid, should they ever realize that their belief is incorrect, they would have no way of effectively reacting, unlike strong right-brain directors or socializers, who have other interactive opinions to react with. This is why strong left brain analyzers, especially those who are weak right-brain directors and socializers *must* consider their left-brain beliefs as correct, emotionally compelling their conformation through rationalization.

It's like walking on eggshells

Distressed analyzers go beyond defending (rationalizing) their beliefs by forcing them on others in seemingly innocent everyday situations—this is mostly what makes them invalidating (see page 48). For example, when driving with a distressed analyzer that is our copilot, they tell us when to turn or stop before we get a chance to do it, which we had fully intended to do. This pre-judging of our actions can be very demeaning when it happens frequently. But we can live with and ignore it if we assume that the strong analyzer has no control over his or her remarks and that they mean well. Of course, constant invalidations does try our tolerance, compelling us to ask them to reign in their fears and control their remarks—unfortunately, this has its price if we have to live or work with them—causing us to "walk on eggshells" when around them.

Every analyzer is his or her own worst enemy

Analyzers doubt much of what they do; for fear that, they made a mistake. So, when *we* say or do anything that might remind them of their possible flaws, they become fearful and either rationalize and retreat or blame us for "always belittling them," instead of realizing that they are overly sensitive to nonexistent invalidation and in fact are invalidating. This is difficult to live with and the only solution is to have them get over those fears using the techniques in Chapters 13 through 15. It also helps strong analyzers to frequently, repeat "nothing's perfect" to themselves and truly believe it, when fearful of their mistakes and the possible mistakes of others.

Hedging analyzers rain on our parade

Analyzers speak in a precise, detailed, logical, one-step-at-a-time, hedging manner, rarely fully committing to what they say unless sure. When unsure of a subject they hedge, for example, if they really love something they will mostly describe it positively, but will not go so far as to say wonderful, fantastic, or awesome. When sure of a subject analyzers leave out nothing important and since everything is important, they leave nothing out. Unfortunately, their thoroughness is too tedious for strong directors who want them to get to the point and for strong socializers with limited attention spans.

Analyzers sometimes say what is best left unsaid. For example, they might make the comment, "It's a perfect spring morning with a fresh smell of flowers in the air and a sun shining through a beautiful blue sky" and then negate that beautiful thought with, "too bad it's going to rain and get colder this afternoon." They are accurate and complete; it is a beautiful day and it will rain this afternoon, but why spoil a beautiful morning with thoughts of a dismal afternoon?

Think of the last time you spoke to an analyzer who was too complete in what he or she said, didn't it "rain on your parade"? The next time you're with an analyzer, don't let them rain on your parade; give them an umbrella of hope!

A step in time saves nine

Analyzers listen to understand; they concentrate on the logic and details of the topic. They become lost when others leave out details, fearing that they cannot proceed until they understand each step in the explanation, requiring you to back up and insert the missing information. For example, when it is crucial for a strong analyzer to understand and the speaker leaves something out of their logical explanation, analyzers can't follow; they need to ask for the missing step before the lecture can continue.

Strong analyzers prefer to listen to one subject at a time, although they can handle a tangent or two off the subject, as long as they can get back to the subject quickly and get all of the pertinent details. They become confused if the speaker goes off on too many tangents, diverting them from the subject and making them anxious about getting back to it—if they can't fully understand, they would rather drop the subject altogether. Analyzers find it difficult to listen to directors, who skip a lot of detail and who tend to mumble. They also find it difficult to listen to socializers who go off on many tangents, barely taking a breath between phrases and rarely ever getting back to the main subject.

It's all about fear and correctness

It isn't easy dealing with strong analyzers, especially if they are weak socializers, but if we understand them better, we can learn to better communicate with them, thereby lessening the stress that provokes most of our problems with them.

It is hoped that the above outwardly viewed analyzer gives you more insight into how strong analyzers think and react, but it is more important to re-

85

member the survival purposes behind those reactions. Fear memories "alert them to danger or risk" for physical survival and analyzer memories identify real and erroneous danger to rationally react if necessary "to unerringly proceed." By knowing a strong analyzer's inner emotional and rational purposes, we know that they have no choice but to act the way they do, especially when distressed; it's part of their million-year-old inner survival system. And by knowing that most of a strong analyzer's fear is erroneous, we are in a position to help them calm down and deal with the situation in a more appropriate manner, assuring them and us that all is well.

Chapter 7

Joy and its Symbiotic Socializer Style

Joy and the Socializer Style
Inner-World of the Socializer Style—*Addressing Our Connections*
Outer-World's View of the Socializer Style
Style Strengths Revisited

If *YOU* are a Strong Socializer

F
I
N
E
S
S
I
N
G

J
O
Y

When you express joy...

Identify it as positive or negative...
Identify the connection's importance...

You will be free to think and act otherwise!
Your manic joy will disappear and...
You will react more appropriately!

Eventually...

You will know your erroneous (unimportant) connections!
Your manic joy will no longer control you!
You will annoy others less!
You will *interact* better with others!

Joy isn't happiness, but it can alert us to it!

Joy and the Socializer Style

Surviving our joys

The purpose of joy is "to alert us to *our connections*" to physically survive; the purpose of the socializer style is "to address our connections" to socially survive. Together they form the joy-socializer symbiotic cycle that helps us to identify and address what we are connected to, when it is important to our survival. When we sense someone or something that may be an important connection, those sensory memories trigger joy followed by sensorially attached socializer memories that try to identify the connection—one symbiotic cycle. If not identified, joy is re-expressed with refreshed sensory memories triggering refreshed socializer memories that try to identify the connection—it may take many symbiotic cycles to identify a connection. Once identified, the PFC (pre-frontal cortex) turns off the joy and instantly records the experience as a new socializer memory made up of sensory, joy, and other rational memories chronologically attached to memories of similar situations.

π   This technical "symbiotic cycle" diagram should be familiar to you by now.

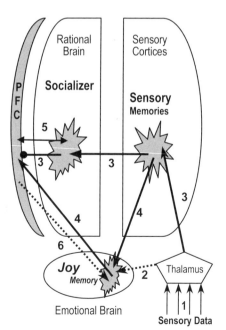

Joy/Socializer Symbiotic Cycle

1. The thalamus receives sensory data.
2. Scant sensory data *preconditions* a joy memory in 20 milliseconds (ms).
3. The sensory memories excite attached socializer memories that are made available to the PFC (Pre-Frontal Cortex).
4. Sensory memories then excite the joy memory in 60 ms, creating a joy alert that focuses the attention of the PFC on the excited socializer memories (3).
5. The PFC uses attached sensory and socializer memories (3) to identify the cause of the joy.
6. If identified, the PFC quells the joy; but if not, the symbiotic cycles repeat.

I never met a connection I didn't like

We might be going to a 25-year class reunion and notice someone familiar, expressing joy, but unable to identify him. Being unidentified, joy is re-expressed, compelling us to ask someone about that person. We learn that he was on our gymnastic team, making him more familiar, but still unidentified, re-expressing our joy. We finally greet him and ask his name, making it all come back, quelling the joy, and compelling us to mutually address our common connections as we record that experience with new memories.

Joy can't buy happiness

It is important to understand that emotionally triggered joy is *not* synonymous with happiness; it simply alerts us to our connections, which may bring us happiness once we rationally identify the connection. Any happiness we may later feel is not from joy (since it was quelled), but from love (elevated oxytocin brain levels) as we share bonding relator thoughts with that connection. It may also come from elevated brain dopamine levels when re-expressing joy about mutual connections. The perceived happiness may come from that telltale surge of noradrenalin that excites our heart, or it may come from our "reward system," which is activated when dopamine blood levels increase, as they do with joy. The higher levels of dopamine make us want to reward ourselves with that positive important connection. For a physical example, we see a delectable dish of ice cream and feel joy, identify that connection as an ice cream we really love, which quells the joy, but not the urge to eat it, and so we eat and enjoy it. Bottom line, joy is not happiness, it connects us to it.

It takes one to know many

It's obvious that joy alerts us to our living connections, for example, family, friends, colleagues, pets, etc., or even to non-living things such as ice cream, but it is also obvious that joy also alerts us to *experiential* connections. For example, we may go to a vintage car show and see a car that evokes joy, but we don't know why, which re-evokes joy and a second symbiotic cycle. We may then remember that our dad had a car just like that when we were very young—he used it to take us to the beach and to many other fun places in that car. This identification quells the joy, allowing us to rationally relive many of those positive experiences etched into our rational memories, most likely producing oxytocin and loving thoughts.

The key here is that sensory input triggers sensory memories of something that may be an important connection of ours, which needs to be identified by socializer and other memories, otherwise we are in a quandary about how we feel and its effect on our survival. This of course is true of *all* emotional alerts; they trigger a need to identify the cause of the emotion to "put our survival mind at ease" before rationally reacting to the situation to survive.

Spontaneity is in the style of the beholder

It is not so obvious when joy alerts us to our *spontaneous thoughts* about things that are important to us. For example, I'm a strong result-oriented director, and when I get a spontaneous thought that will resolve a yet unresolved situation I experience joy, heralded by a surge of noradrenalin in my heart. The surge is intense if the resolution is very important, for example, a way of handling a very complicated situation that has long eluded me. The surge is mild if the spontaneous resolution is important and under consideration, but not yet decided on. This kind of joy-evoking thought also applies to spontaneous memories of strong relators, socializers and analyzers, not just by result-oriented directors.

Emotional heart twinges alerted us to hundreds of exciting thoughts daily, although we may not be sure why, unless it's obvious. A strong relator gets joyful twinges about important people connections. His or her joy is mild if alerted to what seems to be an important connection, for example, someone that *looks* something like an important connection. The joy is intense and quickly changes to sorrow if disconnected from them, or changes to loving thoughts if connected.

A strong analyzer also gets joyful twinges, probably when recognizing a missing step in a task. His or her joy is mild if triggered by spontaneous thoughts about similar situations. His or her joy is intense, quickly changing to fear if being wrong in that situation has had severe negative repercussions.

Strong socializers get many joyful twinges, typically not mild, because of their hair-trigger joy emotion—they should ignore most twinges as erroneous. A strong socializer's sensory input also triggers many thoughts daily of when he or she made a cleaver or humorous remark or did something noteworthy.

Bottom line, all of our connections give our hearts a mild to strong tug to make us aware of them; once aware, our strongest emotion and its symbiotic rational style takes over.

A connection of beauty is a joy forever

We sense all that is important to us, all that we are connected to, whether the connections are living, non-living or spontaneous thoughts—likewise, all that is important to us is by definition a connection of ours. Our sensory memories alert us to these connections, our emotional memories *quantify* their importance (the more intense the joy the more important the connection), and our rational memories *qualify* the connection (as positive, negative or unimportant).

A negative connection is also a joy forever

It is difficult for some of us, especially those of us with a weak socializer style, to believe that joy alerts us to our negative connections—we can't believe that when alerted to someone we despise that we are feeling joy. Joy alerts us to that despised connection in tens of milliseconds; our rational brain identifies it in hundreds of milliseconds, possibly triggering strong anger, fear or sorrow, displacing the momentary joy that alerted us. Later, we usually only remember the anger, fear or sorrow and forget the momentary alerting joy that they displaced. Bottom line, when joy alerts us to a negative connection other emotions will override that joy, but this doesn't negate the purpose of joy—to alert us to *all* of our connections.

Smile for the connection

Our positive and negative connections define what is important to us, producing a joyful smile and allowing us to identify and address them. When we have a positive important connection, we continue smiling and interact as the mood of joy ebbs or as we address our common connections. When we have a negative important connection, we morph our smile and proceed to avoid him/her/it.

Don't lead with your chin

Our positive connections include family, friends, colleagues, pets, daily acquaintances, home, possessions, community, *our* beliefs, knowledge, skills or anything that we hold dear—we are drawn to these positive survival connections. Our negative connections include, enemies, things that harm or threaten us, lack of knowledge or skills we desire, or anything that must be avoided for whatever reason—we are repelled by these negative survival connections and avoid them.

It's obvious what our positive connections are; we express joy when alerted to them and express sorrow when disconnected from them. It's also obvious what our negative connections are; we express joy when alerted to them and express anger, fear or sorrow once identified, making us confront, avoid or try to reconnect with them. But nature didn't intend emotionally triggered joy to be fun; it intended it to alert us to *all* of our connections, especially when we must avoid connections that are physical or social threats. One example of a negative connection is when someone is trying to quit smoking and smells a cigarette, creating great joy and the urge to light up, which might kill him or her if he or she has emphysema or asthma.

All great minds think alike

Joy works hand in hand with the other emotions of strong relators, directors and analyzers who are very weak socializers. Joy alerts strong relators to their connections, and once identified the relator style may elevate brain oxytocin and feel love, or lower oxytocin levels if there is a disconnection, compelling the strong relator to reconnect. Joy alerts strong directors to an important task (connection), after which they complete the task, possibly triggered by anger if confronted about completing it. And joy alerts strong analyzers to identify a step in a procedure or schedule, after which the analyzer may feel fear if the situation is dangerous or risky.

I think I made my point! We all feel joy no matter how weak our joy/socializer style, to alert us to our important connections, identify whether they are positive or negative, possibly express another emotion, and decide how to deal with that connection.

Another day, another connection

We can make a list of our important connections, identifying them as positive or negative, but this would take a lifetime since we add or edit our connections every day. Our list might start with our living connections (family, pets, friends, colleagues, etc.), but it would also include important inanimate connections that bring us great joy. For example, my wife's important connections include her purses; she has scores of them in all colors, shapes and sizes, and they bring her great joy to purchase, look at and wear. My important inanimate connections include my sports cars, computers, and tools that I create things with, all of which bring me great joy to identify, own and operate. Other additions to our connections list include restaurants that provide wonderful food and service, audio and video systems that entertain us, holiday gatherings with family and friends—anything important in maintaining our lifestyle, and everything important to our physical and social survival.

A connection can be something as simple as a beautiful sunset or as complicated as an important task we accomplished or a complicated social situation in which we prevailed. Our connections exist because our sensory memories detect them, our emotional memories alert us to them, and our rational memories identify and address them. But, no matter what our connections, the degree of joy that we feel is directly proportional to our connection's importance to us.

The possibilities are endless—their importance is finite

Like mild sorrow that alerts us to indifference (or *possible* disconnection) or mild anger that alerts us to hindrances (or *possible* confrontation) or mild fear that alerts us to risk (or *possible* danger), mild joy alerts us to possible connections (*possibly* important to us). These include living, non-living connections and spontaneous thoughts, which may turn out to be important, but most of the time they are unimportant (erroneous connections). If you reminisce, you can easily identify your important connections—the fact that you remember them makes them important. It's impossible to remember unimportant connections—the fact that you can't remember them makes them unimportant. We do, though, express mild joy when alerted to unimportant connections.

To sum it up, mild joy alerts us to *possible*, but mostly unimportant, connections. Strong joy alerts us to *important* connections, and extreme joy alerts us to *extremely important* connections that can have delightful consequences (important positive connections to address) or dire consequences (important negative connections to avoid).

Once burnt twice shy

Mild joy alerts us to both positive and negative connections, but we sometimes mistake a negative connection for a positive one. For example, years ago I ordered a pizza at a conveniently close pizza parlor and recently, not wanting to drive the long distance to our usual pizza joint I remembered the convenient one and sensed joy. I ordered for pickup, and when I got there I realized how cold and unfriendly the personnel were (as before), and when I got home I realized how lousy the pizza was. Thus, my joy was alerting me to a negative connection of lousy service and lousy food, but I couldn't identify it at the time (the attached socializer memories were weak), so I figured it was a positive connection, much to my dismay. This second experience has allowed me to strengthen my socializer memories of my negative experiences with them and will be available should I ever consider that pizza parlor again as I experience joy and identify it as a negative connection to be avoided.

Getting all doped up

One research group[1], among others, has concluded that when alone our brain's dopamine levels decrease and when in a crowd they increase, citing possible reasons why—I interpret this research differently. When we are around people that we're connected to they trigger joy and higher dopamine brain levels; when no one is around to be alert to, the lack of joy results in lower dopamine levels. Also, we must consider the style strengths of the subjects tested: Strong socializers would show larger decreases and increases, while weak socializers would show smaller increases and decreases.

As an aside, much of the conflicting personality research is probably due to not taking into consideration the strong and weak emotions/styles of the subjects tested. Research needs to factor in the true personalities of the research subjects to make the research more accurate and better interpreted.

Laugh and the world laughs with you—but not for long

Joy automatically leads us to the concept of laughter, the vocal and physical extension of a smile—like when someone tells a joke. Laughter is defined as "a series of spontaneous, usually unarticulated sounds often accompanied by corresponding facial and bodily movements." But many have found this definition wanting and have tried for decades to define why we laugh, starting out with dozens of reasons, eventually reducing it to seven and finally to one—surprise—defined as "to encounter suddenly or unexpectedly."

Surprise is a *rational emotion* requiring rational thought, and when the surprise is not a physical threat there is no need for anger, fear, joy or sorrow. Unidentified surprise though, may cause fear in analyzers, anger in directors, sorrow in relators, and joy and laughter in strong socializers. You might have noticed that strong socializers laugh at surprises that most of us wouldn't; for example, they may laugh when surprised by someone slipping and falling on an icy sidewalk. They laugh because it is their natural response to surprise, even if they were the one who fell. A strong relator may naturally respond by feeling sorrow for the person who fell, and a strong analyzer may naturally respond with the fear that the unfortunate person was injured. A strong director may naturally respond with anger because the ice wasn't salted, especially if that director or a close friend fell. But getting back to laughter, we try to sort out the punch line of the joke or situation using applicable rational memories and find it so absurd that it provokes harmless surprise and laughter.

Weak socializers—are distracted by and from joy

Strong socializers create many joy memories in the emotional brain and socializer memories in the rational brain that causes them to express joy, which compels them to address that connection. Those of us with a weak socializer style still recognize our connections, but don't continue to express joy unless the connection is positive—negative connections cause our stronger emotions to displace that joy. Those of us who are weak in the socializer style have fewer socializer memories to react with, even when alerted, making it difficult to use a socializer style and all of its positive social interaction attributes.

Strong analyzers are easily distracted from using their weak socializer style. For example, we may be joyfully sharing our mutual connections with our family when we notice an obnoxious in-law enter, triggering fear of having to deal with her, based on analyzer memories of the last uncomfortable get-together. Strong directors are easily distracted from using their socializer style when they notice an aggravating person, triggering anger and director memories of previous confrontations with him or her. Strong relators are also distracted from their weak socializer style when they identify someone that they are disconnected from, replacing their joy with sorrow and the need to reconnect if possible.

Bottom line, even when we use our weak socializer style, with its attached joy and socializer memories, it doesn't guarantee that we won't be distracted from it by our stronger emotions.

Uneasy beats the heart that feels the joy

Another problem is that weak socializers, especially strong analyzers, feel uncomfortable or embarrassed using their outgoing socializer style. For example, should a popular friend enter a room and be surrounded by others, the strong socializers instantly identify him or her and are compelled to jump into the thick of it, while a strong analyzer stays in the background, waiting for a lull before interacting with him or her.

In a heartbeat

In summary, sensory input and emotional memories alert us to our important connections (people and things) through strong or extreme joy, or alert us to possible (mostly unimportant) connections through mild joy. This triggers the PFC to use attached sensory and socializer memories to identify that connection and quell the joy. Should we continue to use our socializer style, we will address those connections using our outgoing socializer attributes (see Chapter 9 and Appendix B), aided by a natural smile and a joyful heart.

Up to this point, we have mostly discussed strong joy triggered by positive and negative *important* connections or dismissed joy caused by unimportant but known connections. To be complete, we need to address rationalized erroneous joy that can cause mania in strong socializers.

Every socializer is his or her own worst enemy

Before moving on, we should address an important aspect of strong socializers—their obvious mania about seemingly unimportant things. You have probably noticed that strong socializers strongly voice their love or hatred of something giving illogical, if not ridiculous reasons why—and the younger they are the more absurd the reasons. This is because when the strong socializer identifies the connection he or she is not sure whether the connection is positive or negative, important or unimportant—this causes uncontrollable rationalization to identify the connection, escalating the joy. But, if the strong socializer can identify the connection that triggered their joy, they might better understand its importance and whether to address or dismiss it as erroneous.

For example, when my strong socializer daughter discusses a TV show she likes, she may state unequivocally that she hates a particular character in the show. In doing so, from the telltale expression on her face, she is expressing joy and not anger. She may express this opinion on numerous occasions, but when asked why she hates that character she gives irrational reasons, typically referring to how that character mistreats another character in the show that she likes—but in my opinion not enough to elicit such dislike. When I inquire further as to why she hates something and she realizes that she really doesn't know why, it seems to make that connection unimportant, dismissing it from future conversations. But, when I inquire and she identifies why that connection is important, she will refer to it in future conversations, but not manically.

Thus, by helping a strong socializer to identify the cause of his or her manic joy of erroneously voiced "love" or "hate" of that connection, they can get past it and label the connection as important (rarely) or as unimportant or as erroneous and to be ignored (typically). This would make those of us listening less bothered by that unnecessarily repeated manic reaction.

Where there's a joy there's a survival

Bottom line on joy: Our connections are our lifeline to the outside world—we need to identify them as important or not. When they are important, we need to address them. When they are unimportant, we need to ignore them. We need to do this for our physical and social survival.

Inner-World of the Socializer Style
Addressing Our Connections

Smile and the world smiles with you

What is the one thing that all humans possess that makes them attractive to all other humans? It's the *naturally* contagious smile that our joyous memories naturally evoke and that others naturally return. A natural joy-evoked smile has obvious survival value for *positive* human connections; it puts us all at ease with non-threatening connections. Since joy alerts us to all of our connections we also smile when alerted to negative connections (threats)—this gives our smile even more survival value. When our joy heralds a *nega-*

tive human connection, it instantly produces a smile that our adversary automatically returns, putting them off guard until we can make a physically or socially appropriate exit—we've all done it! Our genetically wired in instinctive emotional memories, located in the caudate nucleus of the emotional brain, give us our natural tendency to mimic the smiles of others. And, only this emotional brain can produce a *natural* smile by activating unique facial muscles around the eyes.[2] The next time someone smiles at you, think about your facial expression, it probably mimics his or her smile.

The eyes are the mirrors of the smile

A natural smile truly "makes our day" as we bask in the warmth of its positive emotional energy. Unfortunately, not all smiles are natural since *forced* "smiles of the mouth" do not contain joy like *natural* "smiles of the eyes"— it is interesting to note that we also mimic forced smiles of the mouth, which we probably force too. None-the-less, when we naturally smile we produce joy in others, momentarily making them important to us until we identify their importance and quell our joy. This may lead to a glowing smile and positive interaction with a positive connection or a fading smile and a quick departure from a negative connection.

Natural ADD

A major problem for naturally strong socializers is distraction, causing their short attention span (usually misdiagnosed as Attention Deficit Disorder). Sensory input, lack of visual focus (they tend to constantly "scan the room"), and an overly sensitive joy emotion, easily distracts them. For example, while at a convention selling my books and services to one customer, I found myself joyfully scanning the room between eye contacts with that customer for other potential customers. When the joy was absent, I found myself concentrating on the one customer instead of scanning the room.

This is the reason why strong socializers need to be alone when doing tasks; their joy triggers a compelling need to identify and address their connections, distracting them from their tasks and causing delay or incompletion. This is disappointing or annoying to others relying on them, who have to work around them or do their work for them. For example, I have a strong socializer daughter who could be neater than she is. When I tell her to clean up her room she cheerfully says that she will as soon as she gets off the phone or emails her friend back or whatever. Later, when I find her room still a mess I usually pick up obvious trash and throw it away; I then demand that she tidy up her room *now*, as I stand there to make sure she gets started. Once started and with no distractions, she gets the task completed.

It's not what you say, but how you exaggerate it

In their zeal to address their connections, socializers tend to exaggerate. This is partially because we rarely retain all of an experience since some of it never becomes permanent memory, and when recalling it we "fill in the blanks" for what was lost—we *all* do this. Socializers, being non-detailed right-brain interactive thinkers, don't have sufficient detail to supply their long-winded monologues, so they fill in the blanks with what *seems to be* or *should have been* what they experienced, feeling confident that it is correct—unfortunately, their fill-ins may conflict with the understandings of others, especially strong analyzers, sometimes causing conflict.

Do shoot the messenger

We all enjoy listening to a socializer excitedly telling a good story, even when we know they are exaggerating (filling in). But we also like to tell our own story, which is difficult when we can't get a word in edgewise, as the strong socializer jumps from one story to another with hardly a breath in between. We eventually lose interest in and possibly disconnect from that overbearing socializer, using the first chance we get to depart.

If the strong socializer were more appropriate, he or she would use his or her sorrow to detect possible disconnection and trigger the relator style to reconnect by becoming a listener instead of a talker. Then, when the other person is finished speaking, the talkative socializer can acknowledge them for their story and start talking. But, should the talkative socializer interrupt and tell his or her story before the other person has finished, disconnection will occur, and that person will probably depart.

Outer-World's View of the Socializer Style

One hand waves the other

Our inner-world reacts to the outer-world we sense—those in the outer-world interpret these reactions as our personality. Thefollowing descriptions, along with the outwardly observed attributes detailed in Chapter 9 and Appendix B, should help you to better identify strong socializers and to better understand how others interpret you when using your socializer style. If you are a weak socializer, this should match memories of your experiences with strong socializers. If you are a strong socializer, these descriptions should confirm what you already know about yourself.

Scatterbrain thinking

Socializers think in a right-brain interactive manner with sensory, joy and socializer memories as illustrated in the diagram below.

π   This technical diagram is a variation on the "thinking" diagrams on pages 71 and 82.

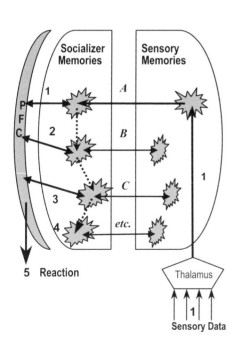

Socializer Thinking

1. When asked something, the socializer starts discussing subject **A** and its sensory memories.

2. When finished discussing subject **A**, attached interactive memories make the socializer switch to subject **B** and its sensory memories.

3. When finished with subject **B**, attached interactive memories make the socializer switch to subject **C** and its sensory memories.

4. This continues until someone or something distracts the socializer who never got back to subject **A**.

5. The reaction is the enthusiastic, excited socializer style formatting each discussion, along with a record (memory) of that *interaction*, but not much detail.

The never-ending story

As shown in the diagram on the previous page, a socializer's interactive thinking allows them to seamlessly branch from topic to topic, explaining that topic's memories before branching over to a related topic and spilling out all of its memories, before moving on, ad nauseam.

This ability also allows socializers to quickly respond to any social situation, sometimes getting themselves out of tight situations. Their right-brain interactive awareness allows them to do many things almost simultaneously, although not very well. So, when they have to unerringly proceed with their tasks, they use their detailed left-brain analyzer memories, or when they have to stay connected with people, they use their detailed left-brain relator memories.

Anything *but* a quiet life

Socializers speak in a boisterous, enthusiastic, exaggerative and random manner, using many superlatives, which help them to entertain others. It is difficult to moderate their enthusiasm, which makes boisterous socializers stick out in a crowd (it's part of the package). They're always ready to tell an inspiring story, exaggerating when needed, using words like wonderful, fantastic, unbelievable, the greatest, awesome and the like. The various topics they speak on tend to have little connection, branching off in a random and entertaining manner, rarely ever making a point. When speaking, they care more about entertainment value than they do accuracy, and every time they tell a story it becomes less accurate and more entertaining, much to the dismay of analyzers or directors who are aware of those inaccuracies, but still enjoy the show.

Time and tide wait for no socializer

Socializers feel uncomfortable when there is more than a one-second gap in any conversation, thus feeling a need to fill it with conversation. Have you ever noticed that when two strong socializers are addressing common connections that it never seems to end as they simultaneously talk, not listening to each other, mutually jumping from subject to subject? When my youngest daughter and her even stronger socializer friends are talking about (addressing) TV shows that they like, they simultaneously talk very fast and loud, jumping from character to character and show to show as they excitedly address (like children in "parallel play") those common connections.

It goes in one ear and out the mouth

Socializers listen to respond—frankly a phrase that rings in the ears of all socializers since birth is, "You don't listen!" Actually, they do listen, but only long enough to get a sense of it, as they prepare their response. Unfortunately, they usually respond before we can complete our statement, interrupting us and never getting the entire message. Sometimes they actually listen until they can speak, as they prepare their response, thereby negating a full understanding—we can't listen and respond simultaneously.

For example, when someone explains a task to them the strong socializer only listens long enough get the gist of it and then says something like, "Oh, I know what you want." and take off to do it. If the task is repetitious, they usually do it well, but if the task is new, they rarely get it right having missed some of the instructions. Their attention span is limited, typically less than 20 seconds, curtailing their ability to fully listen.

And since they listen to respond, they tend to answer questions before we ask them—they assume that they know where the conversation is going. For example, if they think someone is about to ask them a question they know the answer to, they answer the question *before* asked. It's great fun for them, but it sometimes backfires, confusing, frustrating or annoying others. Another frustration with them is their automatic responses.

Don't jump the gun

When requesting something of them, strong socializers instantly respond and then ignore the request. For example, while asking my strong socializer daughter to clean her room she automatically answers "I know, I'm going to do it now!" without missing a beat from what she was doing, as she quickly dismisses it before entertaining the thought. She never got the message since she automatically reacted with a stock phrase, involved elsewhere.

There is a way to get around this and force strong socializers to listen: First tell them not to say anything, and then tell them what you want them to do. If they speak, again tell them not to say anything and repeat the request. By not letting them automatically respond, yet having their limited attention, they are open to listen to the request, especially if immediately repeated. Communicating with strong socializers is usually a one-way situation, but with perseverance, they will hear you and maybe even do what you want.

I never met a socializer I didn't like—initially

It is easy to identify strong socializers, but it isn't easy dealing with them, especially for strong analyzers. But, if we understand them better, we can learn to better communicate with them, lessening the stress that provokes most of the problems we have with them and allowing ourselves to enjoy their delightful approach to life!

The above outer-world view of a strong socializer gives you insight into why strong socializers react as they do. It's fun to know how strong socializers visually think, listen and speak, but it is more important to realize the survival purposes behind those reactions. Joy memories alert them to possible connections for physical survival, and socializer memories identify important and unimportant, positive and negative connections for social survival by enthusiastically addressing important positive connections and by avoiding negative connections.

By knowing a strong socializer's inner purposes, we know that they have no choice but to act the way they do, especially when distressed; it is all an important part of our inner survival system. It is also important to understand that *we* are important connections that cause the joy strong socializers express, compelling them to share their joyous connections with us.

Style Strengths Revisited

Until now, we defined style strength as the amount of daily usage; unfortunately, this doesn't tell us how it came about, but two studies done on socializer strength might point the way.

π This section is a bit technical, *but well worth the effort.*

Survival of the fittest [gene]

It is a fact that the main driving force in evolution is the survival of the genome and that the genome adapts to the environment for the organism to survive. For example, chimpanzees have only one gene copy that produces the "salivary amylase" enzyme to digests starch, while humans have up to 10 copies, allowing them to produce up to 10 times more salivary amylase.

103

Taking this one step further, research has shown that low starch-eating societies have fewer copies of this gene, whereas high starch-eating societies have many copies to satisfy the greater need for this digestive enzyme. Multi-copying of a gene also accounts for our emotion/style strengths.

The more the merrier

Two identical independent studies, one in Israel and one in Bethesda, MD, produced the same result. The study identified 500 human subjects with varying levels of socializer traits from very weak to very strong. The study analyzed each subject's "D4-dopamine receptor gene," which essentially produces the "joy" brain chemical. Their results showed that weak socializers had one to three copies, whereas "strong socializers" had closer to 10 copies; moderate socializers had about four copies. Thus, strong socializers produced much more "joy" brain chemicals than did weak socializers.

The more, the stronger

The research indicates that the more copies of this D4-dopamine receptor gene we have the more excitable is our joy emotion—and thus, our socializer style. This same logic should hold true for the strengths of the anger, fear, and sorrow emotions in their respective areas of the amygdala. This simple mechanism can be responsible for our amygdala's various emotional strengths. In the developing brain, genes first lay out the amygdala's inhibitory neural structure with many more GABA (inhibitory) dendrites than glutamate (excitatory) dendrites (see page 154). Next, each emotion's gene copy (e.g., *D4-dopamine receptor gene* for joy/socializer) modifies the inhibitory neurons by adding more glutamate excitatory dendrites. The more gene copies there are the more excitatory dendrites added and, thus, the stronger the emotion in that area of the amygdala. Well, it works for me.

REFERENCES Interpreted as Support for My Conclusions:

1. Andreas Bartels and Semir Zeki, "The neural correlates of maternal and romantic love," *NeuroImage. 21*(3). March 2004. 1155-1166

2. Paul Ekman, "Facial Expression and Emotion," *American Psychologist, 48*, 1993, 384-392

Chapter 8
Extreme Symbiotic Cycles

Extreme Symbiotic Cycles

Double, double toil and trouble senses burn and emotions bubble

Have you ever wondered what causes your extreme outbursts? Some call it having your rational brain held hostage or hijacked by your emotional brain[1,3]—I call it *Extreme Symbiotic Cycles*. They override naturally healthy symbiotic cycles. Normal, noticeable symbiotic cycles start with sensory information and emotional memories that trigger a strong primary emotion that we quell with that emotion's symbiotic rational style's identifying memories. If not identified and quelled, we go through more symbiotic cycles until quelled. Normal, virtually unnoticed symbiotic cycles occur when we express mild emotions. The cause of mild fear (risk) is quickly identified and quelled by the analyzer style, the cause of mild anger (inhibition) is quickly identified and quelled by the director style, the cause of mild sorrow (indifference) is quickly identified and quelled by the relator style, and the cause of mild joy (unimportant connections) is quickly identified and quelled by the socializer style. Abnormal, extreme symbiotic cycles also occur, involving intense emotion that we cannot rationally identify the cause of that holds our pre-frontal cortex (PFC) captive.

It's emotionally triggered—quick and dirty

Emotionally triggered symbiotic cycles are best understood in terms of the time it takes for them to occur. Symbiotic cycles take about 60 milliseconds to express mild and moderate emotions and to alert the PFC to resolve something, leaving plenty of time for rational processing in about 500 milliseconds, before attempting another symbiotic cycle. Extreme symbiotic cycles take about 20 to 60 milliseconds to express an intense emotion that alerts the PFC to something emotionally intolerable. Unfortunately, the emotion does not allow the PFC its hundreds of milliseconds to rationally sort it out since the emotion is re-expressed in tens of milliseconds.

For example, our eyes vibrate at about 20 cycles/second creating new visual images for the visual cortices to process every 50 milliseconds. The re-expression of an intense emotion triggered by that vision essentially *resets* the PFC, which now has to process the new sensory data. Thus, we cannot sort out the intense emotion until the PFC can process the sensory data, which the extreme emotion is not allowing it to do.

For example, we may see a large rattlesnake a few feet away and express intense fear. We may not be able to move as we fixate on that deadly snake, watching its every move as we experience unrelenting fear that we cannot rationally sort out. Eventually, the snake bites us or the snake slithers off, giving us a chance to identify and quell the fear and hightail it off in a safely chosen direction, hopefully avoiding any other snakes.

Or rationally triggered—escalating and dirty

Unrelenting rationalization of a strong emotional outburst is the other cause of extreme symbiotic cycles. For example, someone may degrade (invalidate) us, as they have done many times in the past, angering us. That anger memory is attached to other memories of past incidences of invalidation, quickly setting off an even angrier symbiotic cycle. This will repeat and escalate to rage as long as we rationalize it, rehashing many attached memories of intolerable past invalidations. The prolonged, rationalized rage ends when it ends with whatever repercussions it creates, which is usually not very pleasant for anyone involved.

And usually impossible to control!

An important aspect of emotionally triggered extreme symbiotic cycles is that they are impossible to control; you just have to work your way through them. An important aspect of rationally triggered extreme symbiotic cycles is that we can eventually reduce them as detailed in Chapter 15. Each primary emotion has its own extreme form, which we emotionally trigger or rationally escalate; they are:

- The Extreme Symbiotic Cycles of *Terror*—involving fear
- The Extreme Symbiotic Cycles of *Rage*—involving anger
- The Extreme Symbiotic Cycles of *Despair*—involving sorrow
- The Extreme Symbiotic Cycles of *Ecstasy*—involving joy

π   This technical diagram is a variation on the diagram on page 17.

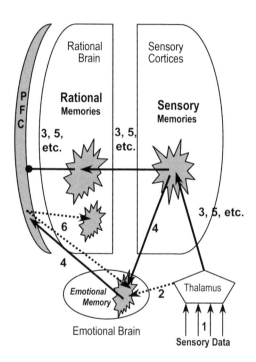

Extreme Symbiotic Cycles

1. The thalamus receives sensory data.

2. Scant sensory data *preconditions* an emotional memory in 20 milliseconds (ms).

3. The sensory memories excite attached rational memories that are made available to the PFC (Pre-Frontal Cortex).

4. Sensory memories excite the emotional memory in 60 ms, creating an emotional reaction that alerts the PFC, which requires about 500 ms to identify and quell.

5. Within 60 ms, another set of sensory data re-triggers that emotion, resetting the PFC, which again needs 500 ms to react.

6. Once the extreme symbiotic cycles end, the PFC quells the emotion and rationally reacts, recording the entire experience as a new memory for future reference.

Extreme Symbiotic Cycles of *TERROR*

Intense, overpowering fear

Fear is a primary emotion (its purpose is "to alert us to danger"); our analyzer style (its purpose is "to unerringly proceed") uses its memories to identify the cause of the fear and quell it. But, if we allow this fear to escalate through extreme symbiotic cycles, it can result in debilitating terror. The dictionary defines terror as "intense, overpowering fear." The extreme symbiotic cycles of terror involve rapid re-expression of intense fear and an elevated, extended emotional mood—analyzer memories do not have enough time to identify the cause of the fear. For example, consider a previous example of a large snarling dog running towards you.

Every dog has his prey

Assume that as a child a dog attacked you. Also, assume that you have not been in this neighborhood before and that an unfenced snarling pit bull is running toward you baring his pointed teeth. The moment you hear it your emotional memory of being mauled quickly produces an intense pulse of fear. The intense fear heightens your senses, providing refreshed sensory information that is to rapid too be sorted out, like a glimpse of the dog's position, no fence, possible escapes, but no decisions. As you sense the dog getting closer and closer with its deafening snarl, its foamy, drool-covered, bared teeth and glaring bloodshot eyes, intense re-expressions of fear trigger more extreme symbiotic cycles, almost paralyzing you with fear, unable to decide how to avoid the attack. These extreme symbiotic cycles of terror may culminate in realizing that the dog is tethered and cannot reach you, quelling the fear—or by being mauled—not all examples have happy endings.

In conclusion

Emotionally triggered Extreme Symbiotic Cycles of Terror involve intense expressions of fear that we cannot quell since intense re-expressions of fear are too rapid to rationally identify and quell. *Rationally* triggered terror caused by rationalization can be quelled with analyzer memories that identify its cause and quell its escalating fear.

Extreme Symbiotic Cycles of *RAGE*

A violent, explosive fit of anger

Anger is a primary emotion (its purpose is "to alert us to confrontation"); our director style (its purpose is "to get resolution") uses its memories to identify the cause of the anger and quell it. But, if this anger is uncontrolled, it can escalate into the Extreme Symbiotic Cycles of Rage. The dictionary defines rage as "a violent, explosive fit of anger." We can better define it here as "emotional memories that cause uncontrollable, elevating anger."

The extreme symbiotic cycles of rage involve rapid re-expression of intense anger and an elevated, extended emotional mood—director memories do not have enough time to identify the cause of the anger. The cycles of rage end after director memories sort them out, or they end when distracted by another emotion or related thought. For example, consider "road rage," which is a misnomer since roads don't get angry, although, they can have some mean potholes. Potholes aside, road rage can be provoked by someone giving us an angry epithet, "flipping us the bird," cutting us off, or when confronting a distressed strong director in any manner.

Road rage is not the exclusive domain of strong directors; weak directors can exhibit it too. For example, an oncoming car cut in front of our minivan at an intersection, threatening (confronting) our children's lives, as we came to a screeching halt inches away from a collision. My weak-director/strong-relator wife instantly became enraged as she literally hovered above her seat screaming politically incorrect remarks at the other driver. Her face was red and contorted with rage, but the rage quickly subsided as her strong relator style took over her PFC with concerns about our kids' safety.

"We wish you a merry Christmas"

Rage is not always instantaneous, rationalized anger can escalate to rage through attached anger memories that evoke even stronger anger, eventually escalating out of control into rage. For example, an argumentative family member always ruins our Christmas dinners by verbally attacking some family member; this time, to his dismay, he confronted me. His first comment angered me, but I ignored it, as did everybody else as usual. But, with each negative comment I became angrier until I exploded in an extremely loud long fit of rage that made him painfully aware that I would no longer tolerate his behavior, ever—it shut him up! Unfortunately other family members were, taken aback by my explosive rage, having never experienced anyone putting the loudmouth in his place.

If you are weak in the director style, you probably have had at least one experience in your life involving the Extreme Symbiotic Cycles of Rage. If you are naturally strong in the director style, you've probably had more experiences than you care to remember.

In conclusion

Emotionally triggered rage involves intense expressions of anger and an attempt to identify its source, but to no avail, since intense re-expressions of anger are too rapid to rationally identify. Rage can also escalate from anger through rationalization with continued intense hatred or rage until the director style can rationally identify its cause (unlikely) or until eventually distracted by some other thought, emotion or action.

Extreme Symbiotic Cycles of *DESPAIR*

To lose all hope: to be overcome by a sense of futility or defeat

Sorrow is a primary emotion (its purpose is "to alert us to our *disconnections*"); our relator style (its purpose is "to maintain our connections") uses its memories to identify the cause of the sorrow and quell it. But if this sorrow escalates through the Extreme Symbiotic Cycles of Despair, it will become debilitating.

The dictionary defines despair as "to lose all hope; to be overcome by a sense of futility or defeat." Desperate thoughts trigger despair and make us feel cut off from our connections, defeated, alone. Despair may be triggered by sensory input and desperate emotional memories that produce intense sorrow, making us feel disconnected from: a loved one (for example, the death of a family member), good health (for example, we are told that we have AIDS), a feeling of usefulness (for example, we are fired from the only job we are good at), etc. Despair can also come from extreme rationalization of a possible disconnection from an important connection (for example, not being contacted any more by a loved one for whatever reason).

Abandon all hope ye who enter here

The extreme symbiotic cycles of despair involve rapid re-expression of intense sorrow and an elevated, extended emotional mood—relator memories do not have enough time to identify the cause of the sorrow.

As an example of despair, let's assume that as a small child your mother abandoned you to a foster home, making comments that convinced you that she didn't love or want you and was never coming back. In that devastating realization, you disconnect from your most important connection. Years later, and throughout your life, when you hear, see, smell something that triggers that devastating emotional memory you feel intense sorrow. Your relator style tries to identify its cause, but fails since it needs about 500 milliseconds to identify it and the sorrow repeats every 20-60 milliseconds.

In this example, rationalization may also trigger extreme symbiotic cycles by evoking memories of your mother's love and protection before she abandoned you, alerting you to the disconnection and triggering intense sorrow. Eventually, some other thought, distraction or possibly some medication distracts you from that despair, halting the extreme symbiotic cycles and allowing the elevated extended mood of sorrow to ebb—without any hope of feeling love.

In conclusion

Emotionally triggered Extreme Symbiotic Cycles of *Despair* involve intense expressions of sorrow that we cannot quell since intense re-expressions of sorrow are too rapid to rationally identify and quell. *Rationally* triggered despair caused by rationalization can be quelled with relator memories that identify its cause and quell its escalating sorrow.

Extreme Symbiotic Cycles of *ECSTASY*

An intense state of joy or delight carrying one beyond self-control...

Joy is a primary emotion (its purpose is "to alert us to our connections"); our socializer style (its purpose is "to address our connections") uses its memories to identify the cause of the joy and quell it. But, if this joy escalates through the extreme symbiotic cycles of ecstasy, our glee will take control of our rational brain. The dictionary defines ecstasy as "a state of joy or delight so intense that one is carried beyond rational thought and self-control," which exemplifies the extreme symbiotic cycles of ecstasy.

From the sublime to the ridiculous is but many joys

Emotionally triggered extreme symbiotic cycles of ecstasy involve rapid re-expression of intense joy and an elevated, extended emotional mood—socializer memories do not have enough time to identify the cause of the joy. Our ecstasy ends when distracted by another thought or emotion, after which the elevated extended mood of joy ebbs.

For example, many of us have had experiences of intense joy when something happened way beyond what we expected. It might be finding out that the person you are in love with is secretly in love with you, or it might be getting a great, high-paying job that you never expected to get, or it might be winning the lottery. Whatever your experience, the joy you felt was so intense that you couldn't rationally deal with it. Rapid re-expressions of joy took control of your consciousness making it impossible to react rationally; you could only express glee. Your joy was eventually quelled by another thought or sensory input—possibly the jaw pain caused by a long-lasting uncontrollable smile that stretched from ear to ear—halting the extreme symbiotic cycles and allowing the elevated extended mood of joy to ebb.

In conclusion

Emotionally triggered Extreme Symbiotic Cycles of *Ecstasy* involve intense expressions of joy that we cannot quell since intense re-expressions of joy are too rapid to rationally identify and quell. *Rationally* triggered ecstasy caused by rationalization can be quelled with socializer memories that identify its cause and quell its escalating joy.

REFERENCES Interpreted as Support for My Conclusions:

1. Joseph LeDoux, *Synaptic Self,* (Viking, 2002)
2. Rita Carter, *Mapping the Mind,* (U of CA Press, 1999)
3. Daniel Goleman, *Emotional Intelligence,* (NY, Bantam, 1995)

Chapter 9
Outer-World's View of Style Attributes

Motivations of a Rational Style
Sensory Attributes of Rational Styles
Attitudes of a Rational Style

We all have a unique *inner-world personality*—defined by our genetics and memories. We also have an *outer-world personality* that can be described in terms of motivation, sensory and attitude attributes. We live in the outer-world and observe what seems to be the inner-world of others who also live in this outer world and observe what seems to be our inner-world.

Motivations of the Rational Styles

Are we motivated yet?

How many *rational* motivations do you think exist? Are there hundreds, dozens or just a few? And which ones do you think apply to each of the four rational styles? Well, according to Neurolinguistic Programming (NLP), which has accurately predicted certain outer-world personality traits for over half a century, there are essentially 12 genetic motivations, which they call "Meta Programs." I organized and listed these 12 motivations as six *opposite pairs* below. I chose the names of the motivations to express the nature of their motivation. The quotes applied to them are not their definitions, but what comes to mind as we try, as an outer-world observer, to understand the inner-world of others.

Pain/Loss, the "I avoid pain or loss" motivation
Pleasure/Gain, the "I seek pleasure or gain" motivation

Necessities, the "I do what I have to do" *obligation* motivation
Possibilities, the "I do what's gratifying" *choice* motivation

Differences, the "half-empty glass, distrusting" motivation
Similarities, the "half-full glass, trusting" motivation

Self-directed, the "only my opinions are valid" motivation
Others-directed, the "only other's opinions are valid" motivation

Self-concerned, the "only my needs count" motivation
Others-concerned, the "only other's needs count" motivation

Decisive, the "I must make a decision" motivation
Indecisive, the "I must avoid making decisions" motivation

One style's loss is another style's gain

The 12 motivations of our outer-world personality are defined below, grouped into opposite pairs—which do you think strongly apply to you?

- **Pain/Loss** motivates us to avoid any experience that can result in pain or loss. The pain can be physical or mental, and the loss could involve anything we hold dear (an important connection).
- Conversely, **Pleasure/Gain** motivates us to embrace situations that will give us pleasure or gain. The pleasure can be physical or mental, and the gain can include anything we desire.

- **Necessities** motivation makes us feel *obligated* to go to work every day, to follow the rules and care for our family and friends. Unfortunately, the necessities motivation tends to lock us into our present situations, making us feel obligated to put up with them, even though we know that they are not what we want or what is good for us.
- Conversely, **Possibilities** motivates us to change our jobs, friends or spouses from what we have to whatever is out there that might be new, exciting or different. The possibilities motivation gives us new insights and alternatives, making us creative, but can also makes us "chase rainbows," abandoning our obligations and important connections.

- **Differences** motivates us to dwell on what's wrong with the situation, making us distrust it and the actions of people involved in it, ignoring what is right with it: we can even distrust our own actions.
- Conversely, **Similarities** motivates us to think about what is right with the situation, making us trust it and the actions of people in it, even when it may be potentially hazardous.

116

- **Self-directed** motivates us to *reject* the beliefs of others, ignoring their opinions when they don't agree with ours, causing problems with authority figures or people that we think are confronting us.
- Conversely, **Others-directed** motivates us to *embrace* the beliefs of others, momentarily believe that only the opinions of another are valid while ignoring our own opinions, even when they are opposite.

- **Self-concerned** makes us reject the needs of others, since only our needs are valid, no matter how petty they may be or how important the needs of others may be. This motivation angers us when we are not meeting our needs, especially when others inhibit us.
- Conversely, **Others-concerned** motivates us to embrace the needs of others, sometimes forgetting our own needs and turning us into martyrs, not in control of our lives, if we are too strong in this motivation.

- **Decisive** motivates us to *make* decisions, demand that they are correct, and not change the decision once made, unless we see the folly in the choice and need to change it.
- Conversely, the **Indecisive** motivation causes us to avoid decisions and be at the mercy of the decisions of others.

All good motivations come in threes

Twenty-five years ago, I thought that each rational style had varying degrees of all 12 motivations. Now I realize that each rational style has just three unique motivations that can also be reduced to their style's purpose (as described on pages 157 to 159). The following tables categorize the styles and their unique motivations.

Analyzer Style	**Socializer Style**
"to unerringly proceed"	"to *address* our connections"
Pain/Loss "we avoid pain/loss"	Pleasure/Gain We seek pleasure/gain"
Necessities "doing what's proper"	Possibilities "doing what's gratifying"
Differences "noticing what's wrong"	Similarities "noticing what's right"

Director Style	Relator Style
"to get resolution"	"to *maintain* our connections"
Self-Directed "only my beliefs are correct"	Others-Directed "others beliefs are correct"
Self-Concerned "only my needs count"	Others-Concerned "only other's needs count"
Decisive "I must make decisions"	Indecisive "I must avoid making decisions"

Motivations support their style's purpose

Each style's motivations are critical to attaining its purpose. For our ana-lyzer style, "to unerringly proceed" we must do what we know works for us (necessities), to distrust whatever doesn't seem right (differences), and to avoid mistakes (pain/loss). For our socializer style, "to address our connec-tions" we must accentuate positive connections (pleasure/gain), consider new and exciting connections to talk about (possibilities) and branch form one related connection to another (similarities). For our director style, "to get resolution" we must consider only our beliefs valid, rejecting others when they disagree (self-directed), focusing on attaining a result without being distracted by the needs of others (self-concerned) and making a deci-sion to attain the result (decisive). For our relator style, "to maintain our connections" we must embrace the beliefs of others (others-directed), to make their needs crucial (others-concerned), and to avoid making decisions that may upset others (indecisive).

Motivations beget opposite styles

Reviewing the relationships between the motivations of the four styles, it is evident that the analyzer style and socializer style share opposing pairs of motivations and that the director and relator styles share opposing pairs of motivations. This is a main reason why the analyzer and socializer styles are opposites as are the director and relator styles; they have opposite moti-vations—but back to the other outer-world personality attributes. The next section, which presents another NLP Meta Program, describes what I refer to as the "sensory attributes," which are also specific to a rational style and are observable from an outer-world vantage point.

Sensory Attributes of Rational Styles

We sense, therefore, we think

Rational memories are stored in the frontal and temporal cortices of the brain, utilizing memories stored in the sensory cortices (visual, auditory, tactile, olfactory and taste). More than a half-century ago NLP identified three ways of thinking to store and retrieve memories. They found that the majority of the population "thought" *visually*, less were *auditory* and even less were tactile (called *kinesthetic*). We can determine which NLP's visual, auditory and tactile ways of thinking we are strongest in with a simple yet accurate test. But, before describing the test, let's explore these sensory attributes and their application to the four rational styles.

Our natural pace

Have you ever met people whose speech and manner were so slow that they acted like a movie or audiotape in slow motion? Or have you met people whose actions, speech and manner were so fast that they seemed to be in "fast forward"? Natural *pace* is a very noticeable aspect of these sensory attributes. For example, people who are "visuals" live at a fast pace whereas people who are "tactile" live at a slow pace and people who are "auditory" live at a moderate pace. Think about friends and relatives who are noticeably fast-paced or slow-paced and those in between to help you to better understand the validity of our sensory attributes.

One picture is worth a thousand memories

When we think *visually,* we think in visions or pictures. When we "visually remember" we compare what we are looking at to pictures (memories) stored in our visual cortex. If there is a match, we remember what we are looking at and if there is no match, we may store the new picture for future reference. There are actually two visual sensory attributes, we think in *visual pictures* and we think in *visual words* (reading). Those of us who think in visual pictures store dynamic pictures in the visual cortex, while those who think in words store pictures of words in the occipital area that are attached to memories in the "temporal cortex" language areas.

One word is worth a thousand memories

When we think auditorially, we think in terms of sounds and the sounds of words; we compare what we hear to the sounds (memories) that are stored in the auditory cortex and the sounds of words stored in the language areas. When there is a sound or word match, we recognize (remember) it and when there is no match, we may or may not store the new sound or word.

One feeling is worth a thousand memories

When we think kinesthetically (tactilely) we think in terms of non-visual (things seem to be darker with more tunnel vision) and non-auditory (sounds seem to be muted) sensations, just concentrating on what we "feel" (it is hard to describe, but obvious to us when we think tactilely). The feeling would then produce a tactile memory (in the parietal cortex, the top part of the head). When we experience that culmination of tactile sensations again, we compare it to the ones in memory and if there is a match, we remember it; if there is no match, a new tactile memory may or may not be stored.

To each his own

There is a high correlation between the four rational styles and the sensory attributes. We use *interactive visual-pictures* to think with the director and socializer styles, we use *visual-words* (writing) to think with the analyzer style, and we use *auditory* sounds of words to think with the relator style. We also use *tactile* thinking with the analyzer style. The table below summarizes the rational styles and their sensory attributes.

Analyzer	Relator	Director	Socializer
Visual (words) Or Tactile	Auditory (sounds of words)	Visual (action pictures)	Visual (action pictures)

The eyes have it

Now that we understand which sensory attributes we use with each rational style, let's discuss how to determine anybody's strongest sensory attribute. It's a lot of fun at parties or with friends, and even children can effectively use the "Eye Movement Charts" on the next page. To use the charts, first position yourself in front of someone so that you can see their eyes. Next, ask a thought provoking, if not a startling question that he or she doesn't readily know the answer to or was not expecting, for example, "What did you have for lunch last Tuesday?" When his or her eyes move, match this eye movement with the eye movement charts on the next page for their strongest sensory attribute; this also gives you a clue to their strongest rational style as indicated in the table on the next page.

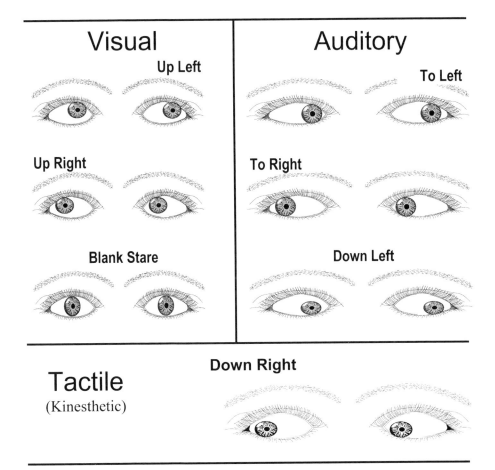

If you want to know your prominent sensory attribute, have someone ask *you* a thought-provoking question while he or she watches your eyes.

There's more to it than meets the eye

You might wonder what your strongest rational style is when strongest in the visual-pictures sensory attribute, since it applies to both the director and socializer styles. The answer is simple; if you are people-oriented, your socializer style is strongest and if task-oriented, your director style is strongest.

I'm sure that you'll find that your strong sensory attribute matches your strongest rational style, although, you may use a different sensory attribute if you have two strong styles. For example, you can be fast, visual-pictures oriented with your strong director style and slow, tactile-oriented with your strong analyzer style—you probably know or may be a person like that.

Birds of a feather think together

Once you know your own strongest sensory attribute and style, you may notice that you communicate better with those who have the same strong sensory attribute as you do (visual people communicate better with other visuals than they do with tactile people, etc.). You may also notice that you seem to conflict with those opposite to your style (directors conflict more with relators and analyzers conflict more with socializers), although some of us seem to conflict with everybody.

Appearances are deceiving

Although accurate, most people don't usually refer to the above Meta Programs (motivation attributes and sensory attributes) to describe another's inner-world personality; they tend to rely on what I call "Attitude Attributes," which form the basis for most personality analyses used today.

Attitudes of Rational Styles

We have met the attitudes and they are ours

A person's "attitudes" are the most common traits used to describe someone's personality. A style's attitudes, like a style's motivations, help us to attain the purpose of the style—and there seems to be thousands of them. I've identified hundreds and condensed them down to those listed in the table below by style.

Style	Purpose	*Attitudes*
Analyzer	"to unerringly proceed"	cautious, conventional, diligent, disciplined, introspective, logical, modest, negative, preparative, reserved, respectful, self-conscious, self-controlled, shy, tactful, tedious, thrifty, touchy
Director	"to get resolution"	adventurous, aggressive, arrogant, assertive, competitive, critical, distant, dominant, faultfinding, independent, persistent, pioneering, temperamental, tenacious

Relator	"to maintain our connections"	amiable, empathetic, gentle, humble, kind, lenient, loyal, obliging, patient, protective, sensitive, submissive, sympathetic, tolerant, worrisome
Socializer	"to address our connections"	boisterous, capricious, carefree, careless, charming, creative, enthusiastic, exaggerative, exciting, expressive, fickle, generous, impulsive, inspiring, inquisitive, persuasive, playful, positive, talkative, teasing

The way to a motivation's heart is through its attitudes

The relationship between a style and its three motivations, sensory attributes and attitudes is obvious; we see it every day. But, could a style's three motivations and attitude attributes be a function of each other; simplifying personality? Let's assume that they are and that the analyzer/socializer styles are opposite as are the director/relator styles and see what shakes out. Below are the attitude attributes of the analyzer and socializer styles collapsed into opposite motivations for these opposite styles.

Analyzer Motivations	Supporting Attitudes "to unerringly proceed"
Necessities "I do what I'm *obligated* to do"	(1) conventional, (2) diligent, (3) disciplined, (4) modest, (5) reserved, (6) tedious, (7) respectful, (8) tactful, (9) touchy/self-conscious/introspective
Pain/Loss "I avoid pain/loss"	(10) cautious, (11) preparative, (12) self-controlled, (13) shy/soft-spoken, (14) thrifty
Differences "I *distrust* other's actions"	(15) negative

Socializer Motivations	Supporting Attitudes "to address our connections"
Possibilities "I do what's gratifying"	(1) creative, (2) capricious, (3) inquisitive, (4) boastful, (5) enthusiastic, (6) exciting, (7) fickle, (8) teasing, (9) playful/carefree/talkative
Pleasure/Gain "I seek pleasure/gain"	(10) careless, (11) impulsive, (12) expressive, (13) boisterous, (14) generous
Similarity "I *trust* other's actions"	(15) positive

To relate the opposite motivations of the opposite styles, I use the numbers (1), (2), etc., to refer to the possible matching of opposite attitudes. For example, the analyzer style's (1) conventional attitude of the *necessities* motivation oppositely matches the (1) creative attitude of the *possibilities* motivation; just like the (11) preparative attitude of the *pain/loss* analyzer motivation oppositely matches the (11) impulsive attitude of the *pleasure/gain* socializer motivation. As you can see, some opposite pairs of attitude attributes fit their opposite pairs of motivations very well, whereas others seem a stretch.

Similarly, the opposite director and relator style's motivations also line up with their attitude attributes as indicated in the table below. For example, the director style's (1) independent attitude of the *self-directed* motivation oppositely matches the (1) loyal attitude of the *others-directed* motivation.

Director Motivations	Supporting Attitudes "to get resolution"
Self-Directed "I reject other's beliefs"	(1) independent, (2) critical/faultfinding/sensitive
Self-Concerned "my needs are crucial"	(3) distant, (4) arrogant, (5) domineering, (6) competitive
Decisive "I get results"	(7) assertive/aggressive, (8) adventurous/pioneering, (9) temperamental

Relator Motivations	Supporting Attitudes "to maintain our connections"
Others-Directed "I embrace other's beliefs"	(1) loyal, (2) lenient/protective/tolerant
Others-Concerned "other's needs are crucial"	(3) amiable/sympathetic/empathetic, (4) humble, (5) submissive, (6) obliging
Indecisive "I leave decision-making to others"	(7) gentle/kind, (8) worrisome, (9) patient

These exercises explore the relationship between a rational style's outer-world motivations and its attitudes. From this point forward, we can ignore the attitude attributes since we reduced them to a function of each style's three motivations. On pages 157 to 159, we will further condense each style's sensory attributes and three motivations into the style's purpose, while considering brain structure and excitability.

To not decide (consciously) is to decide (unconsciously)

Before moving on, it's important to have a clear view of decisiveness since it determines how our inner-world will react to the outer-world.

We all make decisions every day, but in reality, most of them are made for us, by us. There are two kinds of decisions: conscious and unconscious. Unconscious decisions maintain the status quo and conscious decisions create change by overriding unconscious decisions. We make unconscious decisions all day long; they are the name brands we buy, the routes we take to and from work, and the things we say and do without thinking, for example, saying hello to someone we like or avoiding eye contact with someone we dislike. With this in mind, we might want to revisit the notions above that directors are decisive and that relators are indecisive—but for completeness, we will consider the decisiveness of all four rational styles.

Strong directors are decisive! Yes, but are they consciously or unconsciously decisive? Being a very strong, very decisive director I can assure you that every first attempt at a decision is not well thought out; its unconscious and automatic. If the decision is challenged or unworkable, the conscious brain kicks in, weighs more possibilities and comes up with a more workable, conscious decision. Of course, if I base the decision on what I've done in the past, that second decision is also unconscious—a totally *new* approach would be a conscious decision. Bottom line, although decisive, most director decisions are unconscious—we make conscious decisions when challenged by new, important situations or when we need to clean up our act after making an unworkable decision. But the fact is, we *do* make a decision—we can't help it. Weak directors are also decisive when using their director style—they can't help it—even if they are strong relators.

Strong relators are indecisive, mostly for "inhibitory" reasons explained in Chapter 12. Strong relators who are also weak directors seem incapable of making a conscious decision. Have you ever noticed/wondered why your strong-relator/weak-director spouse, child, etc., never gives you a decision when it involves something new (not part of their experience memories)? Isn't it frustrating when you let them decide what to do and they can't decide, even when given options? And forget about asking them for an opinion on something totally new; they don't have one. I've given up asking my strong-relator/weak-director daughter for an opinion on anything she is not familiar with since I know that she is incapable of making a decision about it; she'll simply wait for and acquiesce to my decision. It's not because she is afraid of disconnecting from me or afraid of seeming dumb—it's because her brain can't decide!

We can say the same thing for strong analyzers who are weak directors—they're indecisive when it comes to something new! It's not because they're afraid of erring or afraid of looking dumb—it's because their brains can't decide! As explained in Chapter 12, their inhibited decision-making pre-frontal cortex only allows them to make *unconscious* decisions. When not weak in the director style, their conscious decisions are not lacking, but you might grow old waiting for them to decide on something new or important.

And what about strong socializers? They seem very decisive—hell, they have an opinion on everything! And if they're also *not* weak in the director style, forget it! Like strong directors, strong socializers are excitatory right-brain people who automatically make decisions. And like directors, off-the-cuff decisions are not necessarily realistic, but that doesn't matter since they will probably branched off on another subject before the decision proved unrealistic.

Bottom line—weak directors are indecisive, especially strong relators—most decisions are unconscious, based on the status quo—conscious decisions go against the status quo.

Chapter 10
Natural Compatibility with the Outer-World

Genetic Compatibility
Self-Incompatibility

π   The first part of this chapter is technical in that it explains the basis of compatibility—if not technically interested, skip to page 130.

Genetic Compatibility

Less irritating is more compatible
Have you ever wondered why you are naturally comfortable with certain people and naturally irritated by others? Do you have a family member that you love very much that easily irritates you, and you don't exactly know why? The reason is genetic compatibility, or incompatibility, depending on your point of view. Genetic or *natural* compatibility is the compatibility or incompatibility between our rational style *pattern*'s strong and weak styles, especially when the styles are opposite.

Opposites don't attract
When we compare the director and relator style's motivations in Chapter 9, we notice that they are opposite; the same is true for the opposite analyzer and socializer style motivations, as summarized in the following tables.

Analyzer Style	Socializer Style
"to unerringly proceed"	"to *address* our connections"
Pain/Loss "we avoid pain/loss"	Pleasure/Gain "we seek pleasure/gain"
Necessities "doing what's proper"	Possibilities "doing what's gratifying"
Differences "noticing what's wrong"	Similarities "noticing what's right"

Director Style	Relator Style
"to get resolution"	"to *maintain* our connections"
Self-Directed "only my beliefs are correct"	Others-Directed "others beliefs are correct"
Self-Concerned "only my needs count"	Others-Concerned "only other's needs count"
Decisive "I must make decisions"	Indecisive "I must avoid making decisions"

Attitudes and motivations…you can't have one without the other

The attitude attributes were also shown to be opposite, as a function of the motivation attributes, further emphasizing the opposite relationship between the director and relator styles and between the analyzer and socializer styles.

One man's task is another man's person

Another aspect of genetic compatibility/incompatibility is the task-orientation or the people-orientation of the rational styles. The analyzer and director are task-oriented styles, and the relator and socializer are people-oriented styles. Those who are task-oriented usually work well together and those who are people-oriented usually interact well together. People who are task-oriented usually do not work as well with people-oriented people.

Thus, the criteria for calculating our level of compatibility or incompatibility with others includes task/people orientation our strongest style and the motivation/attitude attributes of our strongest and weakest styles. The following table shows the genetic compatibility between any two people (1st person and 2nd person).

People with opposite strongest styles have –2 incompatibilities, while two people with the same strongest style have +2 compatibility; other style mixtures have between +1 and –1.

Opposites doubly repel

A final aspect of compatibility or incompatibility is our *pattern* of strong and weak styles.

128

Strongest Style of:		Task- vs. People-Orientation of Style	Motivation/Attitude Compatibility	Basic Compatibility Level
1st Person	2nd Person	Same = +1, Opposite = -1	Same = +1, Opposite = -1 Neutral = 0	
Analyzer (A)	Analyzer (A)	+ 1	+ 1	+ 2
Analyzer (A)	Director (D)	+ 1	0	+ 1
Analyzer (A)	Relator (R)	− 1	0	− 1
Analyzer (A)	Socializer (S)	− 1	− 1	− 2
Director (D)	Director (D)	+ 1	− 1 *	0
Director (D)	Relator (R)	− 1	− 1	− 2
Director (D)	Socializer (S)	− 1	0	− 1
Relator (R)	Relator (R)	+ 1	+ 1	+ 2
Relator (R)	Socializer (S)	+ 1	0	+ 1
Socializer (S)	Socializer (S)	+ 1	+ 1	+ 2

* The self-concerned & self-directed motivation attributes of the director style, along with its anger emotion and attributes make strong directors conflict with each other.

When we have two oppositely strong styles, for example, if strong in both the director and relator styles, the use of one style moderates the use of the other style through its opposite motivations and attitudes, balancing each other out. The same is true for the opposite socializer and analyzer styles. Conversely, if we are strong in one style, the director style for example, and weak in its opposite relator style, we are doubly weak in the weak style and double strong in the strong style since they can't balance each other out.

Strongest / Weakest Styles		Basic Natural Compatibility	Strong/Weak Effect Same = +1 Neutral = 0 Opposite = -1	True Compatibility Level
1st Person	2nd Person			
Strong-A/Weak-S	Strong-A/Weak-S	+ 2	+ 1	+ 3
Strong-A/Weak-S	Strong-D/Weak-R	+ 1	0	+ 1
Strong-A/Weak-S	Strong-R/Weak-D	− 1	0	− 1
Strong-A/Weak-S	Strong-S/Weak-A	− 2	− 1	− 3
Strong-D/Weak-R	Strong-D/Weak-R	0	0	0
Strong-D/Weak-R	Strong-R/Weak-D	− 2	− 1	− 3
Strong-D/Weak-R	Strong-S/Weak-A	− 1	0	− 1
Strong-R/Weak-D	Strong-R/Weak-D	+ 2	+ 1	+ 3
Strong-R/Weak-D	Strong-S/Weak-A	+ 1	0	+ 1
Strong-S/Weak-A	Strong-S/Weak-A	+ 2	+ 1	+ 3

The above table is a quick reference for our basic natural compatibility with others, enhanced by either person having a weakest style opposite to his or her strongest style.

In general, people with opposite *strongest* and weakest styles have a −3 incompatibility (for example, a Strong-**A**/Weak-**S** and a Strong-**S**/Weak-**A**), whereas two people with the same strongest and weakest styles have a +3 compatibility (for example, a Strong-**A**/Weak-**S** and a Strong-**A**/Weak-**S**). In summary, +2 or −2 compatibility increases to +3 or −3 when the one or both people have a weakest style opposite to his or her strongest style and others stay the same.

Genetic Compatibility Chart

It takes two to make a compatibility

Below is a quick reference chart to determine your compatibility from +2 (very compatible) to -2 (very compatible) with others. Just pick out the strongest style of **Person #1** (yourself) in the first *column* on the left and then go along that *row* to the right until you reach the *column* of the strongest style of **Person #2** to determine your compatibility/incompatibility. *NOTE:* if the other person has, a weakest style that is opposite your strongest style the compatibility is **+3** or the incompatibility is **−3**, instead of **+2** or **−2**.

Person #2 → ↓ Person #1	Analyzer	Director	Relator	Socializer
Analyzer	**+ 2** (or + 3)	**+ 1**	**− 1**	**− 2** (or − 3)
Director	**+ 1**	Always = **0**	**− 2** (or − 3)	**− 1**
Relator	**− 1**	**− 2** (or − 3)	**+ 2** (or + 3)	**+ 1**
Socializer	**− 2** (or − 3)	**− 1**	**+ 1**	**+ 2** (or + 3)

It's still all about irritation

Genetic or natural compatibility (**+1** to **+3**) or incompatibility (**−1** to **−3**) is a function of *irritation*. When we have a genetic incompatibility of **−2** or **−3** with another person we tend to irritate each other when we are together. The irritation is not instant and overwhelming, it is subtle and cumulative.

Thus, the more time we spend interacting with that person the more irritation we accumulate until we reach an intolerable level. Strong directors will get angry and try to resolve the problem, unfortunately, there is no problem except natural incompatibility, which they can do nothing about. Strong relators will become sorrowful, sense disconnection and try to reconnect by placating the strong director, irritating him/her even more. Analyzers will express fear, back off and remove themselves mentally and/or physically from the situation. Socializers express joy that turns on their socializer attributes, which irritates strong analyzers even more.

Or the lack of it

The other aspect of genetic or natural irritation, or more accurately the lack of it, is when people have a natural compatibility of **+2** or **+3**. These people can be together all day long and accumulate very little natural irritation; you probably see it in your own family.

For example, I have two daughters with a strongest socializer style. They can play together all day long and rarely get annoyed with each other, except on holidays or during vacations when they spend too much time together and accumulate enough irritation to become upset. In contrast, I (a strong director and weak relator) have a **−1** incompatibility with them and we become naturally irritated with each other after being together for a few hours. My wife, a strong analyzer/relator with weak director and socializer styles, has a **−3** incompatibility with our strong socializer daughters and can become highly irritated with them if together for too long. Fortunately, my wife's strong relator style helps her to deal with it when the upset triggers her sorrow emotion causing her to ignore the irritation and reconnect.

It takes two to make a quarrel

People with an incompatibility of **−2** or **−3** with others should limit their time together. They should never work hand in hand throughout the day if they want to limit their accumulative natural irritation, which can result in an upset that both parties do not want. This is especially true of married couples with a –2 or –3 compatibility, who probably shouldn't get married.

For example, I had a client with a very strong analyzer and very weak socializer style. His spouse had a very strong socializer style and very weak analyzer style; their compatibility was –3. They had a wonderful relationship for 10 years, after which it fell apart. She was an airline attendant who was away more than she was home, reducing the accumulation of their natural irritation. Then they decided to have a child; she decided to stay home to take care of her. Thus, they interacted with each other daily, and with the distress of a newborn, they were constantly using their strongest styles. Even though they loved each other, it took less than a year to file for divorce, because they couldn't live with the natural irritation.

Strong socializers with weak analyzer styles who marry strong analyzers with weak socializer styles probably have the highest divorce rate of any combination of rational patterns. Yes, strong directors with weak relator styles who marry strong relators with weak director styles also have a −3 compatibility, but the strong relator tries to ignore the excessive irritation to stay connected, which tends to hold the couple together. It is usually the strong director of the pair that seeks the divorce, driven by anger to seek what seems to be the only resolution to the never-ending and thus, intolerable irritation. In general, a marriage that comprises mates with a −3 compatibility have an uphill battle to stay together.

It takes one to know one

There is another aspect of genetic compatibility, referred to in Chapter 9, which makes us more or less irritated by others; I call it *sensory attribute* compatibility. In general, visuals communicate best with other visuals, auditories communicate best with other auditories, and kinesthetics communicate best with other kinesthetics. In fact, visuals conflict with and try to avoid kinesthetics, and vice versa, whereas auditories conflict little with either visuals or kinesthetics. To reduce irritation, fast visuals should slow down *a lot* for kinesthetics and kinesthetics should speed up *a lot* for visuals.

When communicating with someone you love, try to use his or her prominent sensory attribute. If he or she is the visual-action type, *demonstrate* how you feel. If he or she is the visual-writing type, *write* him or her a card or letter to tell them how you feel. If he or she is auditory, *tell* them how you feel. And if he or she is kinesthetic, touch them and let them touch you, or *hold* them a long time.

Knowing your strongest sensory attribute and that of others can go a long way in helping you to learn, or to better teach others (see page 121 to determine what your strongest sensory attribute is). If they are a visual-writing person, use mostly written material such as books and charts to teach them. If they are a visual-action person, use videos, take trips, or do whatever it takes to *animate* what you teach them. If they are an auditory person, have them listen to tapes, CDs, lectures or whatever is available in audio form—recording their own tapes and then listening to them is also a great study aid. If they are kinesthetic, have them get involved in hands-on studying techniques; have them touch the things that you are studying if possible, or have them make models to aid them in learning.

If *you* are teaching others, determine their strongest sensory attribute and plan your presentation to include aids that allow each person to learn *their way*. If teaching many at a time, incorporate all types of visual, auditory and kinesthetic aids to help all of your students to learn. Giving projects and allowing them to present their results in a video, audio or model format will help them to learn and their projects will be much more interesting for them.

All good things in moderation

When we have a *strong* rational pattern we have, one strong style that we use most of the time and, thus, our other styles are moderate to weak. When we have a *moderate* rational pattern, we have two moderately strong styles that we use much of the time, leaving either two moderately weak styles or one moderate and one weak style. Two people with a moderate pattern irritated each other less, and their level of compatibility is +1 *higher*—+3 is +4, +2 is +3, -3 is −2, -2 is -1—than in the "Genetic Compatibility Chart" on page 130.

Self-Incompatibility

When we irritate ourselves

Self-incompatibility refers to the natural irritation we feel with ourselves when our rational style pattern is conflicting. For example, if we have a strong-director/strong-relator style pattern, we irritate ourselves for not staying connected when using our director style and we irritate ourselves for not getting results when using our relator style—we can't win. The level of irritation increases with the length of time we use one strong style. The longer we use the director style the more it irritates the relator style and vice versa, making it difficult to live with ourselves.

A moderate style pattern helps

Since we must have a moderate pattern to have two strong styles, the two-patterns that produce the greatest self-irritation are the Director/Relator or Relator/Director (depending on which style is the strongest) and the Analyzer/Socializer or Socializer/Analyzer patterns. In contrast, the Director/Analyzer or Analyzer/Director or the Relator/Socializer or Socializer/Relator pattern with less incompatibility would produce less self-irritation. Unlike irritation caused by others, which we can reduce by spending less time with them, we can't spend less time with ourselves. But unless we get our self-irritation into prospective, our mental health and happiness can suffer.

Director and Relator style—a catch-22

When we spend a lot of time using our relator style, our director style will become highly irritated and vice versa.

For example, assume that we have a strong director/relator pattern and that we need to plant a garden by noon, when we have to leave for an appointment. Also, assume that our four-year-old daughter wants to help plant. If you prefer, think of your own child or someone you love in place of the daughter in this example. While planting, the child comes into the front yard and asks to help. When pressed to complete the planting by noon, our strong director style might prompt us to say, "I don't need any help, I have to get this done, so why don't you go and see if your mother needs help!" Once said, we look into her tearful eyes, lit up just seconds before with a radiant smile, evoking our sorrow and compelling us to reconnect with our strong relator style. We walk over to her, kneel down and take her into your arms saying, "I'm sorry sweetheart, of course you can help." We assign her a task, but find it difficult to complete our own work since she wants more attention than job fulfillment, so we end up doing her work with her, nurturing our relationship as we work. As time progresses, our director style becomes irritated because we'll never be finished by noon, prompting assertiveness that causes us to switch to our director style, ignoring our daughter to complete the task. Unfortunately, our daughter makes us aware that she is in need of attention, too, irritating our relator style and expressing concern and the use of our relator style. This switching between styles continues until noon when we have to be somewhere else and end up with either an unfinished garden or an unhappy child or both. If our director style was strongest, it would probably win out; the garden would end up planted by noon and the child ignored. If our relator style is strongest, it would probably win out; the child would feel nurtured and happy and the garden unplanted.

Notwithstanding, no matter which style is our strongest, there will always be natural irritation and self-incompatibility when strong in both the director and relator styles. The only way to reduce this self-irritation is to be aware that it exists and try to better plan the use of our time between getting results and staying connected.

Choose between tasks and people

It is best to decide beforehand what the most important aspect of the situation is—task or people. For example, if planting the garden were a task situation, planting the garden by noon would take priority over nurturing the child, who should be distracted, but promised equal time, possibly later that day. But if it were a people situation, staying connected with the child would take priority over planting the garden, which should be rescheduled for completion later, possibly when the child is taking a nap.

But, who determines whether it is a people or task situation? We do! We decide that the garden must be planted and that the child must be distracted from bothering us, or we decide that the garden doesn't matter as much as our connection with our child. Whatever we decide is appropriate as long as we follow through with our decision. Sometimes it's easy to decide between the task and the person and sometimes it isn't, but if we prepare for and stick with our decision, it will reduce our natural self-irritation and its repercussions. If you know ahead of time which style would be the most appropriate, use Mindset (as discussed in Chapter 14) to prepare your mind to use the appropriate style without becoming highly irritated by your other strong style.

Analyzer and Socializer style—a catch-22

When we spend a lot of time using our analyzer style the socializer style is highly irritated and vice versa. For example, suppose we have an Analyzer/Socializer or Socializer/Analyzer pattern, and we are at a party. Our strong analyzer style inclines us to find someone like us and cautiously discuss topics we know. It also inclines us to stay away from crowds for fear that something can go wrong. While acting this way with our analyzer style, our socializer style becomes irritated because we are dull and boring, and not interacting with others. This turns on our socializer style to engage others and be the center of attention, doing whatever strikes our fancy. Eventually, our analyzer style becomes mortified at our behavior and urges us to behave in a proper manner and stop making a total fool of ourselves. We go back and forth, trying to fulfill the purpose of each conflicting rational style.

If we have an alcoholic beverage, our socializer style will usually take over, but if we don't drink alcohol, the conflict will endure until we leave the party. After we leave, we will probably feel guilty or uneasy about either acting foolishly or being uninvolved—we can't win.

Another example of this analyzer and socializer self-conflict is when we are at work and we need to complete an important project. We can be working alone with our analyzer style to unerringly proceed, until others enter the room. After a while, our socializer style becomes irritated with our analyzer style, which is still trying to unerringly proceed with the project, but getting nowhere because everybody else is talking about anything but the project. Thus, the socializer style takes over and has a great time with the others. This irritates our analyzer style making it want to get back to our important project. We do, but after a while, our socializer style becomes irritated again and we switch back and forth until the others leave or we leave to complete the project.

Again, choose between tasks or people

It is best to decide beforehand what the most important aspect of the situation is—task or people. When it is an activity situation and you need to proceed unerringly, you must use your analyzer style and ignore the uneasy feeling you get from your socializer style's natural irritation. When it is a people interaction situation you must put aside the project and ignore the uneasy feeling you get from your analyzer style's natural irritation. When you have to use both styles, such as in a presentation, you may have to cycle back and forth between the styles as needed, trying not to get stuck using just one style for too long.

No matter which style you choose, use it without guilt for whatever time interval you deem appropriate. If *you* have an Analyzer/Socializer or Socializer/Analyzer pattern think of a recent situation when you experienced much self-conflict when trying to decide whether to use your analyzer or socializer style. Also, think of whether it was a people or activity situation and whether you handled it appropriately.

Those of us with the above **−2** incompatibility patterns, with two strong *opposite* styles find it difficult to lead daily lives because of the constant irritation from one style when using the other. This irritation also exists at a lesser level for those of us who have **−1** incompatibility pattern such as the Socializer/Director or Director/Socializer or the Relator/Analyzer or Analyzer/Relator. Again, this is a conflict between a task-oriented and people-oriented style, and all we need do is choose whether to handle the situation as a task or as a people situation. If you know ahead of time which style would be the most appropriate, use Mindset (as detailed in Chapter 14) to prepare your mind to use the appropriate style without becoming highly irritated by your other strong style.

Relator and Socializer style with moderate self-incompatibility

They have a compatibility of **+1** in the "Genetic Compatibility Chart" above, but still provide enough inner irritation to cause us concern about how we react. When we are using our relator style and sorrow to stay connected, our socializer style becomes irritated with not attracting and interacting with others, turning off the relator style and turning on the socializer.

For example, we may be at a wake, using our relator style, its attributes and sorrow to support the bereaved family members. After a while, our socializer style becomes irritated and decides that they need a little joy to distract them from their pain. When we do, our relator style becomes irritated because we may seem phony, unconcerned and non-supportive, which turns on our relator style. After a while, our socializer style becomes irritated because we are being too serious, especially if someone else lightens up first, turning on our socializer style. In happy situation, such as a celebration, the socializer style would take over, but if an unhappy situation, our relator style would probably take over. No matter which style wins out, it still irritates the other style and frustrates us.

Choose by propriety

The best way to deal with self-irritation when we have two strong people styles is to determine which style is more appropriate, and then use that style without feeling guilty or uneasy.

In general, when people need help to get through something, you must use your relator style and ignore the socializer style's irritation. However, if you decide that the socializer style is more appropriate you should use it and ignore the irritation of the relator style. If you know that you will be in a situation that requires a certain style, you can use Mindset (see Chapter 14) to turn off the inappropriate style and turn on the more appropriate style. If you have a Relator/Socializer or Socializer/Relator pattern think of a recent situation when you experienced irritation when trying to decide whether to use your relator or socializer style. Also, think of whether you handled it with the appropriate style.

Analyzer and Director style moderate self-incompatibility

They have a compatibility of **+1** in the "Genetic Compatibility Chart" but still provide enough inner irritation to cause us concern about how we react. When we are using our director style to get results, our analyzer style fears that we may be leaving out something important, takes over, and unerringly proceeds towards the result already determined by the director style. In the process, we are not attaining results quickly enough so the director style becomes irritated and makes us take short cuts to get results. Again, fear switches us back to the analyzer style as we go around and around as the following example shows.

I have a friend with a strong analyzer/director pattern who is in charge of the design and manufacturing of telephone answering machines for his small company. He must properly design his product, since imperfections cause manufacturing, sales and warranty losses in that tight low-profit market. While he painstakingly designs new products with his analyzer style, his director style irritates him that he is not getting the product on the market fast enough. He needs to have the new product designed and on the market quickly or the product may become obsolete before it is even manufactured. He thus decides to use his director style to speed up the process, leaving little time to check and recheck for design and manufacturing flaws. This causes concern and the use of his irritated analyzer style to assure a quality result. This eventually irritates his director style, which intercedes to quickly get the product on the market. Thus, he's torn between the designs of a minimal maintenance, desirable, easily manufactured product and the need to reach that product market before it disappears. His solution to the problem is to work night and day to satisfy both his analyzer and director styles for a quality, timely result.

Choose between quality and time

One way to deal with strong-analyzer/strong-director irritation is to place a priority on quality or time. Most everything does not have to be done with both a time *and* quality priority as in the example above, so a choice can be made. When time is of the essence, use your director style and ignore the irritation of the analyzer style. When high quality is mandatory, use your analyzer style and ignore the irritation of the director style. If both are required, forget about the daily routine of eating, sleeping, etc., and work on the project with your analyzer style until it is completed in a timely manner.

If you know ahead of time which style would be the most appropriate, use Mindset (see Chapter 14) to prepare your mind to use the appropriate style without becoming highly irritated by your other strong style.

Give peace of mind a chance...

If you use the above guidelines for reducing your self-irritation, you will find it easier to live with your natural style pattern For those of you who are not sure whether you have a two-strong-style pattern, a good indication is that you experience the kind of irritation mentioned here daily. When you have a highly self-irritating rational pattern be aware of it, reduce your conflict as much as possible by sizing up the situation as either people-oriented or task-oriented, or whatever, and then proceed accordingly. "Mindset" is also helpful when you need to use just one of your two strong styles when you will be in a situation that requires that only one style and definitely not the other is appropriate.

Chapter 11
Who's In Charge Here?

Who's in Charge Here?
Reacting Appropriately

Who's in Charge Here?

Don't wear your heart on your sleeve

Take a moment to reflect on the following. What typically controls your reactions; your emotional brain (feelings) or your rational brain (logic)? Well, let me put it another way; does your heart or your head typically control your reactions? You would probably answer "heart" if you were a strong relator or socializer and more concerned about people. You would probably answer "head" if you were a strong analyzer or director that is more concerned about tasks. The fact is you are controlled by your emotions, whether people-oriented (sorrow and joy) or task-oriented (fear and anger), since they erupt before your rational brain can do anything about them. So I guess the answer to the question is emotional—but we do gain rational control, belated as it may be, making it rational—so the correct answer is *both*.

Our rational brain might be working for our emotional brain

Our rational brain is in control when our conscious pre-frontal cortex (PFC) is free to work with our unconscious rational memories. This rational control is lost when an emotional alert pauses the PFC to sort out an emotional outburst and then regain rational control. But if we rationalize that outburst, our rational brain is now working *for* our emotional brain, erroneously trying to justify the inappropriate outburst. Only after rationalization ends does the PFC regain rational control and quell the emotion. Thus, if we want to know "who's in charge here" it helps to know whether we control our reactions rationally or emotionally, and if emotional, whether our emotional brain has hijacked our PFC through inappropriate rationalization.

Variety is the reaction of life

There is absolutely nothing wrong with emotions; they are the spice of life. But, when emotions become inappropriate or we have negative outbursts we need to rationally clean up the destruction they cause. This is why it is important to know whether our rational brain is in control or whether our emotional brain has hijacked it. The ideal social interaction is rational with a sprinkle of positive emotions, but this isn't easy especially if we are distressed.

Count to 10...but whose counting?

When distressed, our emotions and rationalizations control our reactions. When this occurs we need to be aware, pause, and count to 10 to allow the emotional mood to ebb as we avoid rationalization. In doing so, we are distracted from rationalization and can regain rational control over an emotional outburst. Unfortunately, it doesn't mean that the other person is rationally in control. If they are, we can have a productive interaction, but if not, they may thwart our efforts.

Most of the time, the emotions of others are obvious, but some times, they are subtle, creating confusion and problems. When the emotions of others are imperceptible their reactions seem rational and under control, but this may not always be the case. Their PFC can be emotionally distracted causing momentary loss of rational control. There is, though, a clue to subtle emotional reactions—their response is illogical. For example, you may want to know the answer to a question that they are not emotionally willing to provide because of fear, anger or whatever. *Their* emotion is pausing their PFC so that they can't rationally respond to your question. You may pose the question in a different manner, but still get an irrational or non-response. When was the last time someone gave you an obvious irrational or non-response? How did it make you feel? How did you deal with it?

We are all guilty of these irrational or non-responses. When was the last time you remember giving an irrational or non-response to the questions of others? How did it make you feel? How did you deal with it? How did they deal with you? It's important to understand how our subtle emotions can take control of our rational reactions that we need to socially survive.

Reacting Appropriately

Waste not want not

Let's face it, the rational brain evolved for the expressed purpose of sorting out and controlling our primary emotions in order to socially survive—that is, to react in an appropriate manner so as to be acceptable to the community we choose to live in. Fortunately, along with the ability to control emotional reactions, the rational brain also gave us the ability to express *rational* emotions (love, etc.). Unfortunately, it also gave us the ability to rationalize inappropriate emotional outbursts. Rationalization is a rational brain gone astray, caught in a loop that hijacks our rational brain. But if we avoid rationalization, we can use our rational brain as nature planned—to socially survive.

Since the rational brain evolved to give us a social edge and control our emotions, it would be foolish to waste it. For example, we may be angry with our boss for not giving us a deserved raise and show our anger, but this may not be conducive to social survival (making a living). As an aside, one theory for getting along (socially surviving) is to use our analyzer style to interact with strong analyzers or use our director style to interact with strong directors, etc., which may or may not work. What usually works is to use our people-oriented styles in people-oriented *situations* and use our task-oriented styles in task-oriented situations, but this doesn't guarantee that we will react appropriately, especially when we have erroneous emotional outbursts.

Erroneous emotions negate rational control

The erroneous emotional outbursts of others have nothing to do with the present situation and may even trigger an emotional outburst in us, negating our rational control. For example, during a rational conversation something may trigger anger in the person we are talking to, startling us and making us inappropriately react in kind. When this occurs, we must quell *our* emotion, get back our rational control and then try to distract them from their anger, possibly by changing the subject. Most importantly, we must not rationalize our own anger; we must get back our rational control and move on.

In general, avoid situations that cause negative emotional reactions whenever possible, and if unavoidable, clean them up and get back to a rational interaction, hopefully sprinkled with positive emotions. And if you know that a future situation might cause you to have an emotional outburst, use "Mindset" to head it off as explained in Chapter 14. Strange as it may seem, strong emotional outbursts are easier to identify and deal with than are subtle emotional expressions that insidiously creep into a conversations and take control.

Insidious emotions negate rational control

Subtle emotions can insidiously creep into a conversation, reducing rational control. For example, one day my wife and I were trying to resolve an important issue in a civil, rational manner and were doing fine at first. But when I was not getting my point across I became frustrated and noticed that my voice was getting louder and my pronunciation more stern—anger (due to being hindered) was creeping into my conversation, and I didn't even realize it. Likewise, being a strong analyzer, fear was creeping up on her and she started to avoid me—we were not making progress. We were moving further and further away from an understanding. We realized this and parted for a few moments to allow our emotions to ebb and to calm down. Then we discussed it more calmly and rationally and reached an understanding we could both live with. Can you think of discussions that you have had in the past that started out rational and insidiously turned emotional, possibly escalating out of control?

It gives us pause

Subtle emotions that don't escalate out of control can also cause confusion, but there is a simple clue that makes us aware of them; there is an *emotional pause*. A subtle emotion hijacks the PFC to sort it out, causing a half-second pause, before the PFC can gain control and rationally continue. This has nothing to do with a *rational* pause when we need to reflect for a moment before continuing, usually saying "Uh." When others have an emotional pause, it gets our attention and tells us that they have emotional issues with what they're discussing. This is a warning to us to cautiously, rationally proceed and not become involved with or exacerbate their emotional issues.

(Don't) do unto others as they do unto you

We tend to mimic those we are with and get caught up in the emotions of others. But when we are in a rational discussion that becomes emotional, especially when rationalization rears its ugly head, it can easily escalate out of control. When others show emotion it is natural for us to respond accordingly, joining in their sorrow, fear, joy or anger to some degree. But it is best to avoid rationally supporting their emotionally evoking discussion, unless it is our purpose to do so. Instead, guide them away from any rationalization that elevates their emotional reaction, probably by changing the subject. And, should it elevate out of control, don't support it, say nothing, don't react, wait for the person to get back their control and then continue your rational interaction, possibly laced with positive emotions.

Emotions are the spice of life

There is nothing wrong with emotions; they serve a physical survival purpose and they can be a wonderful expression of our feelings. They are also needed to support others in an emotional crisis, for example, expressing mutual sorrow for a lost friend or loved one, or expressing assertiveness when helping a friend resolve something important, or expressing caution when someone important to us is risky. The only time we need to avoid emotional reactions is when they get in the way of what we are rationally trying to accomplish, when they are getting in the way of our appropriate reactions.

Simply apply common sense

Notwithstanding our emotional outbursts, we need to appropriately react to the emotions and rational reactions of others to maintain rational control. We can deal with most people's obvious emotions to some degree, but when not obvious, emotions can get in the way of a meaningful conversation. There are, though, clues to help us if we're observant:

1. People's responses are obviously emotional when they say nothing while their facial expressions displays anger, fear, joy or sorrow. They may even emanate negative emotional energy from fear or anger or positive emotional energy from joy or sorrow (see pages 230 to 232).

2. When it is not obvious, ask yourself "Is this a rational way to react?"

3. If you conclude that they are reacting in a rational manner, respond in a rational manner.

4. If you conclude that they are reacting in an emotional manner:
    a. Don't expect a logical response.

b. Say nothing and wait—count to 10—for their emotional chemicals to ebb and their emotional mood to subside before responding in an appropriate manner.

c. Whatever you do, don't become emotional yourself.

So, the next time somebody asks you "Who's in charge here?" You can answer "why it's little old rational me."

Chapter 12
The *Inner-World's* Symbiotic Brain

Location of the Symbiotic Styles
Cell Biology 101
Processing of the Symbiotic Brain
The Location of *the SELF*

π This chapter is highly technical and is thus, intended for those who need more of a scientific basis for all that passes in this book. Should you not be that technically interested, skip to page 160 on "The Location of the Self" or just skip this chapter altogether.

Location of the Symbiotic Styles

It's not a no-brainer

It is *not* my purpose to provide incontrovertible proof that the four styles and their symbiotic emotions are located in specific areas of the brain, that's the job of neurobiologists and others in the field. It *is* my purpose to suggest where this neurology might logically exist, sighting why. But first, we need to understand rational and emotional neuron processing in simple terms.

It is my belief that the left and right *rational* brains are the sites of specific rational styles. The right brain contains the processing for and the memories of the director and socializer styles and the left brain contains the processing for and the memories of the analyzer and relator styles.

A simple "split-brain" example might help to illustrate this claim, although I will present more evidence. A man suffering severe seizures had his 80 million axons between his right and left brain severed—it reduced his seizures, but left him with a dilemma. He lovingly caressed his wife with his right hand followed by a punch to her face with his left fist, which is a mystery to many[2], but explainable with symbiotic personality. He caressed his wife with his right hand because his left brain, where love, sorrow and relator

147

memories are stored, controls it. He punched her with the left hand because his right brain, where anger and director memories are stored, controls it. Without this separation, there would be communication between the left and right halves, modifying his reactions. Other proof exists, such as sensory preferences, brain structure and neural excitation, so let's move on to how the genetic predisposition of our primary emotions and rational memories create symbiotic personality.

Strong emotions have many memories—weak emotions few

Up to now, we based our definition of rational style strength on daily usage; the more we used it the stronger the style. But daily usage is a function of the number of memories we have for a style, otherwise we couldn't react in so many more situations with one style than with another. Thus, our strongest style should contain the most rational memories and our weakest styles should contain the least—but how would this come about? The answer is simple, genetics and neural excitation.

The emotional brain is indeed more inhibitory than excitatory[1] otherwise, most anything would trigger an emotion, negating the value of this physical survival. We can use this inhibitory fact to show why we have genetically stronger or weaker primary emotions. In our inhibitory amygdala, our genetically *least inhibitory* emotion would be our *most excitatory* and, thus, our strongest emotion. Likewise, our genetically *most inhibitory* emotion would be our *least excitatory* and our weakest emotion. This leaves us with two other primary emotions that are genetically more inhibitory (less excitatory) than our strongest emotion, and less inhibitory (more excitatory) than our weakest emotion, making them moderate to weak.

For example, I have a strongest anger emotion, a moderate joy emotion, a weak fear emotion, and a weakest sorrow emotion. Thus, my anger is the most excitatory, my sorrow is the least excitatory and my fear is more excitatory than sorrow but less excitatory than joy. This simple, plausible explanation of primary emotional strength, based on the emotion's level of inhibition (excitation) also explains rational style strength.

Emotional memories beget rational memories

Bottom line, sensory memories create emotional memories that create rational memories. Sensory data excites sensory memories that trigger attached emotional memories that trigger an emotional alert. The cause of the emotional alert is then identified by attached sensory and rational memories and quelled by the PFC, with the entire experience being recorded in the frontal cortex as a new rational memory—a memory is born.

For example, if a car backfires next to us, that frightening noise triggers analyzer "backfire" memories attached to auditory "backfire" memories that analyzer memories quickly identify and quell. A new analyzer memory is then created in the analyzer area of the frontal cortex to record that new "backfire" experience, making it available to recall all of the sensory, emotional, and analyzer memories from that and past "backfire" experiences. The point is, the emotional alert needed to be sorted out (identified, quelled and the situation recorded) with symbiotic rational memories, some of which were recalled and some newly created.

Thus it follows: our strongest (most excitatory and most expressed) emotion would create a greater number of new rational memories than would our weaker emotions, making more memories available to sort out our sensed daily experiences, whether an emotion is expressed or not. Now that we have a plausible means for creating style memories, lets unlock the mystery of where the style's rational memories are stored in the rational brain.

Location by sensory attributes

As indicated on page 120, each style usually prefers one type of sensory input, although it may use all types depending on the situation. The director style prefers visual-action sensory input about task-related experiences. The socializer style also prefers visual-action sensory input, but about people-related experiences. The analyzer style prefers visual-word sensory input about task-related experiences and deciphers those words using the language centers. The relator style prefers aurally sensed spoken words about people-related experiences and deciphers them in the language centers. With this in mind, the fact that the right brain does most of our visual processing[2,3] and the fact that the left brain temporal area does most of our language processing,[2,3] we can draw some conclusions.

It is functionally more efficient to have the visual-action director and socializer memories located in the right frontal "visually-oriented" right brain. It is also functionally more efficient to have the written language analyzer and the spoken language relator style's memories located in the "language-oriented" left brain. While this supports our style location theory, it is not enough; we also need to consider left and right brain neuron structures.

Location by neuron attributes

The right brain mostly contains sparsely packed neural clusters interconnected by long axons.[2] The left brain mostly contains densely packed sequential neural clusters with few long interconnecting axons.[2] Strong result-oriented directors and strong people-oriented socializers require right-brain interactive thinking to visually interpret and rationally react to daily situations, switching over to left-brain for more detail. Conversely, strong task-oriented analyzers and strong people-oriented relators rely on detailed left-brain memories to react with daily, switching over to right-brain director and socializer interactive memories as needed.

Everybody uses all four styles, storing left and right brain memories and switching between them as needed. For example (refer to the diagram on the next page), when scanning written text for specific information we automatically use right-brain interactive director (task-related) and socializer (people-related) memories to scan what is written and left-brain language details to determine what was scanned. When looking for a concept described by a word or group of words, our PFC "holds onto" the memories of the word(s) stored in the left brain language centers (through hippocampal looping) to compare them to right-brain images of the scanned written words. Once the desired words are found, the PFC switches over to left-brain analyzer (task-related) and relator (people-related) memories to read it in detail, using written language center memories and other relevant memories scattered throughout the brain to identify what is being read. Once read, the details of it are stored as new mid-term left-brain memories. Once stored as mid-term memory they have to go through the usual processes to become long-term memory a described in detail in Chapter 3.

Experiences are complicated memories

A rational (non-emotional) experience involves the memories of many areas of the right and left brains attached to a newly created rational memory of that experience, which provides another access to that group of memories.

π   This diagram is a variation on the "thinking" diagrams on pages 71, 82 and 100.

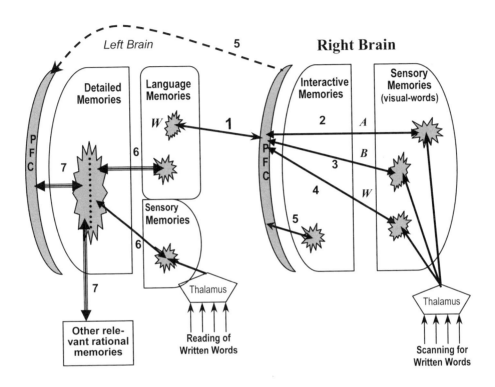

Scanning/Reading Example:

1. The right PFC (Pre-Frontal Cortex) attaches itself to left-brain language memories (*W*) of the words visually scanned.
2. The PFC compares the visually scanned words' sensory memories (*A*) to the language memories (*W*). If no match, the scanning continues.
3. The PFC compares the newly scanned words' sensory memories (*B*) to the language memories (*W*). If no match, the scanning continues.
4. This continues until the PFC compares the scanned words' sensory memories (*W*) to the language memories (*W*) and gets a visual match.
5. After we find the (*W*) words, we stop scanning, leave a memory of that scanning experience in the right frontal cortex, and the PFC switches to left-brain analyzer (task) and relator (people) memories.
6. We then read it in detail, matching known language center memories and storing new language center memories, while understanding what we read using whatever defining rational memories apply.
7. In doing so, we create a new sequential mid-term analyzer memory of what was read, which is attached to word memories stored in the language centers and relevant rational and sensory memories scattered throughout the brain, which were used to understand what was read.

When there is an emotional component involved, for example, when we express sorrow when reading a sad passage, that sorrow pauses the PFC to identify the cause of the sorrow before getting back to the reading, and that sorrow memory becomes attached to that group of memories for that reading experience. And that sorrow re-appears in the future when thinking about that passage.

As you can see any one experience contains many sensory, emotional and rational memories scattered throughout the right and left emotional and rational brains for any one experience.

Music and math experiences

When we are dealing with experiences that involve math or music, we use the right temporal area for numbers (similar to left temporal *written* words) and for the sounds of musical notes (similar to left temporal *spoken* words), and the experiences with these numbers and sounds are stored in the right frontal cortex. This is interesting since subtraction, multiplication, and division—even calculus—are just variations of addition, which is the *interaction of* numbers (memories). Music is the interaction of musical sounds that is best processed in an interactive right brain. If you are a *weak* left-brain analyzer and relator, like me, you can still be an avid reader, but it's a struggle. If you are a *weak* right-brain socializer and director, like my wife, you can still be good at math and music, but it's a struggle.

Getting back to the right and left brains, it seems that their dense sequential left-brain clusters and sparse interactive right-brain clusters coincides with the type of sensory input they process, which also supports our style location theory. It would be helpful if a researcher mapped the axon connections between the symbiotic areas of the emotional brain and the rational brain.

Location by emotional axon mapping

Many axons go from the emotional brain to the rational brain and back again to perceive, identify the cause of, and quell an emotion. There are many more axons going *from* the emotional brain to the rational brain than there are coming back.[1] The axons terminate on numerous areas of the PFC but not the decision-making *lateral* PFC. For structural efficiency, something obvious throughout the brain, the area of the PFC where an emotion's memory axons terminate should be intimately attached to the part of the rational brain where that emotion's symbiotic style's rational memories are stored.

For example, the area of the PFC where "fear axons" terminate should be immediate to the area for storing analyzer memories. Likewise, anger axons should terminate near stored director memories; the same holds true for joy and sorrow axons and memories. Should this be the case, our emotional brain would literally map out our rational brain, determining where its symbiotic rational memories are stored. And, given each *emotion's* level of excitability (or inhibition), it would determine the volume of the rational memories that are stored for each symbiotic emotion.

For example, my strong anger neuron axons would terminate on the PFC adjacent to my many director memories; my moderate joy axons would terminate on the PFC adjacent to my socializer memories; my weak fear axons would terminate near my fewer analyzer memories; and, my weak sorrow axons would terminate near my even fewer relator memories. We can probably verify all of this by research, should anyone care to trace these emotional axons from the amygdala to where they terminate on the PFC, where the rational memory neurons are attached.

In a skullshell

We have provided justification for the right brain to contain the director and socializer styles (memories) and for the left brain to contain the relator and analyzer styles (memories). The next step is to show how each rational style's *purpose* and *motivations* (see pages 117-118) are a function of *where* each style resides in the rational brain. But to do this we need to digress for a moment to summarize synaptic processing—the basis of all memory.

Cell Biology 101

Simply—how neurons work

In its simplicity, a neuron is a building block of memory containing: a cell body (with a nucleus), dendrite receptors (to *receive* neurotransmitters from other neurons) and an axon with terminals (to *send* neurotransmitters to other neurons).

When a neuron gets enough neurotransmitters from other neurons to make it "fire," it sends its own neurotransmitters from its terminals across a synapse (gap) to the dendrite receptors of other neurons. The firing of many neurons in an established neural pattern *is* a memory. Without neural firing, no memory can be established nor remembered. Whether neurons fire or not depends on the quality and quantity of the neurotransmitters it receives at its dendrite receptors.

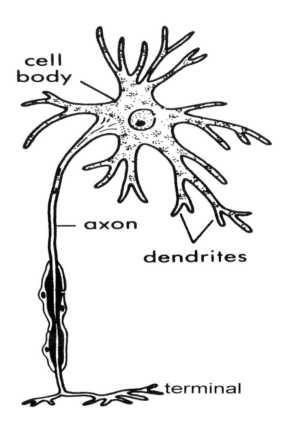

The neurotransmitter can be either excitatory (trying to make the neuron fire) or inhibitory (trying to keep the neuron from firing). Glutamate is the body's main excitatory neurotransmitter and Gamma-Amino-Butyric-Acid (GABA) is its main inhibitory neurotransmitter. All neurons have excitatory and inhibitory receptors and the more excitatory receptors it has the easier it is to fire a neuron. The more inhibitory receptors it has, the more difficult it is to fire a neuron—if *many* inhibitory receptors the neuron will only fire when strongly excited by many other neurons.

Their action is modulated

Special dendrite receptors are scattered throughout the brain that react to peptides, monoamines, and hormones (classified as "modulators"); they affect the excitability of the neuron.[1] When we express an emotion, it dispenses modulators, changing brain chemistry and the way we react. We create memory when there are permanent changes in the various dendrite receptors; this memory will fire in the same pattern when its dendrite receptors are later re-excited in the same manner. For example, when a specific smell is part of an experience, that smell memory makes us remember that experience. Although simple in function (neurons either fire or they don't), their many physical structures make neurons react differently, especially in the *special processing areas* of the brain.

Now getting back to the rational styles, it is my opinion that a style's outwardly observed purpose, motivations and attitudes are a function of neuron excitability in the sparse interactive or dense information structures of the right and left brains respectively, with some consideration given to the special processing areas of the rational brain.

Processing of the Symbiotic Brain

Naturally inhibited emotions require much sensory input

As mentioned, neurons in the emotional brain have many more inhibitory than excitatory receptors.[1] If this were not the case, even the slightest sensory input would trigger an emotional outburst, thereby negating the physical survival value of that emotion (the neuron that cried wolf).

For example, the purpose of fear is "to alert us to danger." If the amygdala were not inhibitory, everything would be a danger thereby negating the value of fear to alert us to *real* danger. Bottom line, it takes strong sensory input to excite enough neurons to trigger an emotion. It is my belief that this inhibitory trait of the emotional brain is applicable to the rational brain, especially the *specialized processing areas* that are more excitatory in the right brain and more inhibitory in the left brain. For example, there is more unique decision-making "spindle neurons" in the right orbito-frontal cortex and anterior cingulate cortex than in the left,[4]

This brings up an ongoing annoyance with research. It would be nice to know which side of the brain the research was done on, as much research measures one side and assumes that the opposite side to be the same. Obviously, this is not always the case since even though the right and left temporal cortices have similar structures; they process different information, processing language on the left and math/music on the right.

If the OFC is inhibited—we can't decide

The specialized processing areas in the brain have special functions that allow us to react differently with each emotion and style—these areas give us impetus or not to make decisions. One specialized area is the left or right "orbito-frontal cortex" (OFC), which is located behind the eyes in the frontal cortex. This area is responsible for sorting out the urges triggered by the emotional brain. A more inhibitory left-brain OFC would stifle most urges by *not* firing (unless the urges were irresistible), negating the excitation of other areas of the brain that would act upon that firing (urge).

Conversely, a more excitatory right-brain OFC would fire, exciting other neurons to act upon those urges, even if they weren't irresistible. For example, if we have an urge to eat ice cream, the more inhibited OFC would stifle that urge by not firing if we weren't hungry, but the more excitable OFC might act upon that urge and excite our pre-motor area to get a cone, even if we weren't hungry. Our ability to resist or give in to urges is obvious when we consider spontaneity. Strong left-brain analyzers and relators lack spontaneity while strong right-brain directors and socializers personify it.

If the ACC is inhibited—we can't decide

Another specialized area critical to rational processing is the "anterior cingulate cortex" (ACC), which resides in a middle layers of the multi-layered PFC. It contains the terminals of axons from emotional and rational memories that the outer layer of the PFC uses to decide with.[1] Since the right *brain* has many interactive neurons with far-reaching axons, the right ACC should too. It seems[2] that the ACC is naturally excitatory, except when fear is expressed and it becomes inhibitory. This inhibition supports my theory that the left ACC can be naturally inhibitory—at least when fear is expressed—and that the right ACC can be naturally excitatory. Thus, sorrow should also cause the left ACC to become inhibitory.

If the Dorsolateral PFC is inhibited—we can't decide

The final specialized area that we will consider is the "dorsolateral PFC," which resides in the outer layers of the PFC. This area is responsible for making decisions with attached rational memories held in the ACC and then acting upon those decisions by exciting the pre-motor cortex. A more inhibited left dorsolateral-PFC would not excite enough of its neurons to fire (to make a decision), which would account for the obvious reluctance of strong analyzers and especially strong relators to make *new* decisions.

Conversely, a more excitable right dorsolateral-PFC would easily excite enough of its neurons to make a decision and act upon it; accounting for the obvious ability of strong directors and socializers to make very quick decisions—maybe too quick—it helps to think first. In summary, a more excitable (right) dorsolateral PFC promotes decision-making, while a more inhibited (left) dorsolateral PFC avoids making decisions.

Our inner-world personality is simple—unlike the outer-world's view of it

Now that we know each style's relationship to the left and right brain structures and specialized areas, let's collapse each style's motivations and attitudes into its purpose. On pages 123 and 124, we collapsed the many *attitudes* of a rational style into its three motivations. Now let's take those three motivations and collapse them into the rational style's purpose by taking into consideration the excitatory and inhibitory natures of the right and left brains, their sparse and dense neural structures, and their more or less excitable specialized processing areas. Thus, we will show how succinctly we can biologically account for the complicated, bewildering outer-world's view of our inner-world.

Our inner-world's analyzer style

The analyzer style's purpose "to unerringly proceed" is supported by three outer-world motivations: "fear of loss/pain," "differences," and "necessities." The "fear of loss/pain" motivation is a direct consequence of its symbiotic fear emotion, avoiding anything that evokes fear or risk. The "differences" motivation is a function of strong left-brain beliefs, which *are* detailed task-oriented sequences about how to proceed. Thus, our left orbito-frontal cortex compares these sequences to what we are doing, indicates any "differences" and makes corrections to unerringly proceed. The "necessities" motivation causes us to stay with the status quo, which is also a function of our detailed left-brain task-oriented beliefs and their comparison to what we are doing by the OFC. We must do what we are used to doing—no changes.

Since fear naturally inhibits the ACC, a variation from the status quo would probably produce fear and shut it down, inhibiting all decisions. In addition, a naturally inhibited dorsolateral PFC would not get excited enough to actually decide on changing the status quo. In conclusion, fear creates left-brain rational beliefs to "unerringly proceed" and supports them with inhibited specialty processing areas that resist change. This creates an outer-world view of an analyzer style that "unerringly proceeds" with its "fear of loss," "differences," and "necessities" motivations and attitudes.

Our inner-world's socializer style

The socializer style's motivations are opposite to the analyzer style. The socializer style is located in the right brain, has the purpose "to address our connections" and is supported by its three outer-world motivations of "desire for gain/pleasure," "similarities," and "possibilities." The "desire for gain or pleasure" is a direct consequence of the socializer style's joy emotion, which activates the "reward centers" of the brain, making us reward ourselves with a pleasurable connection. Unlike the analyzer "differences" motivation that keeps us from acting contrary to our left-brain beliefs, the socializer "similarities" motivation has many similar interactive right-brain memories to decide to react. Unlike the analyzer "necessities" motivation, which demands that we follow our strong left-brain beliefs, the socializer "possibilities" motivation allows us to *choose* how to react among many right-brain possibilities. This choice is initiated by an excited right-brain OFC that makes us act upon our urges aided by an easily excited ACC with its many interactive right-brain axon terminals that gives us many choices to satisfy that urge and quickly decide with an easily excited dorsolateral PFC.

As you have probably noticed, socializers make quick decisions as they interact with others, quickly jumping from one thing to another as the urge arises. In conclusion, joy creates right-brain concepts about how "to address our connections" and initiates these actions with its excited specialty processing areas. This provides others with an outer-world view of the socializer style as it "addresses our connections" with its "desire for gain/pleasure," "similarities," and "possibilities" motivations and attitudes.

Our inner-world's director style

The three outer-world motivations: "decisive," "self-concerned" and "self-directed" are a consequence of the director style's inner-world purpose, "to get resolution." The "decisive" motivation is a consequence of an excited right brain OFC that initiates an urge to get a result, an excited "anterior cingulate cortex" rich with axon terminals from many interactive memories (choices), and an excited dorsolateral PFC to quickly make the decision to attain resolution and act on it by activating the pre-motor areas. The "self-concerned" motivation (i.e., only I have concerns; nobody else) and the "self-directed" (i.e., only my opinions count, nobody else's) is a consequence of the fact that the director style does not store memories about people, only about resolving situations—any people involved are just variables affecting the all-important decision. Also, there are many interactive resolution memories attached to the excited ACC to quickly react.

In conclusion, anger creates right-brain concepts about how to "get resolution" and supports them with its excited specialty areas. This provides others with an outer-world view of the director style as "getting resolution" with its "decisive," "self-concerned," and "self-directed" motivations and attitudes.

Our inner-world's relator style

The three outwardly observed: "indecisive," "others-concerned," and "others-directed" motivations of the relator style are opposite to the director style and support the relator style's purpose "to maintain our connections." The "indecisive" motivation is a consequence of an inhibited OFC that suppresses urges, an inhibited ACC that focuses on "staying connected" memories, leaving the dorsolateral PFC with nothing new to decide unless it is about supporting or reconnecting. The "others-concerned" motivation (i.e., only others concerns count) and the others-directed (i.e., only others opinions are valid) is a consequence of a left-brain ACC that is naturally inhibited or inhibited by oxytocin, making us focuses on sensed concerns and opinions of others instead of our own. Once the concerns and opinions of others are sensed, the relator style's left-brain beliefs dictate how we *must* proceed to reconnect or stay connected, nothing else matters since no other type of memories are stored there.

In conclusion, sorrow creates left-brain memories about how to "maintain our connections" and supports them with inhibited specialty processing areas that resist decisions, allowing us to focus on others needs and opinions. This provides others with an outer-world view of the relator style, as it "maintains our connections" with its "indecisive," "others-concerned" and "others-directed" motivations and attitudes.

In construction

The inner-world neural structures of the right and left brains, their excitability, inhibition, specialized processing areas, and symbiotic emotion's neurotransmitter modulators, account for the outer-world view of each style's purpose, motivations and attitudes. Other theories may exist, but they don't negate this one in which the right brain processes the director and socializer styles and the left brain processes the analyzer and relator styles—this theory can also be used to explain the location of the "self."

The Location of the SELF

It's not easy to locate

No discussion of personality would be complete without considering the concept of "self." The dictionary defines *self* as "1) the total, essential or particular being of a person [personality?]; 2) the essential qualities distinguishing one person from another [personality?]; 3) one's consciousness of one's own being or identity [the ego?]; 4) one's own interests, welfare, or advantage [survival?]." A fifth definition would obviously include our DNA coding, which is unique, except maybe for some identical twins. Philosophers and scientists for thousands of years have attributed the "self" to everything from glandular disorders to spirituality. Except for one definition of self, based on synaptic processing[1], almost all definitions consider the outer-world view of the self. Like personality, which is misleading when viewed from the outer-world view, the outer-world view of self is also misleading—others cannot define *our* inner-world self, only we can.

Is it in our accomplishments—or lack of them?

To attain an adequate measure of self we must define its components and their importance to us. One component is how well we think our physical appearance fits in with our lifestyle, which is something that may be overly important for some. Another component is our accomplishments, which we are rightfully proud of, positively contributing to self. A third is our *lack* of accomplishment, because others have imposed unrealizable standards on us, negatively contributing to self—outer-world views unfortunately have an affect on how some of us define our self.

The most important component of self is our genetic/learned personality and the integrity with which we react. If we maintain our integrity (see page 50), we positively contribute to self by consistently reacting according to those strong integrity beliefs (memories)—this consistency is crucial to defining the self.

Is it in the ego—or in the mirror?

When consulting the dictionary, one of its "self" definitions includes "*ego*— 1) the self as distinct from the world and other selves [self-recognition], and 2) an exaggerated sense of self-importance." Definition 1, the "face area" of the brain[3], just behind the ear allows us to store memories of faces so that we can match those memories to visual sensory input and "recognize" someone. This is an important aspect of social and physical survival since we need to be able to recognize friend from foe.

One important face to remember is our own, as seen in mirrors, pictures, videos, etc.—this visually reinforces the belief that we exist. By noticing that nobody else looks exactly like us, we fortify the belief that what we see in the mirror is unique. People who have a damaged brain "face area" can't recognize others; they can't even recognize themselves in a mirror. And since they can't recognize themselves, they have no memories attached to the sensory representation of that face. Those afflicted have no name, no identity, no personality, nothing to distinguish them from everybody else in the world—they have no self.

Is ego a right brain resident?

Ego Definition 2, "an exaggerated sense of self-importance" many believe, resides in the right brain for which there is justification. As discussed above, the director and socializer styles and their attributes reside in the right brain. The socializer's contribution to ego is its purpose "to address our connections," requiring a false sense of self-importance to believe that our positive and negative connections naturally want to interact with us. The director style's contribution to ego is its "self-concerned" and "self-directed" motivations putting the director's opinions or concerns above all others. This combination of right-brain socializer and director thinking *is* "an exaggerated sense of self-importance."

It is our inner-world—nothing less—but maybe more

Our unique genetics, facial recognition, learned mental and physical skills and learned personality (memories), which reside in every aspect of our physical and mental being make up the self—self is the sum total of us.

Whether a spiritual or ethereal component to self exists or not is difficult to prove unless you believe in ghosts. The spiritual self can simply be an unrealistic, emotionally excited belief or it may actually exist. Those of us who've had experience with telepathy, telekinesis or mediums (spirits) are more likely to believe in a spiritual component than those of us who haven't.

Lastly, the goal of every living entity from the simple blade of grass to the complex human is gene survival, which involuntarily places great value on propagating its unique DNA—its "self."

REFERENCES Interpreted as Support for My Conclusions:

1. Joseph LeDoux, *Synaptic Self,* (Viking, 2002)

2. Rita Carter, *Mapping the Mind,* (U of CA Press, 1999)

3. Rita Carter, *Mapping the Memory,* (Ulysses Press, 2006)

4. J. Allman, A. Hakeem, N. Tetreault, "The spindle neurons of frontoinsular cortex (area FI) are unique to humans and African apes," Society for Neuroscience Abstract Viewer & Itinerary Planner. 2003. Abstract No. 725.5.

Chapter 13
Finessing the *Inner-World's Memories*

Personality *Imbalance*
Finessing *Memories*
My Personality Evolution

Personality *Imbalance*

Time and evolution wait for no man

It took billions of years to evolve from bacteria to animals and hundreds of millions of years for mammals to evolve into rational humans. A single human life span is indeed very short in comparison, but it still offers an opportunity for further evolution with our highly evolved rational brain.

Nature has gifted us with purposeful emotions and rational styles, but not equally. Every emotion is important to our physical survival and every rational style is important to our social survival—thus, our weak emotions and styles put our survival in jeopardy—we need to resolve this imbalance. Unfortunately, our imbalanced personality is all we have to work with, but it is up to the task if we are!

The long and the short of it

There are at least three techniques for balancing our personality, two are short-term and one is long-term—kind of like types of memory. One technique deals with short-term finessing of strong emotions, another deals with short-term finessing of weak styles, and the third deals with long-term finessing of all strong and weak emotions and styles. A short-term finessing technique called "Mind-set" can help you reduce the use of strong emotions; refer to Chapter 14. Mind-set involves the creation and fortification of memories to automatically identify the cause of and quell an emotional alert at an upcoming event. For example, if we need to effectively work with others tomorrow and know that they will probably provoke our anger, we can mentally create director memories to identify the cause of tomorrow's possible confrontation and quell the anger as it builds, *before* externally expressing it.

Mind-set is very effective, I've successfully used it for decades, but it is just a quick patch on a predictable emotional outburst. Another short-term technique involves "role-playing" for more appropriate use of a weak rational style; refer to Chapter 14 for details.

Nothing succeeds like Mind-set

Mind-set also allows us to use a more appropriate style once we quell our strongest emotion. For example, if I (a strong-director/weak-relator) am going to a family reunion where I am sure to encounter family members I dislike, I use Mind-set to repress my anger *and* to enhance my role-playing by including in my Mind-set the memory that "I will love all and all will love me at tomorrow's family reunion." Then, at the family reunion, I role-play as a relator to bond with others and possibly even clean up some past issues. This effective two-step short-term approach always works, except when we are distressed; unfortunately, it does little to permanently improve a genetic personality imbalance.

The long-term personality balancing technique involves avoiding rationalization of strong emotions by identifying their cause and creating emotional and rational memories for weak emotions and styles by finessing memories. This creates mid-term memories that repetition strengthens in future situations.

Finessing *Memories*

Some are born lucky—the rest need help

Few of us are born with a balanced personality that allows for the appropriate use of emotions/styles when not distressed, the rest of us are born with easily triggered (strong) emotions and rarely triggered (weak) emotions with their symbiotic strong and weak symbiotic styles.

There are a myriad of emotional memories to trigger our strong emotions attached to a myriad of rational memories to identify their cause and move on or to rationalize with, thereby blocking the few memories we have for the use of more appropriate emotions or styles. Thus, we need to create emotional memories to trigger our weak emotions, and we need to attach rational memories to them that identify their cause and quell them, allowing us to have a more appropriate reaction using that rational style—but we must do this in an orderly fashion.

First we must stop rationalizing strong emotions; second we must create many more memories for our weak emotions, and third we must create rational memories that identify and record experiences involving them.

Two rationalizations don't make a right

We must stop rationalizing our *strong* emotions—*every* emotion is real, but not necessarily appropriate. For example, if verbally or physically confronted our alerting anger emotion and our decisive director style reaction are appropriate because that's what evolution intended. But if there is no confrontation, the anger is inappropriate. When there is danger or risk, our alerting fear emotion and analyzer style reaction are also appropriate, but if there is no danger or risk, it is inappropriate. Inappropriate, rationalized emotions are of two types—displaced and deluding.

Those who cannot forget the past are condemned to repeat it

Past situations cause rationalization of *displaced* emotions that make us feel as if we are reliving that experience. For example, we may have been abandoned as a child and feel anger, fear or sorrow when someone makes a harmless comment that triggers that strong abandonment memory. The anger, fear or sorrow is very real, but its cause is not in the present; it's in the past—displaced.

Another common example of a displaced emotion is a vicious dog attack when we were young creating a "dog danger" emotional memory that triggers fear every time we see a dog. The dog we presently see is probably not a danger; the erroneously triggered fear memory of that bygone dog attack makes us think it is. Instead of consciously identifying the original attack as the cause of our displaced fear and quelling it, we unconsciously relive the attack and re-express the fear, unconsciously labeling all dogs as vicious and rationalizing that fear. To simply address the fact that the past attack caused the fear may bring up too many painful memories, but it is the only way to avoid rationalization of this experience every time we see a dog.

165

Laboring under a delusion

The *present* situation causes rationalized *deluded* emotions that we can't face. For example, after my fourth glass of wine at dinner my wife gave me "that look" and told me that I was having too much alcohol. I became silently angry, deluding myself that she was the cause of my anger—its true cause was that "she was probably right, but I didn't want to face it"; I just wanted to enjoy the wine. Instead of consciously identifying this and quelling my anger, I quickly rationalized it with erroneous causes such as "who is she to tell me how much to drink" (re-triggering my anger); "I've had more wine than this before and was fine" (re-triggering my anger); "just because she can't tolerate alcohol she thinks nobody else can" (re-triggering my anger)—I was unconsciously deluding myself to avoid the truth.

Another example of how we delude ourselves is at work when our boss makes a negative comment about a report that we had recently handed in. We may express fear, anger or sorrow and unconsciously rationalize it with erroneous causes such as "my boss is always so critical" (re-triggering the emotion); "*he* was wrong the last time he criticized my work" (re-triggering the emotion); "he's not always correct either" (re-triggering the emotion); and on and on, avoiding the real cause of the fear or anger, which was that the boss was right. If instead, we had *consciously* admitted that the report wasn't very good because we had little time to properly complete it, we would have quelled the fear, anger or sorrow and avoided the rationalization.

Most of our rationalizations come from not accepting responsibility for our inadequacies, mistakes or shortcomings, causing us to delude ourselves instead of facing who we are or what we did or didn't do. The rest of our rationalizations are caused by displaced emotions from long past experiences that haunt us and hijack our rational brain. Bottom line, we can't avoid rationalization of inappropriate emotions unless we consciously identify their true cause as either displaced from the past or as a deluding of ourselves and identify the emotion's true cause, which is not always easy to do.

The first step is the hardest

Unconscious rationalizing from displaced emotions of bygone experiences or emotionally deluding ourselves about our inadequacies will not quell an emotion and allow us to move on—we need to consciously identify the true cause of that very real emotion. Strong analyzers need to consciously identify the danger or risk and whether it's real, erroneously displaced or deluding them—most of their danger is erroneous.

Strong directors need to consciously identify what is confronting or hindering them and whether it is real or erroneously displaced or deluding them—most of their confrontation is erroneous. Strong relators need to consciously identify what is disconnecting them and whether it is real, erroneously displaced or deluding them—most of their disconnections are erroneous. Strong socializers need to consciously identify the importance of the sensed connection and whether it is positive, negative or unimportant (erroneously displaced or deluding them). Bottom line, we need to consciously avoid natural unconscious rationalization and take rational control to quell the emotion and loosen its grip on our conscious mind.

Knowing our "hot button" helps

Throughout this book, we have come to realize that most of our emotional alerts are inappropriate; the reason for much of it is our "hot button." By identifying our hot buttons, we can take a major step in ridding ourselves of inappropriate strong emotions that hijack our conscious brain and promote rationalization. It takes much introspection to determine our hot buttons since we're too busy rationalizing to notice them when they're pressed. Strong analyzers need to identify the key danger to their existence that triggers their inappropriate fears, for example, financial insecurity. Strong directors need to identify their key confrontation that triggers their inappropriate anger, for example, rejection. Strong relators need to identify their key disconnection, for example, their broken childhood home. Strong socializers need to identify their key connection, for example, something they are desperately seeking. It isn't easy for us to determine our hot buttons, but those close to us usually have a better take on it—so ask them!

Other's hot buttons are more obvious

It wouldn't take my wife very long to identify my anger hot button—rejection. As a child I was rejected by my mother who hid us away in a foster home for years until she was financially able to "collect us" once remarried. Rejection confronts me with that devastating memory of being abandoned, provoking my anger. I am happy to say that my mother and I reconciled a few years before her death, but I still become angered when I sense rejection, whether it is real (rarely) or erroneously displaced (usually).

By realizing that erroneous rejection caused much of my anger, I was able to do something about it. Now, if I erroneously perceive rejection and express anger I think, "this rejection isn't real, it's a ghost from the past"; this quells the anger and the experience adds a new director memory to my arsenal for future use to identify that erroneous rejection.

An example of how invasive erroneous rejection can be is when somebody has "better connections" than I do (i.e., a better house, car, higher paying job, etc.). Yes, all strong directors confront themselves with this type of *self-invalidation* as described in Chapter 5, but in my case, I usually interpret it as rejection. I now deal with it by avoiding rationalization, identifying the confrontation as erroneous rejection, and quelling the anger. And to rationally complete the experience I consciously accept that they're just doing their thing and that I'm just doing mine. Their connections are not my connections, and as long as I am happy with mine, I have no problems with theirs. This creates an even stronger director memory to identify, quell and react to situations in the future caused by erroneous rejection.

Sometimes we need a shotgun approach

Identifying confrontation/hindrance is not always obvious; sometimes we need much identification when the angry experience is more than one angry outburst. For example, one day I was walking up a ramp to try to catch a train, and there were many others in front of me—a hindrance, but an acceptable one. Then an obnoxious fool and his friends stopped short to take a picture, holding up the crowd that was piling up on me; a definite hindrance, but I got over it. The fool did this twice more, hindering then confronting and angering me. I decided to try to get around them, but their stretching across the walkway prevented it. I then maneuvered around the obnoxious shutterbug, slightly bumping his highly protrusive gut, excusing myself. He remarked, "Why don't you knock me over while you're at it?" to which I replied; "I *said* excuse me." He (a strong director looking for an argument) rhetorically replied, "Oh, so as long as you say excuse me it's OK to knock me over." To which I replied "So it's OK to knock you over if I say excuse me?" Dumbfounded he had no reply, prompting his lanky, brown-tooth mentally challenged friend to spit out "Yeah, I'll knock you real hard!" To which I replied "Oh, my Hero!" We moved on, and that was that except for my ensuing rationalization.

The fools were not worth a thought, but the multifaceted experience showed many unresolved angers. My own self-invalidation caused the initial hindrance, which I acknowledged and which quelled that anger, but when they stopped twice more it re-triggered my anger. After rationalizing for a moment, I realized that from behind that shutterpig reminded me of a bully from my past that I hated—that identification quelled the anger. But I still had real anger to deal with, the confrontation of me bumping him and him confronting me about it. After our altercation and the ensuing rationalization, I realized that the bump wasn't intentional; my inner ear balance problem caused it. That was the final anger to quell, to stop the rationalization of that unpleasant situation. Bottom line, many angers cause many rationalizations *at once* and need individual identification to quell each and move on.

Don't rationalize—quell it—move on

It's difficult to accept our natural personality imbalance and thus, our natural inappropriateness, but if we put it into prospective, we can accept who we are and evolve. Structurally, our strongest emotion is naturally more excitable than our weaker emotions and is erroneously expressed much of the time, so why rationalize it? If sensory input evokes our strong fear, the fear isn't valid;, there is no threat of danger, so why justify it through rationalization; why not just quell the fear and move on? Similarly, if sensory input erroneously evokes our strong anger, that anger isn't valid; there's nothing confronting us, so why try to justify the anger instead of just moving on? The answer is simple; it's easier to unconsciously react than it is to make a *conscious* decision about how to appropriately react.

Modern man has evolved too quickly from mere physical survival to social survival, and rationalization is a fail-safe to unconsciously deal with emotional alerts until we can get them rationally under control. So, either we can wait a hundred thousand years for humans to evolve into erring on the side of appropriateness, or we can do something about it now!

The next step—create new memories

To better balance our personality, we must create emotional memories that trigger *weak* emotions, while simultaneously attaching new rational memories, all recorded as a new rational experience memory for future reference in similar situations. For example, if we are a strong director and weak relator we must create sorrow memories to detect disconnection, relator memories to identify the cause of disconnection (our angry outburst) to quell the sorrow, reconnect, and record that experience as a new *relator* memory containing sensory, anger, sorrow and relator memories of that experience. This newly recoded relator memory is then available for future reference when we have another angry outburst and need to reconnect.

With time and effort, we will establish many emotional and rational memories, for example, for every anger outburst we can attach specific sorrow and relator memories to it for future reference. When we have a sufficient store of emotional (e.g., sorrow) and rational (e.g., relator) memories that emotion and rational style will no longer be weak—we'll have a more balanced personality. Most people don't realize it, but *real growth* is in fact a growth in weak emotional and rational style *memories* that automatically lead to a more balanced personality and not just learning some new task or idea.

Consciousness is the key

Personality balancing relies on one simple principle—that we are *consciously* aware of the emotional alert and *consciously* identify its true cause, thus quelling the emotion, fulfilling its symbiotic style's purpose and recording a rational memory of the experience for future use. For example, if we lose our job, intense fear will alert us to the danger of not providing our family with the ability to physically survive (home, food, etc.). The fear will be rationalized with many analyzer memories of losing our home, starving our family, and changing our lifestyle, prolonging that intense fear for minutes or days. When we have other resources such as savings, retirement, home equity, etc., we can quell that intense fear by balancing the joy of our resources with our fears and storing that experience as a new analyzer memory containing both the problem and solution. Unfortunately, we can't do that until we identify the *real* danger and quell the fear.

The real danger might be that we are terrified of not being able to provide for ourselves because we were poor as a child with a drunken provider that we couldn't rely on. Once we identify this "I can't provide for myself either hot button," we quell the fear. We free ourselves from thinking only with fear and analyzer memories; we allow ourselves to remembering our bank savings to feed our family for many months until we find a new job; we express joy when reminded that "we have enough home equity to cover the mortgage payments to keep a roof over our heads."

Thus, by *consciously* attaching rational memories to emotional alerts that identify its cause we quell the emotional alert. This frees our minds to use rational memories from other styles to react more appropriately and record the entire experience for future reference. And when the rational thoughts that are freed up involve our weak emotions/styles we get a bonus, we increase our weak emotional and rational memories, better balancing our personality—as I did.

My Personality Evolution

In the beginning, there was the imbalance

We start our lives with emotional memories devoid of attached rational memories; we end our lives with countless interconnected emotional and rational memories that no longer do us any good. In between, we establish an abundance of memories with our stronger emotions and styles and a scarcity of memories with our weaker emotions and styles. This abundance or scarcity makes our reactions inappropriate much of the time, especially when we're distressed.

If we're born with a more balanced genetic personality, that is, with four *moderate* emotions and styles, we can react appropriately much of the time—except when distressed, when we react with our strongest style. Unfortunately, only a small percentage of us have this more balanced pattern—most of us have strong and weak emotions and styles and too many of the weak and strong styles are opposite and conflicting as noted in Chapter 10.

The next question that probably comes to mind is: "Is it possible to have a 'perfect personality' that can appropriately react in every situation?" Emotionally, the perfect personality would require equally weak anger, fear, joy, and sorrow emotions (all with highly inhibited neurons) to avoid inappropriate emotional outbursts, which is possible. Unfortunately, that would put our physical survival system in peril, negating that important aspect of our personality. Rationally, the perfect personality would require equally moderate rational styles; this too is possible. But it would also require that each style have sufficient memories to ruminate in order to decide how to appropriately react in every situation. Unfortunately, in doing so, we would waste so much time trying to choose the appropriate style option that the situation would pass us by before we reacted—hey, that sounds like a strong analyzer.

Bottom line, the perfect personality doesn't exist! Top line, we can have a better-balanced personality if we avoid rationalization, reduce the influence of our strong emotions, increase the influence of weaker emotions, and react with the more appropriate style.

A little knowledge is a wonderful thing

We constantly establish new alerting emotional memories and reacting rational memories with our strong emotions and styles, but rarely with our weaker. The first step then towards a better personality balance, would be to increase the use of our weak people-oriented styles and emotions in people-oriented situations and our weak task-oriented styles and emotions in task-oriented situations. The final step would be to use the most appropriate emotion and style in as many situations as possible.

To do this we need to increase our weak emotion and style memories, which is difficult, since our weak emotion's highly inhibitory neurons are naturally inadequate to build them; otherwise they would have already done so. Nature is fighting us, but it has also provided us with the means to prevail, as evidenced by evolution itself. Evolution chose to evolve emotionally first for physical survival and rationally later for social survival; maybe we should do the same. For example, I tried to finesse my weak relator style in people-oriented situations in lieu of my strong director style, using techniques in Chapter 14, but with little permanent success. What did succeed, and it took decades to discover this, was to create sorrow memories to sense disconnection and then attach relator memories to them to identify the disconnection and reconnect—the simplest things tend to elude us.

The leopard can change its spots

At age 29, I took a personality test that was as accurate as it was depressing. I have the common "jerk" pattern—very strong director and very weak relator, compounded by a moderate socializer and a weak analyzer style. My moderate socializer style allowed me to identify and rationally enjoy my important connections. My strong director style made me self-oriented, offending many and causing mistakes. My weak relator style rarely helped me to reconnect to others that I had offended. My weak analyzer style rarely helped me to avoid mistakes and danger. In a nutshell, I was clueless as to how I negatively affected others and frequently put myself in danger or at risk.

The more things change the more they stay the same

After decades of research involving thousands of people and much intro-spection, I discovered Symbiotic Personality, which made me aware that I had a very weak sorrow emotion. I couldn't feel the pain of disconnection from others, and even when I could, my very weak relator style rarely al-lowed me to reconnect, being devoid of relator experience memories.

Now I can feel sorrow (maybe too much at times) and can use my weak relator style to reconnect with others that I have offended or who have of-fended me. I can also use my relator style more often because I am more aware of the thoughts, needs and opinions of others, allowing me to feel "love" (refer to Chapter 4) more often. It took *me* a long time to develop this because I had to figure it out, but you don't have to figure it out so your personality evolution shouldn't take too long.

Over the decades, I have employed many helpful techniques to use my weak relator style in lieu of my strong director style, but they were just short-term solutions (refer to Chapter 14). Once I realized that my lack of sorrow blocked my progress, my goal became its greater use, but rationalization of my anger blocked that sorrow. I had to consciously stop the rationalization and identify the real confrontation to quell the anger and feel the sorrow.

Using brain plasticity to my advantage

Due to the amazing plasticity of the brain, we attach new rational memories (to record an experience) to sensory and emotional memories every time we trigger an emotional memory, which can be to our advantage or disadvan-tage. For example, it is to our *advantage* when we walk by a yard, are frightened by a barking, snarling dog, identify that the dog is fenced in, and record that experience with an analyzer memory of that frightening dog be-ing behind a fence. Thus, when we walk by and are startled again, by that dog, we quickly identify the situation as the dog being behind the fence, re-alizing that the fear is erroneous (the dog presents no danger), quelling the fear and recording that new experience with a new analyzer memory. Eventually, if we walk by enough, we anticipate that fenced-in dog, identify it as not dangerous and quell the emerging fear as we pass.

An example of using brain plasticity to our *disadvantage* is when we use erroneous causes to rationalize angry outbursts, attaching new director memories to that experience and strengthening that anger memory. Thus, rationalization strengthened my many anger memories, impeding my progress—I had to do something about that.

Fighting rationalization with fire

I needed to stop rationalizing my erroneous anger using any method possible. Sometimes I would try to talk myself out of it, even yelling at myself for rationalizing, which didn't help much. I eventually realized that the best way to stop the rationalization was to identify the real cause of the anger, which amazingly quelled it. Eventually, one anger-evoking situation at a time, I avoided rationalization, identified the cause, and quelled the anger, building up useful director memories to deal with future anger.

Now, most of my angry outbursts automatically trigger rational memories that automatically identify the confrontation and quell the anger. Of course, there are times when I am distressed and my anger/rage hijacks my PFC and I loose control—fortunately, those situations are rare.

I needed it like a hole in my anger

Once my anger was quelled, it created an emotional void for sorrow to be expressed. Unfortunately, I had few sorrow-triggering memories to work with—bottom line, I still couldn't sense the disconnection my anger caused. It took me many, many years, one non-rationalized experience at a time, to establish enough sorrow memories to become sensitize to my disconnection from others—reconnection was another matter altogether.

Eventually, even though my sorrow experiences identified the disconnection, quelled the sorrow and allowed me to use my relator style, my strong director style would distract me to resolve some task, recording that experience as a director memory instead of a relator memory. Thus, when I would have an angry outburst in a similar situation, identify the erroneous confrontation and quell the anger using memories of previously recorded experiences I couldn't reconnect because there were no attached relator memories.

Simply put, the sorrow-causing anger only accessed director memories since there were no attached relator memories. Bottom line, even when I avoided rationalization and expressed sorrow I still didn't reconnect. And, since I was not yet aware of symbiotic personality, I didn't know how to resolve it.

Never say never

Initially, one situation at a time, through great conscious effort, I created relator memories to record the reason for the sorrow and how I reacted to it, allowing me to stay with my relator style instead of having it kicked out of my consciousness by my strong director style. What helped was to remove all tasks from my mind and instead, focused on the expressions, opinions and needs of the other person.

Eventually, I began to feel "love," elevating my oxytocin (vasopressin) brain levels and feeling as one with the other person, momentarily making their needs, concerns, and beliefs my own, which is the essence of using the relator style for reconnecting. The more relator memories I attached to the sorrow memories, the more automatically they identified the cause of the sorrow, quelling it, and the more clues (relator memories) I could use to re-connect. And each new experience recorded a new relator memory of what happened and how I rationally reacted, allowing me to do the same in the future for similar experiences.

Today, my sorrow memories alert me to my disconnections, and their attached relator memories help me identify the cause, allowing me to quickly reconnect in minutes instead of hours or days. Bottom line, I'm not a strong relator (there's no excess of relator memories), but I'm not a weak relator (there's sufficient relator memories) to use my relator style as needed.

The above three-step process: (1) avoid rationalization of a strongest emotion, (2) build memories for a weak emotion, and (3) build memories for that weak emotion's symbiotic style, applies to the greater use of my relator style over my strong director style. This process equally applies to any combination of strong and weak styles, for example, non-rationalization of fear along with increasing joy memories can help strong analyzers who are weak socializers to get more joy out of life.

This brings us to the final step in *my* personality evolution: the more appropriate use of my weak fear emotion and analyzer style. To accomplish this I had to create emotional memories to trigger fear and attach analyzer memories to record each experience, eventually allowing me to control my dangerous and inappropriate impulses.

One balanced emotion does not a human make

I have been fearless (reckless) most of my life—I don't know how I ever survived—but I am not alone. Many of us are weak in fear and the analyzer style; it becomes dangerous, though, when they are also strong in the director and/or socializer style. Strong socializers try to push the envelope and explore the "possibilities," ignoring the good sense attached to the "necessities" of avoiding certain aspects of life. Strong directors also test for limits and sometimes exceed them to their detriment. Strong directors also reject concerns and opinions that are not their own, for example, we deal with local traffic laws *impulsively* (some might say repulsively). When we see a speed limit we get an impulse to speed, when we encounter a stop sign we get an impulse to roll through it, when we see a yellow light we get an impulse to speed up and run a red light, when we are stuck behind someone we get a strong impulse to swerve around them, and when passed by someone we get an impulse to pass them. These impulses, caused mostly by self-invalidation (see Chapter 5), can cause problems for strong directors and for society in general. One of my anger "hot buttons" had to do with diving, so it was a good place for me to start. Here is the story of how I became aware of the need for a more cautious life and how I attained that goal for a better personality balance.

One man's loss is another man's license

One evening, upon returning home from a long car trip, I got a speeding ticket, paid the fine and thought little of it—exactly one year later, it happened again. Should it have happened again over the following six months, I would have lost my driver's license; I thought much of it. If I lost my license I couldn't pick up my children after school, I couldn't run necessary errands, and would be wasting $800/month on a leased automobile that I couldn't drive.

I panicked and went to the state's DMV website to look up a safe-driver program to reduce my points. Instead, I found out that my two speeding tickets, besides costing me $300 in fines, would cost me an "assessment fee" of $375. I also found a list of driving infractions and their point value, many of which I was not aware of—it scared the hell out of me. Just one trip to pick up my kids at school could easily generate enough point violations to lose my license.

I was what is called an "aggressive driver," who typically speeds, who constantly switches lanes sometimes cutting people off, who speeds up at yellow lights and ends up running red lights, who slowly rolls through stop signs and right-turns on red, and who is instantly aggravated by other drivers who get in the way. In short, I was an angry driver who was afraid of little—but I couldn't afford to be any more.

Unavoidable

My greatest danger was that almost any infraction could have cost me my license. I not only had to stop speeding, I had to change my entire attitude about driving. Frankly, I hated driving and couldn't wait to get to where I was going—it was boring, and so I made it more exciting. Driving was annoying and frustrating, urging me to quickly get around hindrances. Driving also caused a lot of guilt when I knowingly offended others with my driving (a consequence of my newly strengthened sorrow). But hate it or not, driving is unavoidable.

For weeks, I was fearful, if not paranoid, about all aspects of driving. Every time my speedometer went over the speed limit, I expressed fear, identifying the danger as the possible loss of my license, slowing down and recording that experience with an analyzer memory, including my slowing down to the speed limit. This happened many, many times a day, strengthening that fear memory and its analyzer reaction to slow down below the speed limit.

Although the alerting fear and analyzer reactions served their purpose and made me a less aggressive driver, I still had my aggressive driver impulses to get over. I then realized that I could attain my purpose (to save my license) by changing my driving attitude, which I realized was a consequence of my inappropriate driving *goal*—so all I had to do was establish a more appropriate goal.

Of two evils, choose the lesser

My old driving goal was due to boredom and a strong "get it done" director style to quickly complete any trip. On repetitive short trips, for example, picking up my kids, I would try to get there in minimal time, possibly breaking some previous record. On out of town trips, my goal was to get there by a certain time or average a certain speed (usually speeding). My new driving goal was simple: I would *never* consciously drive over the speed limit. This meant that I would have to constantly keep track of my speed and keep it under the speed limit, which was difficult in town at low speed limits that nobody seemed to follow.

I would constantly keep track of my speed and the local speed limits, and when I accidentally went over the speed limit, I would express fear, identify the danger of losing my license, and immediately slow down—one situation at a time. Eventually, I realized that I could simply set my cruise control for one mile under the speed limit to attain my new driving goal. And although unplanned, my new goal resolved other aspects of my aggressive driving.

A blessing in disguise

By staying below the speed limit, there was no need to switch lanes or cut people off any more; I just stayed in the slow lane and everybody passed me by. There was no yelling and guilt from offending others; now I only offend aggressive drivers impatient with me. I no longer ran yellow/red lights; by the time I reached the intersection, they were already red. I no longer rolled through stop signs and right turns on red; I was going so slow that stopping wasn't much of a change in speed. There was no need to speed up and pass others who were slow—hell, I was the slowest person on the road. And besides, to pass anyone I usually had to go over the speed limit, which was a no-no.

So, instead of getting angry with others holding me up, I just relaxed and thought of other things until I could proceed. There were though, a few instances when I was distressed and got frustrated with and yelled at other drivers whose driving judgment was very poor, for example, very fearful drivers taking a very long time trying to make a left turn in moderate traffic. The yelling did neither me nor the other driver any good and eventually became a rare occasion.

Success is never final

Throughout this process, I automatically reduced my driving anger and weakened my many anger memories attached to driving—talk about reducing rationalization; if there's no anger there's no anger to rationalize. But of course, my patients had limits, especially when I was distressed. Upon occasion, I would get angry at and pass other drivers, negating my driving goal, upsetting them and upsetting myself with strong fear, but this just fortified how inappropriate my old driving attitude was.

Over the six months that I was paranoid about losing my license, I increase my fear memories every time I passed the speed limit or had the opportunity to test a traffic law (i.e., stop sign, yellow light, etc.). I automatically identified the danger as losing my license and automatically created analyzer memories that made me aware of the consequences, thereby dictating my rational reactions. After many months I was able to use my analyzer style to react more appropriately—well, at least when driving.

Damn the paranoia full speed ahead

A special bonus came with this process, my "problem with authority" or more accurately "paranoia with authority figures" reduced significantly. Since I was not violating traffic laws, the police had no issues with me and thus, I had no issues with them. Being a strong director and knowing I was violating some law as an aggressive driver made me paranoid when I noticed an authority figure lurking about. The paranoia manifested itself as rationalization of why the authorities had no right to hassle me (which they did), and how I would confront them if caught—this is no way to live! In time, I zeroed out my driving violation points and my fear of losing my license diminished, but not enough.

No good deed goes unpunished

Since the fear of going over the speed limit was well established, I now had a problem with fear instead of anger. Even with no driving violation points, I experienced fear each time I exceeded the speed limit, but this seemed to naturally sort itself out. Over many weeks and many speedometer viewings, I attached analyzer memories to that fear, by telling myself that there was no immanent danger of losing my license, but that I should probably slow down. After many months, my "going over the speed limit" fear noticeably reduced from strong (danger) to mild (risk). In essence, I established analyzer memories that no longer required fear to alert me to exceeding the speed limit; the sensory input (seeing my speedometer speed) unconsciously slowed me down. This lack of emotion (anger or fear) made driving more pleasant than stressful, but I was tired of just moping along, getting passed by every little white-haired old lady peering through her steering wheel.

I knew that I couldn't go back to my old driving attitude and, thus, had to established a new driving goal, which was to drive near, but not more than 7 mph over the speed limit, which seemed realistic. This new goal eliminated the same problems that never going over the speed limit did, but it also gave me some flexibility to pass slow white-haired old ladies. In general, I still use my cruise control to drive within ± 7 mph of the speed limit on high-ways and ± 4 mph in the city—when I go over my mph goal I experience mild fear that alerts me to the *risk* of getting a ticket, but not to the *danger* of losing my license.

You can't argue with success

The fear triggered by the danger of losing my license spilled over to other aspects of my aggressive driving urges. It now seemed risky to give in to urges to cut others off, not fully stop at stop signs or flashing red lights, not stop at a yellow light as it turns red, and all the other aspects of aggressive driving. Every time I feel one of these urges I express mild fear, identify the risk of getting a ticket (fear) or offending others (sorrow), which quells the fear or sorrow, and the urge, while it records another analyzer memory of that experience for future use. And each time I re-experienced a previous urge those analyzer and relator memories become stronger.

When I drive, I drive with my director memories, both consciously and un-consciously, creating new director memories that record each noteworthy experience. But now, my new analyzer memories interject into each driving experience, attached to the director memories that recorded those experi-ences. Thus, when a driving situation occurs I now have the option to use director memories and give into my urges or switch over to my analyzer memories and quell those urges, which I mostly do. By not giving in to those urges, I create new or strengthen established analyzer memories about not giving in to them, making it easier each time not to give in. These ana-lyzer memories have also attached themselves to other director memories and urges with similar sensory input that has nothing to do with driving— they increase daily.

Fools rush in where analyzers fear to tread

I now find myself less likely to give in to my usual urges and do something dangerous or dumb. Now, before I do something stupid my analyzer memories allow me to proceed more cautiously. For example, my family and I were visiting a museum that had a new exhibit under construction, with walls and signs restricting us from entering that area. In the past, that inhibition would evoke mild anger ("they can't tell me where to go") and urge me to go into the area to see what was going on. But this time I didn't. I seemed to naturally quell that urge and didn't go into the restricted area; it amazed me. The risk of clashing with authority may have caused mild fear, causing my indecisive analyzer left brain to quell the urge instead of giving into it with my decisive director right brain. My urge to confront authority has diminished in all areas of my life, but not because I now fear authority, I just don't feel the need to create erroneous confrontation with it any more, making me much less paranoid and confronted by it. Authority is what it is; it has its purpose just like everything else.

My lack of urges to fight authority weren't the only changes; I now have more analyzer options to unerringly proceed in all aspects of my life. I now plan ahead and give myself enough time to do tasks more comprehensively with my analyzer style instead of giving into my director style's urge to just get them done. This now makes a task a pleasure instead of a nuisance.

Crossing the Rubicon

The bottom line on *my* personality evolution is that the reduction of erroneous anger rationalization has caused a major reduction in my anger and the excessive use of my director style. Concurrently, there has been a significant increase in my sorrow/relator and fear/analyzer memories, making them available to replace erroneous anger and provide me with more than just director options for reacting to a situation. I now have and take the option to use my less weak relator style to stay connected and take the option to use my less weak analyzer style to proceed less erringly. This gives me a more balanced personality and the ability to experience more of the wonderful aspects of life. I am by no means perfect, but I do have a more well-rounded personality that makes me feel better about myself and my approach to others—it is something that anyone can accomplish if they want it badly enough.

You still can't argue with success

Anyone can evolve to a more balanced personality and experience a more fulfilling life, not just angry directors who find it difficult to experience love. For example, strong analyzers with a weak socializer style can stop rationalizing fear and enjoy their connections more. Strong relators with a weak director style can learn to be more assertive and decisive, instead of playing the victim or martyr. Strong socializers with a weak analyzer style can be more effective at completing tasks instead of letting down others who are relying on them.

In fact, we all could use a more balanced personality, no matter what our weak and strong styles. So let's move on to how *you* might best evolve your personality. And please, don't be concerned with how long it takes. Yes, it took me decades to use my weak relator style in lieu of my strong director style, but it only took six months to use my weak analyzer style to keep me from giving in to the dangerous and destructive urges of my strong director style. And each month my personality becomes increasingly more balanced. Yours can too by utilizing the *short-term solutions* in Chapter 14 until you can complete the *long-term solutions* in Chapter 15.

Chapter 14
Finessing *Strong Emotions & Weak Styles*
...Short-Term Solutions

Finessing Strong Emotions...Short-Term
Finessing a Weak Relator Style
Finessing a Weak Director Style
Finessing a Weak Analyzer Style
Finessing a Weak Socializer Style

Finessing *Strong Emotions...Short-Term*

Set your mind to what you want

In Chapter 15, we'll discuss long-term solutions to finesse our memories and attain a more balanced personality than gifted by nature, but short-term solutions are also helpful. There are two short-term solutions: One reduces the use of our strong emotions; the other increases the use of our weak styles.

We can avoid emotional outbursts using a technique that I call "Mind-set." Mind-set allows us to create a rational memory that will automatically sort out and quell a future emotional outburst *as it is happening*—this may sound weird or scary, but it can work for any emotion at any future event. In Chapter 3, we discussed the how we create mid-term memories throughout the day and strengthened them by hippocampal rehashing at night. Thus, we can create an identifying or "sorting out" rational memory today and fortify it overnight to automatically quell an emotional outburst tomorrow. After tomorrow, this mid-term memory will fade unless we recreated and used it another day. I've used this technique for decades—it *always* works!

When you need anger control

When a strong director needs to work with others the next day to attain specific results, he or she must avoid angry outbursts that will stay their pro-

183

gress. Any hindrance of results could elevate to perceived confrontation, producing strong anger or even rage. Thus, to keep the anger from escalating out of control a memory needs to be in place that can quell that anger as it increases. The following anger Mind-set technique allows strong directors to create such a memory.

1. The night *before* the anger-evoking event, find a non-distracting place to do your Mind-set alone before retiring.

2. Visualize the next day and the situations that can evoke your anger and how much you want to avoid it.

3. Say to yourself something like: "I will not get angry no matter what happens; it will be a wonderful day and I will love working with them and they will love working with me"—visualize it—feel it!

4. Repeat Step 3 one or two more times.

5. The next morning, repeat Steps 2 through 4 when alone, usually when showering or dressing.

Step 3 creates, and Steps 4 and 5 fortify, the anger-quelling mid-term memory and overnight hippocampal rehashing makes it available for the next day. By the way, have you noticed that Step 3 also gives you the option to use your people styles once the growing anger is quelled, by assuming that it *will be* a joyful experience (socializer style) and a bonding experience (relator style). If you are a strong director who has already tried this kind of Mind-set technique, then you have experienced the building up and automatic quelling of your anger and possibly the willingness to consider the needs and opinions of others involved as you enjoy working with them. If you have not tried this technique, you are in for a delightful surprise.

When you need fear control

When you (a strong analyzer) have to work with others to attain specific results, your fear can keep you from doing your part. Your fear may be mild if you perceive risk (you missed something important), strong if you perceive danger (you'll look incompetent), or rationalized to terror (you might lose your job). Thus, to have a clear mind to productively work with others you must avoid fear the next day. Your fear is not that obvious to others except when shut down or become overly detailed, stalling a realistic timely conclusion. Thus, if they can set in place a memory that can quell that growing fear, the group can achieve their goals tomorrow. The following Mind-set technique allows you to do so:

1. The night *before* the fear-evoking event, find a non-distracting place to do your Mind-set alone before retiring.

2. Try to experience that next day and the situations that can evoke your fear and how much you want to avoid it.

3. Say to yourself something like: "I will not become fearful no matter what happens; I will not become overly focused on minor or missing details; we will get the results we need."

4. Repeat Step 3 one or two more times, as you picture and feel it happening the next day.

6. The next morning, repeat Steps 2 through 4 when alone, usually when showering or dressing.

Step 3 creates, and Steps 4 and 5 fortify, the fear-quelling mid-term memory and overnight hippocampal rehashing makes it available the next day. Once you quell the growing fear, Step 3 also allows you the option to use your director style to get resolution. If you are a strong analyzer who has already tried this kind of Mind-set technique, then you have experienced the building up and quelling of your fear and possibly the need to attain instead of fearing resolution. If you have not tried this technique, you are in for a pleasant surprise.

When you need sorrow control

For strong relators, avoiding the next day's sorrowful outburst is sometimes vital if they are to avoid erroneous disconnection that distracts them from productively working, possibly with difficult people, to attain their goals. They are prone to trigger erroneous disconnection that compels them to reconnect, which is inhibiting to strong directors and distracting to all. While trying to reconnect, they are distracted from productive interaction with others, especially when a sorrowful outburst stops everybody in their tracks. Like anger and fear, perceived indifference triggers mild sorrow that can grow in intensity through rationalization. Thus, if a strong relator can set in place a sorting out memory that can quell that intensifying sorrow they can achieved their goals. The following Mind-set technique allows them to do this:

1. The night *before* the sorrow-evoking event, find a non-distracting place to do your Mind-set alone before retiring.

2. Try to experience that next day and what others mat say and do that can evoke your sorrow and how much you want to avoid it.

3. Say to yourself something like: "I won't be overly sensitive to what others may say or to their indifference; I will concentrate on the task at hand and will help to get the results we need."

4. Repeat Step 3 one or two more times, as you picture and feel it happening the next day.

7. The next morning, repeat Steps 2 through 4 when alone, usually when showering or dressing.

Step 3 creates, and Steps 4 and 5 fortify, the sorrow-quelling mid-term memory and overnight hippocampal rehashing makes it available the next day. But, Step 3 also opens the door to the use the opposite director style to get resolution once you quell the elevating sorrow. If you are a strong relator who has already tried this kind of Mind-set technique, then you have experienced the building up and automatic quelling of your sorrow and possibly the need to attain, instead of being distracted from, results. If you have not tried this technique, you are in for an invigorating surprise.

When you need joy control

If you are a strong socializer, avoiding the next day's overly joyous outbursts is mandatory when you need to pay attention and avoid going off on tangents that can distract you and others from productively working together. You must ignore mild joy from unimportant connections; addressing them is distracting to others who don't want to hear about it. You must also ignore the great joy from important connections; they will definitely distract you and others from what you're trying to accomplish. Thus, if you can set in place a memory that can quell the intensifying joy you can have a productive day and achieved your goals. The following Mind-set technique allows you to accomplish that:

1. The night *before* the joy-evoking event, find a non-distracting place to do your Mind-set alone before retiring.

2. Visualize that next day and how good friends might distract you and how much you want to avoid that distraction.

3. Say to yourself something like: "I won't be distracted from the task at hand; I will focus on the details, and we will get the results we need."

4.   Repeat Step 3 one or two more times, as you picture and feel it happening the next day.

8.   The next morning, repeat Steps 2 through 4 when alone, usually when showering or dressing.

Like above, Step 3 creates, and Steps 4 and 5 fortify, the joy-quelling mid-term memory and overnight hippocampal rehashing makes it available the next day.   But, Step 3 also opens the door to the use the analyzer style to focus on the details and to use the director style to get resolution once you quell the distracting joy. If you are a strong socializer who has already tried this type of Mind-set technique, then you have experienced the building up and quelling of your joy and possibly the need to focus on and attain the necessary results. If you have not tried this technique, you are in for a sobering surprise.

Finessing a *Weak Relator Style*

It's a labor of love

When we are naturally strong in the relator style, it's easy for us to stay connected and to acknowledge others—we take it for granted. When we are naturally weak in the relator style, preserving relationships and acknowledging others can be a rare and wonderful experience. If you are naturally weak in the relator style, think of the last time that you used it to reconnect with and acknowledge a loved one. Think of the close connection you had and the love you felt as you made what was important to them important to you; also think of the positive energy you shared. Wouldn't you want to experience that more often? Of course, you would, but it isn't easy with a naturally weak relator style, especially when you have a strong director style.

This section gives you two techniques for finessing your naturally weak relator style. The first technique employs the use of the primary sorrow emotion with its quelling symbiotic relator style; the second technique puts you in the "relator mode." If either technique is unproductive by itself, a combination of both techniques should work as long as you are not distressed or distracted. If considering the future, use Mind-set the day before entreating the use of your relator style.

Technique-1: Since the relator style automatically sorts out its symbiotic sorrow emotion you should be able to turn on your relator style by thinking a sad thought about the person with whom you want to share your relator style. This may sound absurd, but it works. First clear your mind of everything except the other person's needs, otherwise forget it! Next, think of a wonderful experience that you shared with him or her. Finally, think of him or her not being around any more, leaving big holes in their part of your day in the life you share. If you succeed with this technique, you will feel an overwhelming expression of sorrow, an emptiness, which will turn on your relator style, causing you to use its attributes to appreciate, acknowledge and nurture your relationship with him or her. What you have done is reacquaint yourself with and focus on the importance of this person in your life, instead of just taking him or her for granted.

Technique-2: If the above sorrow Technique-1 doesn't work for you, probably because you don't have enough relator memories, the following technique might help you to turn on and use your weak relator style. Also, the repeated use of the sorrow Technique-1 above may be necessary when your stronger styles and their symbiotic emotions try to displace your relator style. To finesse your weak relator style, do the following:

Before you meet that special person (anticipation always helps):

☺ **Set aside plenty of time**; you have nowhere else you want to be!

☺ **Remove any tenseness** in your voice; tenseness is obvious and puts others on the defensive. Consciously relax your face and body muscles by taking one or two slow deep breaths.

☺ **Remove all thoughts from your mind**; only think about the other person and the wonderful experiences you shared with them.

When *with* that special person:

☺ **Listen, don't respond**; responses require thought and negates listening.

☺ **Concentrate on what they say**; make their opinions your opinions and their concerns your concerns.

Caution

If you're a strong director or analyzer, try very hard to keep thoughts of pending tasks out of your mind since they will instantly turn off your relator style and turn on a task-oriented style. If you are a strong socializer you will be easily distracted, so remove all distractions (TV, crowds, etc.) and only focus on that person. You do not have enough relator memories to keep your stronger styles from replacing your relator style—so keep using the sorrow Technique-1 to get you back to your relator style.

Using this technique to finesse the use of your naturally weak relator style can help you to better preserve your relationships. If you are a strong director, "listening without responding" will help you to circumvent your natural need to get resolution—results are *never* required when using the relator style.

Finessing a *Weak Director Style*

Go ahead; make my day

When we have, a strong director style we take for granted our ability to make decisions and get results. When we are weak in the director style, making difficult decisions to get resolution can be an exhilarating experience. Attaining results in repetitive daily situations is simple for all of us, whether our director style is weak or strong, but attaining results in new or difficult situations can be a challenge for many of us. If you are weak in the director style, think of the last time that you used it to make a difficult decision or to attain a result that needed resolution for too long. Now think of your exhilaration at getting that situation resolved and finally over with. That result may be a consequence of diligence and a commitment to resolve it, or forced by anger; either way that situation finally got resolved. When we make decisions and act on them, we have more control over our lives, feel less like a victim or martyr, and relish in it.

When we need to make difficult or crucial decisions we need to use our director style. It thus behooves those of us with a naturally weak director style to be able to use it when necessary, especially if we have a naturally strong relator style. This section gives two techniques for finessing a weak director style. The first technique involves the use of the anger emotion and its quelling director style; the second technique is to put you in the "director mode." If neither technique works for you or if you are also naturally strong in the relator style, try using both techniques simultaneously. When considering the future, use Mind-set the day before entreating the use of your director style.

Technique-1: Since the director style sorts out anger we should be able to finesse the use of our director style by generating anger. To use this technique, first clear your mind of everything except the situation you want resolved. Think of how its lack of resolution invalidates you or keeps you from doing other important things. Get frustrated about the kinds of situations that went unresolved throughout your life and how frustrating (not painful) they were. If you do not succeed with this technique to arouse your anger, think of someone or something involved in that situation that is impeding your results and what he, she or it does that frustrates you. This should arouse your anger emotion enough to turn on your director style and decide how to resolve the situation—if you have enough director memories from which to choose.

Technique-2: In order to finesse a naturally weak director style, you need to know how to think and act like a director. While using your naturally weak director style, you must not allow your naturally strongest style to displace it. If you are a strong relator or strong socializer, don't even think about people, just results! If you are a strong analyzer, don't even think of the tedious process, only focus on your intended result. Thus, to finesse your weak director style, do the following:

☺ **"Visualize" the result in your mind** before starting the project, as if it were already done. Unless that vision exists, you cannot use your director style nor directly attain your result; you must "be at the result."

☺ **Only focus on the important details**, if unknown they're unimportant.

☺ **Believe in your visualized result and support it when working with others;** only accept information that supports that result. Ask enough probing questions to support your visualized result, ignoring anything else that may clutter up your mind.

☺ **Work backward from the visualized result** to determine the logical procedure to attain that result; this "back from the future" path is the procedure you will use to attain your result.

☺ **Consider the result more important than the people involved** in attaining the result; the director style does not care about people. If you are caring, you're not using your director style.

☺ **Set aside an unreasonably** *short* **amount of time** to attain your result. If you are an analyzer or relator, allow one-fourth to one-fifth the amount of time you think it would take. Give yourself fifteen minutes to do an hour's task or give yourself an hour to do a four- or five-hour task. If you are a strong socializer, allow about one-half the time it would normally take. Severe time constraints trigger anger (through hindrance) and the natural use of the director style.

Using the above technique to finesse the use of your naturally weak director style can help you attain necessary results. Unfortunately, the lack of sufficient director memories won't keep your strong style from replacing your director style, especially if distressed. When displaced, apply anger Technique-1 above again, but this time give yourself even less time to complete the task; that should get you back to the director style and the resolution you desire. This is especially important if you are a strong relator who tends to let sorrow make you a victim or martyr.

Finessing a *Weak Analyzer Style*

Practice makes perfect

We attain our best results when they are repetitive, whether at home or at work. Unfortunately, when we have a new project to complete, we do not typically attain our best results, except when we use our analyzer style. When we have a naturally strong analyzer style, we dwell on the unerring process; the result is secondary. When we are naturally weak in the analyzer style, proceeding in an unerring manner to a superior result on new projects can be a rare and fulfilling experience. If you are naturally weak in the analyzer style, think of the last time that you used it to unerringly proceed towards a superior result. Think of your attention to detail, how you proceeded in a logical, systematic manner and how much peace of mind it brought you, especially when your livelihood was at stake.

This section provides two methods for finessing a weak analyzer style. The first technique involves the use of the fear emotion and its quelling symbiotic analyzer style. The second technique puts you in the "analyzer mode." If neither technique works for you or if you are naturally strong in the socializer style, try using them together. If considering the future, use Mindset the day before entreating the use of your analyzer style.

Technique-1:   The analyzer style always follows an expression of fear to sort out the reason for that fear and proceed unerringly. Consequentially, by expressing fear, we can turn on our analyzer style. We need not be terrified to turn on our analyzer style; we just need enough fear to "jump-start" it. To evoke your fear just think of the negative repercussions of a poor result. These negative repercussions might involve injury to you or others, a large personal financial loss, losing your livelihood, potential embarrassment, a degrading of your prestige or self-image or whatever pertains to that situation. Dwelling on these negative repercussions will evoke fear, followed by your analyzer style, to avoid them. Unfortunately, the mood of fear will subside and you may have difficulty maintaining the use of our analyzer style, probably because you don't have enough analyzer memories, which is why Technique-2 is very helpful to learn. This is especially helpful for naturally strong socializers with a naturally weak analyzer style.

Technique-2:   To finesse your naturally weak analyzer style you need to know how to think and act like an analyzer while keeping your strongest styles from displacing your analyzer style. If you are a strong relator or strong socializer, don't even think about people, just the process. If you are a strong director don't even think of results, just think about the process used to attain those results. To finesse your weak analyzer style:

☺ **Schedule 3 to 5 times more time than you think you need** to complete the task. For example, if you think it usually takes fifteen minutes, give yourself an hour, or if it usually takes an hour, schedule three to five hours of uninterrupted time to complete the project.

☺ **Seek out all of the details**…for *each* step along the way.

Use a "checks-and-balances system"

☺ To assure an unerring process you *must* learn this discipline; without it you can't use your analyzer style:

  1. Have a detailed logical procedure to follow; complete the first logical step.
  2. Complete the second logical step.

3. Check the results of the second step against the first and correct the first and second steps to make sure that they logically support each other, adding new details as found.

4. Complete the third logical step.

5. Check the results of the third step against the first and second steps and correct the first, second and third steps to make sure that they logically support each other, adding newfound details.

6. Complete the fourth, etc., logical steps in the procedure and check each step against the previous steps to make sure that they all logically support each other, adding newfound details.

7. Add new steps to your initial procedure if warranted.

8. Make sure the result fulfills your criteria for the project and make any final adjustments to better define the result. Review all steps to make sure they all support the adjusted result.

This checks and balances system is time consuming, which is why you need to allow three to five times the usual amount of time to complete the project.

Using the above technique can help you unerringly proceed with your naturally weak analyzer style. If you are a strong relator or socializer, segregate yourself from any people distractions. If you are a strong director, don't even think of short cuts; they will negate your unerring process and produce inferior results. Since you have few analyzer memories, your analyzer style will be replaced with your stronger styles so keep using the fear Technique-1, and give yourself even more time than required to get you back to the analyzer style and an unerring process.

Finessing a *Weak Socializer Style*

Do throw caution to the winds

When we have a strong socializer style, we take for granted our ability to identify and address our connections, which brings us much joy. But when we are weak in the socializer style, its use may be a rare and wonderful experience. If you are weak in the socializer style, think of the last time that you used it to share in the joys of others; more importantly, think of the times that you experienced personal joy. Think of how happy, playful, carefree and excited you were. Wasn't it a wonderful experience? But that's not easy to do with a weak socializer style, especially if you have a strong analyzer style. When we are with others, especially in non-work situations, we tend to use our weak socializer style more, but usually not as much as we would like or need to, in order to enjoy life.

This section gives us two techniques to finesse a weak socializer style. The first technique involves the joy emotion and its quelling symbiotic socializer style that addresses the cause of that joy. The second technique is to put you in a "socializer mode" and naturally act as if we had a strong socializer style. If neither technique works for you or if you are also naturally strong in the analyzer style, try using both techniques simultaneously. If considering the future, use Mind-set the day before entreating the use of your socializer style.

Technique-1: Since the socializer style automatically follows the emotional expression of joy, we should be able to finesse our socializer style by thinking joyous thoughts about a person or the situation. First, clear your mind of everything that has to do with tasks or the needs of that person; next, relive joyous experiences with him or her. If you succeed with this technique, you will feel a strong expression of joy, which will turn on your socializer style, causing you to use its attributes to address that joyous connection (person). Once your socializer style is in use, go with it, enjoy the ride, and don't allow thoughts about tasks turn it off. If this doesn't work for you, probably because you don't have enough socializer memories, use Technique-2 to re-trigger your socializer style.

Technique-2:   In order to finesse a naturally weak socializer style you need to know how to think and act like a socializer. While using your naturally weak socializer style, you must not allow your naturally strongest style to displace it. If you are a strong analyzer or director, don't even think about tasks, just people interaction; if you are a strong relator; don't even think about the other person's needs or opinions. Thus, to finesse your weak socializer style:

☺ **Ignore the clock** (get rid of your watch) don't think about deadlines or schedules; be free and capricious with your time.

☺ **Place yourself in the center of attention**. Don't be timid and stand on the sidelines; "get into the thick of it" and make your presence known.

☺ **Invite conversation.** Make complimentary statements, or ask questions that bring up topics you want to discuss. If uninterested in the present topic, smoothly change it to a topic you find more interesting.

☺ **Speak in an enthusiastic, expressive and inspiring manner**; really enjoy talking about it! Others must get the impression that whatever you are talking about or doing is the greatest thing possible.

☺ **Be quick, witty and creative** and adapt to the situation with off-the-cuff remarks that just pop into our head. Let your mind "flow," and then "go with that flow" to be natural and spontaneous. Don't be afraid to say anything that comes to mind, no matter how absurd you may think it sounds. In fact, don't think about what you are going to say at all! Just say it!

☺ **Let your mind wander, randomly, from topic to topic.** Don't think analytically or logically, just "react" with whatever comes into your mind.

☺ **Draw upon your emotional energy**. When you use your socializer style, you expend a great deal of physical and emotional energy. This is far more energy than you ever use with your analyzer or relator styles. But don't worry; the energy is there. In fact, when you have the energy you know you're using your socializer style.

Using the above technique to finesse the use of your naturally weak socializer style can help you to better express your joys and address your connections. Since you have few socializer memories, your stronger styles will replace your socializer style; so keep using the joy Technique-1 to get you back to the socializer style—have some fun! This is especially important if you are also a strong analyzer who lets fear reduce your life's joys.

The above techniques for using your rational styles more appropriately, in people-oriented and task-oriented situations, are only short-term and dissipate quickly—but they are great while they last! They are not permanent and will not balance your personality and give you a more fulfilling life; that requires a long-term commitment and the use of techniques for finessing memories in Chapter 15—have a great life!

Chapter 15
Your **Personality Evolution**
...Long-Term Solution

Your Personality Evolution
Completing a *Strong Director's* Evolution
Completing a *Strong Analyzer's* Evolution
Completing a *Strong Socializer's* Evolution
Completing a *Strong Relator's* Evolution

Your **Personality Evolution**

Nothing ventured, nothing gained

The final step in your personality evolution started a little after your birth and continues today. This chapter can help you complete that evolution within your lifetime—and the sooner you do it the better the *rest* of your life will be. By evolving, you support the overall purpose of natural evolution to propagate your genes with your children and by socially providing an emulative example to help them to successfully evolve.

Let's face it, many couldn't care less about improving, happy to be just who they are, but this just means that they've completed their evolution. On the other hand, there are those of us less blessed, who find it a constant struggle to live with our "genetic challenges," feeling that something important is missing; we need to evolve to a more balanced state—this chapter can help!

Have faith in yourself. Yes, it's difficult to change; we slip back at times, controlled by negative emotional memories, but that's natural. Our negative emotional memories are like weeds in a garden of memorable delights. It's hard work to weed them out and to keep them out; they need attending. Once you get your garden under control, keep it that way; continuously weed out inappropriate emotional and rational memories, and feed it with ones that are more appropriate.

197

Do open a can of worms

By now you should be aware of your strong, moderate and weak emotions and styles, especially if you evaluated yourself using Appendix-A; if not, you might want to refer to it before continuing. Once you know your strongest emotion/style, you know the emotion you need to stop rationalizing. Once you know your weak emotions/styles you know the ones you need to strengthen, especially if they are opposite to your strongest.

The strong director and weak relator (or strong relator and weak director) rational pattern and the strong analyzer and weak socializer (or strong socializer and weak analyzer) rational pattern require special attention. These patterns are opposite, and thus, being strong in one and weak in the other makes us outwardly viewed as doubly strong in one and doubly weak in the other since they can't balance each other. For example, if we have a strong director and weak relator combination, we are doubly self-directed, self-concerned, and decisive, making us appear egocentric and uncaring to others. Also, when you have one of these opposite patterns, it's much more difficult to: 1) stop rationalizing your strong emotion to quell it and create an emotional void, 2) fill that void with your opposite weak emotion, and 3) build that weak emotion's memories and its symbiotic style's rational memories. This will delay your evolutionary quest, but not block it.

Don't bite off more than you can change

I categorize the four main sections below first by strongest style and then by weak emotions/styles. First, choose the section for your strongest style, and follow it to help reduce rationalization of its symbiotic emotion (for example, the director style and anger). Next, choose a subsection (➲) for the weak style that you want to strengthen. When choosing, it helps to balance the use of your left and right brains, decreasing the usage of the strongest style side and increasing the usage of the opposite side. This is a given when you have opposite strong and weak styles (i.e., right-brain director and left-brain relator styles or right-brain socializer and left-brain analyzer styles) as noted above. When you are a right-brain person that is moderately strong in both the director and socializer styles, you need to build left-brain memories for your weak relator and/or analyzer styles. When you are a left-brain person that is moderately strong in the relator and analyzer styles, you need to build right-brain memories for your weak director and/or socializer styles.

It takes two to tango

The preceding section mostly refers to rational patterns with one very strong style. Before moving on, we need to comment on *moderate* rational patterns with two moderately strong styles. They represent a genetically more balanced personality, which is great, but they may contain one or two very weak styles, which is not so great. If you have a moderate pattern, choose the strong style opposite to the weak style you need to build. If there is a second weak emotion/style, work on that after getting the first one under control. For example, if moderately strong in both the director and socializer styles (right-brained) with too few fear/analyzer memories, start by reducing joy rationalization and build your fear and unerring analyzer memories. Or, if you are moderately strong in the analyzer and relator styles (left-brained) with too few anger/director memories, start by reducing sorrow rationalization and build your anger and decisive director memories.

A bird in the hand is worth two in a bush

Then again, you might be desperate enough and want to choose a weak style that you must strengthen *now* instead of balancing your left- and right-brain memories and rational patterns. Here are some examples:

- If you are a strong analyzer, relator or socializer who is in a position of authority and finds it difficult to be assertive with your staff to get results, choose to build your weak anger and director memories first. Just go to the main section for your strongest style (for example, "Completing a Strong Analyzer's Evolution"), and review it to help reduce rationalization of that style's strong emotion (i.e., fear). Then choose the subsection "➲ If weak in anger/director" within that main section, and proceed to build those weak anger and decisive director memories.

- If you are a strong director and/or socializer who makes too many impulsive, flawed decisions that are putting your life or livelihood in jeopardy, first go to the director or socializer main section to reduce rationalization of your strong angers or joys. Then go to the subsection "➲ If weak in fear/analyzer" within that main section and proceed to build those weak fear and unerringly proceeding analyzer memories.

- If you are a strong director or analyzer who finds it difficult to share time and love with your family, or a strong socializer who gets much more self-centered joy than shared love, first go to the director, analyzer or socializer main section to reduce anger, fear or joy rationalization.

199

Then go to the subsection "➲ **If weak in sorrow/relator**" within that main section and proceed to build those weak sorrow and reconnecting relator memories.

- If you are a strong analyzer who resents strong socializers that seem to get more fun out of life than you, first go to the "Completing a Strong Analyzer's Evolution" section to reduce rationalization of your strong fears. Then go to the subsection "➲ **If weak in joy/socializer**" and proceed to build those weak joy and connecting socializer memories.

Remember to choose your strong and weak styles well; you will be spending the next 6 to 12 months consciously building the memories that will balance your emotions and styles to allow you to consciously, unconsciously and sub-consciously live a more satisfying, fulfilling and evolved life. Once successful, go to the PersonalityFinesse.com website, and tell me your success story—I'd love to hear about it!

The "essence" of a style

In Chapter 14, we suggested using a style's symbiotic emotion to get into the style's mode (to use its attributes), but this doesn't always work. Some weak directors find it unacceptable to be angrier; just ask any strong relator. Some weak analyzers find it unacceptable to be more fearful; just ask any strong socializer or director. Some weak relators find it unacceptable to be sorrowful; just ask any strong director or socializer. And believe it or not, some weak socializers find it unacceptable to be more joyful; just ask any strong analyzer. But then again, availing ourselves of a weak style's attributes is not as fruitful as availing ourselves of our weak style's "essence."

A style's *genetic purpose* is to socially deal with its symbiotic emotion's alert. A style's *essence* is how it helps us to lead a more balanced life. You might find it helpful to memorize the essence of *your* weakest style for it will help dispel your doubts as you try to strengthen it.

- ☺ The analyzer style's essence: **"allows us to make *better* or safer decisions"** (to do a better job or avoid inappropriate or dangerous impulses).

- ☺ The director style's essence: **"allows us to make *more* decisions"** (to be more assertive and have more control over our lives).

- ☺ The relator style's essence: **"allows us to interact *better* with our connections"** (to share more bonding/loving moments and stay connected).

☺ The socializer style's essence: **"allows us to interact *more* with our connections"** (to share more joyful moments).

In for a penny, in for a pound

It is doubly important to strengthen the weak style opposite to your strongest style to avail yourself of that weak style's essence. For example:

- If you are a strong relator that is weak in the director style, you need to emerge from your martyr/victim existence of not being in control of your life and be more assertive and decisive.

- If you are a strong director that is weak in the relator style you need to be more sensitive to your affect on others; you need to share in instead of discarding life's fleeting loving moments.

- If you are a strong analyzer that is weak in the socializer style you need to be more sensitive to your connections, embracing instead of fearing them; you need to share in instead of avoiding life's joyful moments.

- If you are a strong socializer that is weak in the analyzer style you need to quell unwise or dangerous urges to avoid calamity and allow your connections to interact with you.

As you sow, so shall you glean?

If your efforts don't show immediate improvement; give yourself a few months of conscious effort before expecting results—just stay aware of your goals: "to stop rationalization of your strongest style and avail yourself of the essence of a weak style." At first, major efforts will produce minor results, with less rationalization of your strongest emotion and more use of the weak emotion and style you want in its stead. There will come a crossover point, when a little effort produces major results, when your weak emotion/style memories are strong enough to allow you to choose between them and your strong emotions/styles. Eventually it will become natural for you to use that weak style without your strong style displacing it, drawing on its essence to lead a more balanced life—good luck on your quest!

Nothing succeeds like you

As you read, experiences will pop up creating erroneous emotions; stop and allow yourself to dwell on them since it's all part of resolving them. Don't try to justify (rationalize) past reactions as you ponder them. Instead, try to think about what triggered that emotion in that situation. When you have come to a successful conclusion on that issue, read on, again pausing and reflecting as you go, sometimes on the same type of situation and sometimes on another. Go with each reflection to wherever it leads you. Each success-fully concluded thought is but another experience to add to your arsenal of memories that will eventually help you to attain your goals. The fact is, even though musing on erroneous emotions is helpful, giant steps in your success will occur *during* an unexpected emotional outburst, as you avoid rationalization, fill the void with an appropriate emotion, rationally appro-priately react, and rationally record that experience for future use.

The pace of your success is what works for you. Getting through this chap-ter is not your goal—getting something out of it is. From this point onward, ignore all that does not apply to balancing *your* personality (the majority of this lengthy chapter); just skip to and work with whatever does. If you are curious about how this process might work for a loved one with a lopsided personality pattern, then read on. Maybe you can convince him or her to become more evolved, although, *your* success is the proof in their pudding. The next step is to skip to the main section for your strongest style: strong director (p. 202), strong analyzer (p. 210), strong socializer (p. 215), or strong relator (p. 220) to reduce rationalization of your strongest emotion.

Completing a *Strong Director's* Evolution

The first step is the hardest—to stop anger rationalization

Anger rationalization is "a series of misleading identifications of an errone-ous confrontation." It is as natural to rationalize your strong anger, as it is to express it, making it difficult to quell it and move on. Anger triggered by an overly excited (less inhibitory) amygdala heralds erroneous confrontation that gets in the way of maintaining better connections with our relator style, addressing more connections with our socializer style, or making bet-ter/safer choices with our analyzer style. Your main objective is to immedi-ately identify what's truly confronting you and realize that it has little to do with the present. Unfortunately, as hard as you try you will not always be able to immediately identify its cause. But if you work on each type of re-occurring angry outburst separately, you will eventually identify its true cause. Once consciously identified, the anger will stop, recording that experience as a new director memory that includes: your sensory, emotional and rational memories that alerted you to the confrontation, its cause, and how you rationally reacted. This memory record will later allow you to more quickly identify that confrontation, quell that angry outburst and create another rational record. After many experiences, you will unconsciously quell that anger automatically before it becomes an angry outburst—maybe a spousal example will help.

If at last you don't succeed, don't try again

The following scenario is all too typical and probably represents the major conflict between a strong director and a strong relator spouse.

The situation is that your strong relator spouse plays the martyr/victim by not asking for help when overwhelmed, and later he or she blames you for not helping. This confronting blame makes you rationalize and re-trigger your anger with director memories of the last few times this situation occurred, since its cause was never identified.

The solution is to identify the real confrontation, which is *not* "your spouse is making you the bad guy for not helping, when you were never asked," but which *is* "you were insensitive to your spouses needs up to the point of offering help, since they were not as important as your needs."

Once you consciously identify the true cause of the confrontation, quell the anger and create an emotional void, you'll record that experience's sensory, emotional and rational memories for future use. And if you allow yourself to fill the anger void with sorrow, you'll eventually become more sensitive to your spouses needs and less to your own, as future sorrow alerts you to disconnection. And, as you *consciously* identify the true confrontation, quell the anger and feel sorrow on subsequent experiences, you will automatically see the need for and offer help, possibly sharing a loving moment. Of course, if he or she constantly rejects your offer, the desire to offer it will fade. But, at least you won't get angry about it when confronted, just annoyed that he or she prefers to ride the martyr/victim train instead of taking control of his or her life.

Every man is the architect of his future

As previously noted, just because an angry outburst has a cause it doesn't mean that we can readily identify it, leaving us with natural rationalization—but we can change that. We can avoid rationalization as we search for the true cause of the confrontation; we can consciously distract ourselves from considering those rationalizing memories. One way is to remove ourselves mentally or physically from the situation that caused the confrontation and anger, for example, leave the room. We might shake our head or think "nothing's wrong" or "everything's OK" or do whatever works for five to ten seconds to distract us from the anger and allow the re-triggering angry mood to ebb. For example, if your spouse says something that angers you, don't think of what he or she said or did; instead, count to 10 as you picture the last time he or she smiled lovingly at you. This will not only distract you from your anger, it will attach relator memories to the director memory recording that experience.

Once distracted from your anger, think back to the sensory input that just triggered it, which is the key to identifying the confrontation since that same sensory input triggered the anger. Recollect the sights or sounds or whatever you sensed that triggered the anger—the devil is in the details. This will be very difficult at first, but it will become easier with practice, especially since the same confrontation causes each reoccurring situation. Maybe an example about cars (what a surprise) and director self-invalidation will help.

Every man is his own worst enemy

Over the past 35 years, I have owned eight new and two used BMW cars and one new and two used Asian cars; I've had good and bad experiences with both. But every time I would see an Asian car (too many times a day) I would get angry, rationalizing the many aspects of their differences and why my BMW is the better car. This may seem like a dumb thing to do, but strong directors think dumb self-invalidating thoughts like this all the time.

My rationalization would focus on the problems that I had with the Asian cars and the joy of driving "the ultimate driving machine." Never having tried to identify the cause of my anger, its rationalization plagued me. Finally, when I tried to consciously identify its cause I realized that my last thought before the anger was a mental picture of the Consumer Report "Reliability History," indicating that the leading Asian cars had a better reliability rating than BMW. Once I *consciously* identified the true confrontation, good old director self-invalidation (I was self-invalidated because I drove the lesser *rated* car), the anger disappeared, immediately and totally; I was amazed. The next few times I became angry when I saw an Asian car, I consciously identified the true confrontation, told myself that the ratings were their opinion and not mine, and the anger magically disappeared, every time. Eventually, that type of anger disappeared since I *unconsciously* identified and quelled the confrontation before it ever surfaced. Even though I didn't feel or express the anger at first, there was a split-second mental pause (an anger void) after I saw an Asian car. Today, even that anger void no longer exists, indicating that the emotional alert, and thus, the emotional memory no longer triggers my anger—something I didn't think was possible.

Nature abhors a vacuum

For you to succeed in your quest to reduce your angry outbursts you must *consciously* find the true cause of the confrontation, create an anger void, and fill it with a more appropriate weaker emotion. For example, sorrow must fill the anger void of an angry outburst that causes disconnection "to allow you to better interact with your connections" (to share more loving moments). Fear must fill an anger void involving road rage "to allow you to make better/safer decisions" (thus avoiding giving in to inappropriate or dangerous impulses). When we don't consciously try to identify the true cause of the confrontation, natural rationalization will fill in that anger void with more anger—avoid this at all costs!

Bottom line, stop your unconscious anger rationalization and consciously substitute the appropriate weak sorrow, fear or joy emotions if you expect to reduce your anger.

➲ If weak in sorrow/relator

You need to strengthen your weak relator style "to allow you to interact *better* with your connections" (to share more loving moments). To avail yourself of this relator style's essence you need to fill the anger void with sorrow as you build and strengthen your sorrow and relator memories. You probably have a long history of unidentified disconnections and thus, a long history of creating sorrow in others instead of love. But this can be reversed if you consciously fill that anger void with sorrow by attaching sorrow memories to every non-rationalized angry experience—concentrating on the needs and opinions of others is crucial. You must let down your guard, look at his or her face and see *his or her* sorrow, which your anger caused. If you love them more than justifying your emotional outburst, you will naturally *mimic* their sorrow, eventually triggering real sorrow from your own new sorrow memories.

At first, it won't trigger your sorrow (leaving an empty anger void), but with each experience that you focus on their sorrow and understand what disconnected you, you will build and strengthen your sensory, sorrow and relator memories. Eventually, you will be able to sense disconnection and express sorrow and turn on your relator style—unfortunately, you may not be able to hold onto it to reconnect.

Filling the anger-void with sorrow isn't enough—at first

Weak or non-existent relator memories will be overpowered by attached director memories that identified and recorded that angry experience. But, each time this anger-evoked situation is re-experienced and the anger void filled with sorrow and relator memories, you will build and strengthen these sorrow and relator memories, eventually making them more excitable than attached director memories, thereby allowing your relator memories to support your reconnection.

As the sorrow and relator memories consciously pile up, you will no longer be weak in sorrow and the relator style, allowing you to sub-unconsciously (emotionally) detect disconnection with your sorrow memories, unconsciously quell that sorrow and reconnect with your relator memories—hopefully expressing love.

Start with a pet peeve—not a major problem

Since many situations evoke your anger and since you will need to consciously attend to each situation individually, start with a pet peeve; don't start with something that enrages you since you cannot quell rage only avoid it. It is also very helpful to start with something that you experience many times daily, to build those sorrow/relator memories quickly (for example, my many daily oriental car angry reactions). As you get that pet peeve under control, branch out to other angry outbursts and work on them as well.

You will always have these angry outbursts when distressed, but you will be able to repair the damage and reconnect instead of rationalizing and enraging your anger. Eventually, your newly created and strengthened sorrow and relator memories will allow you to interact *better* with your connections by sharing more loving moments with them.

➲ If weak in fear/analyzer

You need to strengthen your weak analyzer style "to allow you to make better or safer decisions" (to do a better job or to avoid inappropriate and/or dangerous impulses). To avail yourself of this analyzer style essence you need to fill the anger void with fear memories as you build and strengthen your fear and analyzer memories.

As a strong director and weak analyzer, anger controls your life and your impulses with little room for fear, which is necessary when we *must* proceed without error or calamity. For example, we all delight in and are proud of the exceptional results that we produce—we do it with our analyzer style. I have completed many projects with my "get it done" director style, and yes, I was happy to get them done, but they are in no way as satisfying and fulfilling as projects that I have completed using my analyzer style. The analyzer style left little room for error because I spent a great deal more time properly designing and working on the project using the analyzer "checks and balances system" (see pages 192-193).

Thus, if you *must* get better results at your job or when on your own, you need to build and strengthen your analyzer memories to keep your director style from taking over and messing it up, which it will always try to do.

Fill the anger-void with fear

Attach fear memories to director-dominated situations where you need to do a better job. It is obvious in "*My* Personality Evolution" in Chapter 13 that I needed to start out with a situation that evoked real fear, even terror. In your case, it may be the fear of losing your job, your family or your health if you don't make some drastic changes now—immediacy is important!

Once you choose to work with that fearful situation your fear memories will increase, filling the anger void and allowing you to eventually attach analyzer memories to identify and quell the fear as you unerringly proceed with your newly established analyzer memories that can keep strong director memories from taking over. After many repetitions your analyzer memories will become strong, allowing you to choose whether to get the task done quickly or to get it done well—it's great to have a choice!

Eventually, your newly created and strengthened fear and analyzer memories will not only allow you to produce better results, it will also allow you to make better/safer decisions and not give in to inappropriate and dangerous impulses.

➲ If weak in joy/socializer

You need to strengthen your weak socializer style "to allow you to interact *more* with your connections" (to share *more* joyful moments). To avail yourself of this socializer style essence you need to fill the anger void with joy memories as you build and strengthen your joy and socializer memories.

When not distressed you can probably use your socializer style and get joy out of a social situation, a *little* alcohol sometimes helps. When distressed, your director style will take over, sometimes evoking anger, which can only be resolved with sorrow and the relator style as noted above. If you are easily angered when in a group, your anger will take over and thus, avoiding rationalization is an important first step and consciously filling the anger void with joy (the recognition of your connections) is the next step. The final step involves repeated experiences of that situation to create and strengthen your joy and socializer memories. Eventually, anger and director memories will not overpower your joy and socializer memories for that type of situation.

Think of a strong positive connection

An important tool for evoking joy in everyday situations is a positive connection that evokes real joy, even ecstasy when recalled; you need to identify that strong positive connection. Think about your day and what creates joy for you; then when in a social situation reflect on that kind of joy to turn on your socializer style and interact with others, attaching those joyous memories to that experience.

For example, a strong positive connection of mine is a wonderful meal at a fine restaurant with a great bottle of wine, so, when I'm in a social situation I evoke my joy by thinking or talking about such an experience. My joy and socializer style is not weak, but the technique works just as well. You can evoke your joy by dwelling on a positive connection of yours, thereby attaching it to the director and socializer memories recording that experience; these recordings will evoke joy as it quells this anger in similar situations in the future.

A life of socializing is a joy forever

Relive your joys in similar but angry situations, strengthening those joy and socializer memories and weakening the anger outbursts. For example, if you are going to an office picnic, don't be angered by negative connections (individuals you don't like), dwell on positive connections (individuals you like); if none exist, think about a strong positive connection of yours (spouse? child?), allow yourself to bath in that joy, and allow it to spill over into your interactions with others at the picnic. After many rational memories of many joyous experiences, even if angrily evoked, will contain increasingly stronger joy and socializer memories that will override director memories, making your life more joyful, and probably more loving as you open yourself up to your connections and feel love by sharing common connections with others.

This will also allow you to choose whether to get a task done or share your connections with others in similar situations. Eventually, your newly created and strengthened joy and socializer memories will allow you to interact *more* with your connections by sharing more joyful moments with them.

Completing a *Strong Analyzer's* Evolution

The first step is the hardest—to stop fear rationalization

Fear rationalization is "a series of misleading identifications of erroneous danger." It is as natural to rationalize your fear as it is for you to express it and unfortunately, rationalization reinforces it. Fear triggered by an overly excited (less inhibitory) amygdala heralds erroneous danger that gets in the way of a being more decisive and assertive with our director style, maintaining better connections with our relator style, or addressing more connections with our socializer style.

Your evolutionary objective, should you choose to accept this mission, is to immediately identify the real danger and realize that it has little to do with the current situation, which should naturally quell that fear. You will not always be able to immediately identify the real danger or risk to avoid rationalization, but if you work on each reoccurring fearful situation separately, you will eventually identify the real danger. And once it is *consciously* identified it will be quelled and an analyzer memory recorded for that experience, including the sensory, emotional and rational memories that alerted you to and identified the real danger or risk and how you rationally reacted.

This record (memory) will allow you to consciously and quickly identify the real danger and quell the fear when that fearful situation reoccurs, creating another rational record each time. Eventually you will automatically identify the fear and automatically quell it before it becomes emotionally noticeable; maybe an example will help.

If you're not part of the solution, you're part of the problem

My wife is a very strong analyzer plagued by fears and their rationalization. One New Year's Day she was on call at Children's hospital and needed to go in for a nutritional consultation with a newly admitted diabetic patient. It was a snowy day (it was Buffalo, what else would it be), and she had little gas left in her Durango. I checked her car and it read 56 miles left in the tank (actually over 100 with the reserve). I told her that she had over 100 miles, and it wasn't a problem. We had planned to fill up later that day at a far-away gas station at a $1.50/gallon savings (about $30 total), something important to my frugal wife. Had she filled up on the way to the consultation she would be late; she would also be late for a planned family holiday festivity immediately upon her return from the consultation.

She became fearful that she would run out of gas and rationalized that she might slide off the road and get stuck in a snow bank—she had a fearful experience in the blizzard of 1977. I asked her how many times that ever happened, and she quickly switched to another rationalization that it is better to be cautious and get the gas instead of taking the risk, which she rationalized once more. I told her that she was erroneously rationalizing, that there was no danger and that she had plenty of fuel to make her trip and be on time—this did not quell her fear and she filled up on the way to work. It wasn't the danger of running out of gas that fueled her fear; it was that she didn't trust my judgment about the miles she had left in the tank. She would have quelled her fears had she realized that the unwarranted distrust, not on running out of gas, caused her fear. This would have recorded a rational memory of the experience that could have been used in future situations to dispel the fear of running out of gas when the tank is low.

Start with a haunting fear—not a terrorizing fear

Since *many* situations evoke fear and since you will need to consciously attend to *each* situation individually, start with a fear that haunts you the most (giving you numerous opportunities to work on it *daily*). Don't choose a fear that terrorizes you since you cannot quell terror—only try to avoid it. Follow a sequence involving: (1) the expression of the fear; (2) its non-rationalization; (3) identification of the real danger to quell the fear and record an analyzer memory of that experience with its attached sensory, emotional and rational memories; (4) filling the *fear void* with another emotion and strengthen that emotion's memories and (5) strengthening that emotion's rational style's memories of the experience through repetition.

As you get that particular fear under control, branch out to your other fears and work on them as well. Over many months or years, you will reduce your fears significantly. Eventually, you can work on the fears that terrify you, using some of the anger, sorrow or joy memories that you created along the way. You'll always have your fears, especially when distressed, but you don't have to give in to them—you can consciously identify their true cause, quell them and move on.

⮩ If weak in joy/socializer

You need to strengthen your a weak socializer style "to allow you to interact *more* with your connections" (to share more joyful moments). To avail yourself of this socializer style's essence you need to fill the fear void with joy memories as you build and strengthen your joy and socializer memories. To stop rationalizing fear in general, avoid focusing on what might go wrong with the situation, and instead, focus on what's great about it. For example, a strong fear of most analyzers is that something may destroy their financial wherewithal even when they are financially well off. To stop rationalizing this fear, rationally tell yourself that all is well and think about your financial strengths (cash, investments, assets, etc.), but don't think about how you may lose them, which *is* rationalization of that fear. If well off, rationally think about the joy of spending that money on the things that you want and love. If you are a self-employed workaholic, think of enjoying some time off in slow periods instead of filling that time with worry and non-productive tasks. Through a constant conscious effort, you will stop rationalizing this financial fear and fill that fear void with joy. This will also turn on your socializer style to allow you create and strengthen socializer memories, which will initially be replaced by strong analyzer memories and other financial fears, but will eventually be strengthened if you consciously acknowledge your assets and what you can do with them using attached socializer memories. Do it *every* time this financial fear arises.

Eventually, as you consciously avoid rationalization and think joyful thoughts every time you trigger this financial fear, it will negate the fear leaving you only with joy. If this occurs in a task-oriented situation, you will quell the financial fear and joyfully return to your task. If this occurs in a people-oriented situation, you will quell the financial fear, express joy, turn on your socializer style and share your connections with others. Eventually, your increased joy and socializer memories will allow you to interact *more* with your connections by sharing their joyful moments.

Overcoming fear at public gatherings

If you become fearful in social situations that you must play an active part in, for example, at a social gathering at work where you must interact with colleagues and clients, then use your joy to stimulate your socializer style. To accomplish this think of a strong positive connection of yours that evokes *positive* joy and applies to these fearful social situations. For example, my weak socializer and strong analyzer wife is a weather nut; she loves the weather channel and loves analyzing the local weather forecasts and is good at it; it is a strong positive connection of hers. So when we're in a social situation that she needs to get more joy out of when stressed, I make some comment about the great weather or beautiful sunset, etc., which turns on her joy and helps her to recognize and enjoy other connections. This brings out an important point—others who know our important connections can help us evolve.

Of course, it is always best to evoke our own joy to evolve more quickly. For example, my wife evokes her own joy by thinking about her most important connections, our children, especially as infants; other infants that remind her of ours are also important connections that evoke her joy. You can also use your important positive connections to create joy and socializer style interaction in the many situations that evoke your fear if you can stop rationalizing the fear. And if you repeat this enough, eventually building sufficient joy and socializer memories, fear and analyzer rationalization won't override them.

➲ If weak in sorrow/relator

You need to strengthen your weak relator style "to allow you to interact *better* with your connections" (to share more loving moments). To avail yourself of this relator style essence you need to fill the fear void with sorrow memories as you build and strengthen your sorrow and relator memories. As mentioned on pages 48 and 49, analyzers are invalidating and cause disconnection. Thus, when your fear invalidates and disconnects you from others, quell the fear and fill the fear void with sorrow memories that will trigger your relator style and allow you to focus on the opinions of others instead of your own.

Strong analyzers fear much, which can invalidate others, for example, a strong analyzer parent may invalidate their adolescent child by not allowing them attend an unknown function for fear that they may be harmed, disconnecting the child from the parent. The parent can either rationalize the fear by thinking of the ways the child could be harmed or the parent can focus on the child's need to attend the function, express sorrow and reconnect with the child, possibly working something out.

Fears are powerful, especially when they involve a loved one, and natural rationalization of that fear is very destructive when no real danger exists. Analyzer invalidations frequently occur for many reasons and thus, your goal as weak relator is to consciously establish an unconscious sequence involving: 1) expressing fear, 2) avoiding rationalization, 3) identifying the cause of the fear and quelling it, 4) triggering sorrow and the relator style and 5) bonding and positive supportive interaction. You need to do this for every situation that triggers invalidating fear that disconnects you from others. Eventually, your newly created and strengthened sorrow and relator memories will allow you to interact *better* with your connections by sharing less invalidation and more loving moments with them.

⊃ If weak in anger/director

Strengthening a weak director style "allows you to make *more* decisions" (to be more assertive and have more control over your life). To avail yourself of this director style essence you need to fill the fear void with anger memories as you build and strengthen your anger and director memories. For example, your dawdling child will be late for school because you can't get her out the door and into the car, and coaxing isn't working. Using mild anger to demand that the child get in the car immediately and possibly helping the child with clothes, books, etc., does get the result desired and may not be too disconnecting. This is an example of mild anger (caused by the *hindrance* of not getting the child in the car and off to school). But sometimes it takes strong anger to get results. For example, if you need to catch a plane and your dawdling child is making you late; it will trigger strong anger since getting her into the car and missing your plane confronts you. This will cause you to physically pick her up and strap her in the car seat and rush to the airport. Although effective, that strong anger also causes disconnection, which you need to clean up with sorrow, the relator style, and love once settled in at the airport.

Although disconnecting, anger does get results and in this example records a rational record of that experience including sensory, emotional and rational memories for *both* the parent and child. Maybe the next time the parent will start out sooner, and the child will be more cooperative, remembering the anger and disconnection from the last experience, getting the desired result sans anger.

Anger can be cathartic

Anger purges strong analyzers from the usual guilt that accompanies getting results; there is no guilt when using the director style, just results. For example, the demanding parent on the way to the airport felt little guilt, but once settled on the plane she felt the guilt and disconnection and hopefully turned on her sorrow, which allowed her to reconnect.

Strong anger is appropriate when being confronted (which is its genetic purpose), but you must clean it up with the relater style once expressed. Mild anger on the other hand is more appropriate for building anger and director memories that make us more decisive and assertive when we need to be. For example, if you are hindering yourself from completing an important task because you are drowning yourself in the details for fear of making a mistake, you need to: 1) stop rationalizing and quell that fear, 2) fill the fear void with anger, 3) identify its cause as self-hindrance to quell the anger, and, 4) be more decisive about which details are important and which aren't. This experience's recorded analyzer memory will contain anger and director memories that made you more decisive, allowing you to complete the task quicker. And when these same fears arise for a similar project, you will have the opportunity to strengthen those anger and director memories and avoid being bogged down in the future.

Eventually, these newly created and strengthened anger and director memories will be available for many other projects that you may get bogged down with—in essence, you will become *more* decisive and get more accomplished, giving you more control over your life.

Completing a *Strong Socializer's* Evolution

The first step is the hardest—to stop joy rationalization

Joy rationalization is "a series of misleading identifications of an *unimportant* connection"—lets face it, if it were an important connection, we would have identified it as such, quelling the joy. Like the other emotions, joy is an alert, but if it has a "hair trigger," it can alert us to everything. And when it is an erroneous connection, it will trigger rationalization to try to identify the connection, but to no avail. Once rationalization is avoided, that possible connection is either important and needs to be addressed (whether positive or negative), or is identified as unimportant and needs to be ignored. Too much time and a great deal of energy is wasted rationalizing joy about unimportant connections, distracting strong socializers from being more assertive/decisive with their director style, maintaining better connections with their relator style, or avoiding dangerous impulses with their analyzer style.

All that glitters is not important

Your goal as a strong socializer should be to avoid rationalization by immediately identifying a connection—the identification of important connections will always quell the joy. But you will not always be able to immediately identify the connection as important or unimportant, and thus, if after one or two unsuccessful symbiotic cycles of *conscious* consideration (not unconscious rationalization) consider it unimportant and move on. By deeming it unimportant and quelling the joy, the socializer memory recording that experience will fade. But if deeming it unimportant doesn't quell the joy, the connection is probably new and possibly important and needs further investigation. When finally identified as important, the joy is quelled and a socializer memory of that experience is stored along with the sensory, emotional and rational memories that alerted you to and identified the important connection and how you rationally addressed it. Should you sense that important connection in the future, the new socializer memory of that new experience will strengthen the memories of this previous experience making that connection even easier to identify the next time—maybe some examples will help.

All the world's a connection—but not necessarily important

We meet many people in our lives; some are important connections and some are not. Co-workers and bosses that we see every day are important connections as are our boss's bosses that we rarely see. Most workers in other parts of our company that we rarely see are unimportant connections, even though we somewhat recognize and smile at them in passing.

Sometimes we meet people in our daily activities, such as our children's favorite teachers or the parents of our child's friends, clerks at our favorite stores, etc. These are important connections that our joy alerts us to.

Sometimes we have dealings with an employee at a store, maybe even more than once and some time later see someone on the street that looks like him or her. We try to identify him or her but can't because he or she is an unimportant connection; we must deem it unimportant to quell our joy.

Bottom line: It's not realistic to be distracted by or spend time with unimportant connections, that's why they're unimportant, especially when you have to be somewhere else or there's work to do. Strong socializers are all too ready to identify anybody that might be a connection, wasting hours each day interacting with both important and unimportant connections when they should be completing their tasks. Instead, they should at least identify the unimportant connections and move on, or at best, identify the important connections and tactfully excuse themselves when there's work to do.

⟳ If weak in fear/analyzer

You need to strengthen your weak analyzer style "to allow you to make *safer* decisions" (avoid inappropriate and/or dangerous impulses and stop wasting time). To avail yourself of this analyzer style essence you need to fill the joy void with fear memories as you build and strengthen your fear and analyzer memories.

Being excitable right-brain individuals, strong socializers give in to dangerous urges all too easily. A typical urge is to interact with someone they recognized as a possible connection, but is actually a dangerous connection or one not in their best interest to be with. When the connection is important and negative, the urge is automatically repressed. If unknown, we must identify them as negative to avoid them now and in the future. Unfortunately, strong urges cause unconscious rationalization that prolongs the joy and the desire to give in to the urge to interact with a negative connection. The increased levels of dopamine from the expression of joy may also urge us to "reward" ourselves by giving in to that urge. To counteract this, we need to: 1) stop unconsciously rationalizing the joy, 2) consciously identify the urge as unimportant or dangerous and quell the joy, and 3) fill that joy void with fear, which will quell the urge. This experience will then create a socializer record that can be used in the future to consciously identify and quell the joy should that dangerous or inappropriate urge surface; eventually it will be unconsciously sorted out and avoided after more *consciously* controlled experiences.

A burning desire

We may see something that we have always wanted, but is very expensive and would place a financial hardship on our family should we purchase it (for example, a new home, Ferrari, etc.). Unfortunately, when alerted to that desire we feel joy and the irresistible urge to reward ourselves by purchasing it. This puts undue strain on *us* because we fear the financial repercussions of purchasing it. If instead, should we consciously identify that object as interesting but unimportant we quell the joy, allowing us to consciously fill that joy void with the fear of financial repercussions. This will attach an analyzer memory to that socializer experiential memory; making it available for consideration the next time we get that same urge. Eventually, if we *consciously* identify that urge as unimportant enough times and express the fear of financial repercussions, the analyzer memories will dominate those experiential memories for that situation and automatically quell the urge long before it can be acted upon. And by applying this technique to other situations, our newly created and strengthened fear and analyzer memories will make *safer* decisions by not giving in to inappropriate or dangerous urges in other areas of our lives.

⮑ If weak in sorrow/relator

You need to strengthen your weak relator style "to allow you to interact *better* with your connections" (to share more loving moments instead of just rambling on). To avail yourself of this relator style essence you need to stop rationalizing joy and fill the joy void with sorrow as you build and strengthen your sorrow and relator memories.

In your rambling zeal to address your human connections, you've probably disconnected from those who couldn't get a word in or whom you cut off when they tried. To resolve this you need to *consciously* fill that joy void with sorrow by attaching sorrow memories to every non-rationalized joy experience as you consciously concentrate on the need to address *their* connections with you. You must stop talking, look them in the face and see *their* sorrow or discontent that your excessive, random and typically pointless discussions have caused. If you love them more than you love rambling rationalization, this will help you to naturally *mimic* their sorrow, possibly producing actual sorrow of your own. At first, it won't trigger actual sorrow (leaving an empty joy and talking void), but as you focus on their need to be heard with each experience, you will build and strengthen your sensory, sorrow and relator memories. Eventually, you will be able to sense disconnection and express real sorrow and turn on your relator style, but you may not be able to use it to reconnect.

It may sound dumb, but fill the joy void with sorrow

At first, weak relator memories will be overpowered by strong socializer memories that identified and recorded that experience. But, as this particular joy-evoked situation is re-experienced and the non-rationalized joy void filled with sorrow, you will build and strengthen sorrow and attached relator memories. Eventually you'll make them more excitable than attached socializer memories, allowing your relator memories to urge you to reconnect. And as the sorrow and relator memories consciously pile up, you will no longer be weak in sorrow and the relator style, allowing you to emotionally detect disconnection with your sorrow memories and unconsciously quell that sorrow and reconnect with your relator memories. In doing so you will learn why these connections are the most important.

➲ If weak in anger/director

Strengthening a weak director style "allows you to make decisions that get tasks accomplished" (instead of socializing when there is work to do). Strong socializers and directors are excitable right-brain people (see Chapter 12) who have little difficulty making decisions, especially when giving in to urges. Strong directors give in to urges to complete tasks even when they are unnecessary; strong socializers give in to urges to interact with others even when they have important tasks to complete.

As noted on page 98, distractions by possible connections plague strong socializers, hindering the completion of their tasks. Thus, by using their weak director style, strong socializers can give themselves urges to complete necessary tasks. To accomplish this they need to: 1) avoid rationalizing joy triggered by unimportant connections to quell the joy, 2) fill the joy void with anger, and 3) identify the cause of the anger as being hindered by distracting unimportant connections, which will quell the anger and allow you to build and use your director memories to complete the task.

It comes with the territory

Unfortunately, at first, you will have few anger and director memories to urge you to complete your tasks; your socializer memories will take control and urge you to continue socializing. But, through conscious repetitive effort, you can strengthen your anger and director memories enough to complete your tasks and prevent your socializer memories from overriding them. Eventually with each consciously controlled experience the anger, memories will increase, as will the director memories. They will unconsciously urge you to complete your task without conscious effort and noticeable anger. Eventually, these new anger and director memories will not only allow you to get more accomplished, they will help you to be more decisive and have more control over your life.

Completing a *Strong Relator's* Evolution

The first step is the hardest—*to stop sorrow rationalization*

Sorrow rationalization is "a series of misleading identifications of an erroneous disconnection." It is as natural to rationalize your sorrow as it is to express it, but that results in the disconnection that you are trying so desperately to avoid (a self-fulfilling prophesy). Sorrow triggered by an overly excited (less inhibitory) amygdala heralds erroneous disconnection that gets in the way of being more assertive and decisive with our director style, addressing more connections with our socializer style, or making safer choices with our analyzer style although, not usually a problem with strong relators.

Your objective is to immediately identify the erroneous disconnection and realize that it has little to do with the current situation; this will naturally quell the sorrow. You will not always be able to identify the erroneous disconnection, but if you work on each reoccurring sorrowful situation separately, you will eventually identify the disconnection for each situation and quell the sorrow. And once consciously identified and quelled, a relator memory recording will be made of that experience that includes the sensory, emotional and rational memories that alerted you to and identified the disconnection and how you rationally reacted. This record will allow you to consciously identify that disconnection and quell the sorrow in the future, creating another rational record each time. Eventually the sorrow will become automatically identified and quelled before it becomes emotionally noticeable creating a sorrow void. The next step is to fill that sorrow void with an appropriate emotion that leads to a more appropriate rational reaction; maybe an example of an all too common situation will help.

The meek will inherit the *anger*

I'm a strong director and weak relator who is typically involved with my own concerns, not paying attention to the concerns of my strong-relator and weak director wife when she voices them—half the time I don't even hear them if she is speaking in a low voice on my deaf ear side. My perceived indifference to her makes her feel that I'm angry with her, causing her to feel disconnected from me and expressing sorrow. Her sorrow is erroneous since I'm not upset with her; the fact is she doesn't even exist at a moment while I'm absorbed in something else. What she needs to do is stop the rationalization, fill the sorrow void with anger and identify the cause of the anger as the *hindrance* of my indifference to her concerns. This will quell the anger and allow her to decide that this was not the best time and leave; it may also make her more assertive and demand that I listen to her. This of course can only occur if her relator style doesn't replace her director style and re-start the whole process, although, it would give her another opportunity to consciously increase those few anger and director memories. That is, the more often she consciously avoids sorrow rationalization and consciously fills the sorrow void with anger, and the more she makes a decision to be assertive about voicing her concerns the stronger those anger and director memories will become.

Eventually, the quelling of her sorrow will be automatic as her director style takes over and she gets her concerns resolved. Actually, this is what has naturally occurred over our decades of our marriage, making her feel less disconnected from me and making me feel more connected to her. It would though, have been better for both of us had she finessed her strong sorrow/relator and weak anger/director personality years ago; the same can be said for me about finessing my strong anger/director and weak sorrow/relator personality. Why wait? Get it done now!

➲ If weak in anger/director

Strengthening a weak director style "allows you to make *more* decisions" (to be more assertive and have more control over your life). To avail yourself of this director style essence you need to fill the non-rationalized sorrow void with anger memories and build and strengthen those anger and director memories.

To build director memories that allow you to be more assertive, make more decisions and complete your tasks, you need to feel confronted or hindered. Being a strong relator, you naturally hinder yourself with indecision. Thus, you need to consciously realize that *you* are hindering your progress with erroneous disconnection instead of making the necessary decisions and acting on them. Lets face it; it's easier for a strong-relator/weak-director to make a decision by not making a decision (let others make it) than by actually making the decision. And to make it worse, when relators finally make a decision with their director style it doesn't mean that they won't renege with their powerful relator need to maintain connections since their director memories just aren't strong enough to resist it.

Again, fill the sorrow void with anger

Once you stop rationalizing the erroneous disconnection and quell the sorrow, you need to fill that sorrow void with anger. Next, identify the cause of that anger as your hindering indecisiveness to quell it, and allow your director memories to urge you to be more assertive, make decisions and act upon them. Unfortunately, at first, you will have few director memories to spur on your decisions; your relator memories will take over and make you indecisive to avoid erroneous disconnection. But through *conscious* effort, you can strengthen your anger and director memories and be more assertive and decisive without your relator memories overriding them. Eventually, your newly created and strengthened anger and director memories will allow you to have more control over your life, no longer at the mercy of the decisions of others.

One final comment

Strong relators that are weak directors don't know how to manage their anger and typically end up rationalizing that anger instead of identifying its cause, quelling it and moving on. Anger rationalization is destructive no matter who does it, even a strong relator who is a weak director. Remember, the anger is just an alert, not a means of accomplishing things, that's the job of the director memories.

➲ If weak in fear/analyzer

You need to strengthen your weak analyzer style "to have *better* task outcomes." Unlike strong excitatory right-brain directors and socializers that need to have their urges better managed, the left-brain relator style naturally quells urges, especially those that may cause disconnection. Thus, you would only need to build your weak fear and analyzer memories if your sorrow and relator memories are negatively affecting your task outcomes, especially if your livelihood is at stake.

Better safe than sorry

To build those fear and analyzer memories you need to stop rationalizing erroneous sorrow, fill that sorrow void with fear, quell the fear by identifying the danger (losing your job), and use analyzer memories and methods to unerringly complete your tasks. Once you have established those fear memories you will need to build up analyzer memories or else your strong relator memories will take over, distracting you, and displacing whatever analyzer memories you have. Unlike most styles, the analyzer style has a built in method for establishing analyzer memories—a "checks and balances system" (see pages 192-193). If you diligently follow this system, it will guarantee an unerring result; all you need to do is provide the details and follow the rules for completing a task. While using the system you will create analyzer memories that will help you to complete any kind of task, whether your job is riding on it or not, making you feel more fulfilled in what you have accomplished.

➲ If weak in joy/socializer

You need to strengthen your weak socializer style "to allow you to interact *more* with your connections" (to share *your* joyful moments, instead of just identifying with others). To avail yourself of this socializer style essence you need to fill the sorrow void with joy memories as you build and strengthen your joy and socializer memories.

To stop rationalizing sorrow in general, identify the disconnection as non-existent, which should quell the sorrow. Next, fill the sorrow void with joy that stems from a shared positive connection, for example, feeling the joy from and identifying an important positive shared connection such as food, friends, or entertainment that you both love. This will quell the joy and allow you to address that shared connection, which will lead into other shared connections and further episodes of joy and addressing them.

It isn't difficult for a strong relator to get involved with and address shared positive connections since the relator style makes us supportive of what others have to say. Unfortunately, all too often strong relators turn joyful interactions into negative ones, for example, mentioning a recently deceased friend, which only triggers strong sorrow and puts a damper on a joyful interaction, something that no one appreciates. But with conscious effort, a strong relator can quell his or her hair-triggered sorrow and replace it with joy to promote positive interactions with others about positive connections.

It's all in a *year's* work

You will find that some of my suggestions will work for you and others won't. This is because we all think with unique memories and mine are different from yours. This is *your* personality evolution, and the only thing that works for you is what works for you. One aspect of your quest is to better understand yourself and what you have to work with. The more you consciously apply what you know works for you the faster you'll progress. There is only one universal aspect of your quest—results.

As you *consciously* eliminate rationalization of strong emotions, consciously fill that emotional void with weak emotions thereby creating more weak emotion/style memories, you will eventually find this happening unconsciously. You will have more loving relationships with your stronger sorrow and relator style; you will get more joy out of life with your stronger joy and socializer style; you will get better results and not give in to dangerous urges with your stronger fear and analyzer style; and you will be more assertive and decisive, getting more resolution with your stronger anger and director style. It all depends on whether you're willing to make a commitment to have a well-balanced personality and a more fulfilling life.

All good things in moderation

Don't overdo it; concentrate on one goal at a time, if not it will overwhelm your brain and you will fail. I started out wanting to experience better relationships with those I loved. Decades later, after I attained that goal through anger-reduction and sorrow-expansion I was ready to take the final step and strengthen my weak analyzer style to better proceed with my tasks, make safer choices and not give in to dangerous or inappropriate urges. In the process, I found out more about myself than I had bargained for, but it's all worth knowing. Likewise, there will be many sobering and wonderful things that you will discover about yourself as you complete your personality evolution, which is something only you can do for yourself—enjoy your quest!

Chapter 16
Beyond Personality

Lacking Personality—*Non-Thinking*
Automatic Personality—*Instinctive Thinking*
Positive and Negative Emotional Energy

Lacking Personality—*Non-Thinking*

What if—it's a no-brainer

When people say, "he or she has no personality," they're usually referring to someone very weak in the socializer and possibly the relator style. But, is it actually possible to have no personality? The answer lies in the definition of symbiotic personality. Symbiotic personality can be *functionally* defined as: "sensory input that triggers rational memories and reactions *plus* sensory input that triggers emotional memories and alerts that are identified and quelled by rational memories." But what if there were no rational reactions? What if there were no emotional alerts? What if there was no sensory input? This would negate this definition of symbiotic personality; or would it?

Have you ever tried to *not have an emotion?*

To *rationally* block, an emotional alert triggered by sensory input is impossible since the emotional brain processes a physical threat and expresses an emotion long before the rational brain knows it has occurred. It is possible, though, especially if you are in a sensory deprivation chamber, to block out sensory input and, thus, not trigger an emotion by sensory input. But does that mean that we won't have an emotional alert? No, since you can't block rational thoughts that trigger erroneous emotions—they're erroneous because they have nothing to do with the sensory-vacant present. Then again, it isn't difficult to avoid having emotions since that is our usual state. But eventually, thoughts will trigger an emotion even if we are in a sensory void. The fact is, we cannot permanently *not* have emotions.

Have you ever tried to *not think rationally?*

That's an easy one! If you weren't rationally thinking, how would you rationally know that you weren't rationally thinking? You couldn't rationally identify that you were in that non-rational think state since it would require rational thought to do so—well, maybe you could emotionally ratify it. When we trigger an emotion, it triggers its symbiotic rational style to rationally identify the cause of the emotion, knocking us out of that non-rational-think state. The fact is, we cannot permanently *not* rationally think.

Have you ever tried to *not sense?*

It's not easy, even in a sensory deprivation chamber. For example, as part of my doctoral thesis I built a "quiet room" for testing. At the end of the day when everybody else was gone and the building was quiet, I would sit in my room's quiet darkness and try to devoid myself of all sensory input —to try to not think. It wasn't difficult to do for a minute or so, but after my timpani settled down to the quieter state, the low hum of the building or the sound of my heart would distract me from non-thinking. On the other hand, it's possible to negate sensory input by just staring or clearing our mind; we do it every day. Unfortunately, it only lasts for a short period, although, with tremendous effort and training, I could maintain that state for longer periods. The bottom line is, we *can* block out sensory input through intense meditation, but not for long.

In retrospect

We can experience states of non-emotion-alerts or non-rational-thinking or non-sensory-recognition, but not for very long and rarely, if ever, all at once. Eventually, our personality will prevail since its genetic mandate is to survive physically and socially—a non-personality state puts our survival in jeopardy. Thus, having no personality at all is impossible, unless we're dead, and if so, we don't need it any more.

Automatic Personality, *Instinctive Thinking*

To socially survive we need the four genetic rational styles and their *learned* rational memories. But there is another genetic component of social survival—*genetic* (instinctive) rational memory.

All animals are not created equal

Modern Man's social-survival rational brain evolved from our 190-million-year-old physical-survival mammalian (emotional) brain. Along the way, mammals developed sensory cortices to store sensory memories to make their emotional triggers and emotional alerts more accurate. The "caudate nucleus" section of the mammalian brain evolved genetic *instinctive emotional memories* to increase the accuracy of instinctive emotional responses (to turn away from bright light, cover our ears for very loud noises, etc.). Concurrently the parietal and motor/pre-motor cortices developed automatic physical reactions that allowed us to better physically react to those instinctive emotional alerts for our physical survival. For social survival, the rational brain also required genetic *instinctive rational memories* for automatic rational reactions.

It's not necessary

It isn't necessary to know how a neuron works in the brain to know how the brain works; all we need to know is what causes our emotional alerts and rational reactions—learned and instinctive memory. It is not necessary to know how instinctive memory works, only that it exists and supports our physical and social survival, but its method of action is very intriguing, if not illusive.

But it's helpful

"Instincts" make us think of the automatic reactions of the rest of the animal kingdom. Non-human animals go through mating rituals that seem neither logical nor taught, but work to propagate their specie's genes. Some animals instinctively hatch a few eggs in creatively designed nests and dotingly care for their young (birds), while others just deposit hundreds of eggs in a sandy hole and move on (turtles). These instinctive patterns of behavior are wired-in neural patterns (memories) that the animal is born with (genetic) and are thus, "genetic memories." Until recently, rational human reactions were relegated to nurturing—learned memories—but humans also have obvious instincts, probably wired into their genetic rational memories.

Human genetic memories

Familiar instinctive reactions usually have to do with physical survival, for example, instantly ducking when an object is hurling toward our head or instantly turning away from noxious fumes. We trigger these physical responses before rational thought can occur. The emotional brain can process an object hurling towards our head by visually sensing that object a certain distance and 50 milliseconds later, noticing that it is much closer, triggering an emotional fear alert and an automatic reaction to duck and protect our head with our arms. These instinctive reactions have to do with the swiftness or intensity of the sensation. For example, if we smell noxious fumes, we instantly turn away from them, and if we eat toxic food, we instantly spit it out or suffer the physical consequences. This requires millisecond timing, which is the emotional brain's timeframe, not the slower rational brain.

Some are wired—some are wi-fi

The lateral amygdala is genetically wired to detect physical danger and alert the rational brain to deal with it. The instinctive examples above account for some dangers, but our *learned* sensory, fear and rational memories account for the vast majority of danger to our survival. For example, emotionally we learn to trigger our anger, fear, joy and sorrow to alert us to what might affect our physical survival, but that's not instinctive. Rationally, to avoid the danger of a car hitting us we *learn* not to walk into the street; that's not instinctive either. We do, though, rationally react more instinctively than we realize; we mimic others without a clue, instinctively smile when smiled at, and take on the unique facial expression of others when they're expressing an emotion. Some people may call this empathy, but it is something else.

Imitation is the sincerest form of survival

There is a new name for instinctive human interaction called "Social Intelligence" that seems to indicate that our brain is genetically wired with "mirror neurons" (bi-polar spindle neurons) that cause us to mirror (mimic) the reactions of others, for example, returning a natural smile.

If someone gives us a natural smile, the sensory vision of that smile activates our motor/pre-motor cortex to contort our facial muscles to also produce a natural smile. These mirror neurons seem to be in abundance in the emotional brain and in the pre-motor and motor cortex that initiates our physical reactions (triggers our muscles); they may also be located elsewhere in the neocortex. This same mirroring applies when seeing others expressing the unique anger, fear and sorrow facial expressions. This mirroring might occur without triggering an emotion, utilizing axons of the mirror neurons that go directly from the emotional brain to the motor/pre-motor cortex. Then again, maybe we trigger this mirroring (same facial expression) by a mild expression of that emotion, which creates the facial expression by sending signals to the motor/pre-motor cortex to contort our face. If so, that emotional expression, no matter how subtle, would require the PFC to identify and quell it. This could trigger rationalization and possibly confusion about why we are feeling this emotion.

Sans emotions

When emotions are *not* involved, the motor/pre-motor cortex mirror neurons would contain rational mirror memories that match sensory input and activate the appropriate muscles. For example, when we are with someone that we trust we might cross our arms or sit or stand, mimicking what he or she does. If we don't trust that person, our emotional brain is in an alerting mode and not dealing with rational mirroring. This trust comes when we use our relator style and we feel as one with another (as discussed in Chapter 4) and thus mirror each other.

Genetic memories—mirror memories

In order to mirror the sensory input you need a genetic memory to match it to—that memory might require a cluster of mirror neurons. That "mirror memory" would need to match some aspect of what is being perceived, for example, mimicking a natural smile would involve a memory that reflects some unique aspect of another's natural smile, possibly the crinkle in the eyes that can only be triggered by the emotional brain. To work, this mirror memory would have to be fixed, not variable, like all other memory. The mirror memory neurons would have to maintain their neural interconnections; never changing, they must never change their dendrite structures nor their axon connections going from the sensory cortices to the mirror neurons in the emotional brain or motor/pre-motor cortices, which must also be fixed for these physical reactions to occur without change.

With this in mind, lets move on to what some may think is "beyond personality"—positive and negative emotional energy—which may be another explanation for instinctive human interaction. We may mimic another's smile by seeing the crinkle in their eyes. We even mimic another by picking up their emotional energy.

Positive & Negative Emotional Energy

Negative Emotional Energy

Unnerving intensity…We've all felt the intense radiation of our emotional energy and that of others—both *negative emotional energy* and *positive emotional energy*. It's easy to identify our own emanations when we express intense emotion. For example, when we express intense anger (rage) we feel the negative emotional energy we emanate, and when we share love, we feel the positive emotional energy we emanate. It isn't as easy to detect the positive and negative emanations of others unless connected to them. For example, if a strong director is irate, emanating high levels of negative energy, you won't feel it unless you are the cause of it. Or, if someone is feeling love for you, emanating high levels of positive energy, you won't feel it unless you are using your relator style or sharing a loving thought with them. Take a moment to reflect on your own past experiences with positive and negative emotional energy to confirm this.

Terminology-wise

The terms positive and negative are not appropriate since they connote good or bad, right or wrong, and since all emanations have, survival value or else they wouldn't exist. On the other hand, positive emotional energy makes us feel "good" and negative emotional energy makes us feel "bad," which compels us to continue using such terms. We sometimes refer to emotional energy as psychic energy, but we'll continue to call it emotional energy since it's part of our emotions—the emanations seem to come from the emotional brain.

Anger and negative emotional energy are a given

So are joy (at the recognition of our important connections) and positive emotional energy, but what about fear or sorrow? What kind of emotional energy, if any, do they emanate? The answer lies in our own experiences, for example, fear. You have probably made at least one "way-of-life threatening" mistake that you were unaware of when reprimanded for, surprising you and causing you to emanate intense emotional energy from your intense fear. If you thought back to when that situation occurred and about the *quality* of the emotional energy, you would find that it's the same negative emotional energy emanated with intense anger. Ergo, both intense fear and intense anger produce the same negative emotional energy. The situation determines whether fear or anger caused the negative energy.

You might also think back to a situation when you were very angry and severely reprimanded someone (emanating negative emotional energy) who in turn expressed intense fear and emanated intense emotional energy back to you. It was the same negative emotional energy—think about it! We might say the same thing about the emotional energy emanated with sorrow.

Orientation is a key

Anger is symbiotic with the *task-oriented* director style; fear is symbiotic with the *task-oriented* analyzer style, and both emanate negative emotional energy—thus, task-oriented styles emanate negative emotional energy. Since joy is symbiotic with the *people-oriented* socializer style and produces positive emotional energy, one could infer that the *people-oriented* relator style's sorrow should also produce positive emotional energy. It's genetically efficient for the people-oriented emotions to produce the same positive emotional energy since the task-oriented emotions produce the same negative emotional energy. This brings up the "Joy-Sorrow Paradox."

The "Joy-Sorrow Paradox"

We all expressed sorrow and joy vicariously when reading a book, seeing a movie or play, etc., but are the tears we shed tears of joy or tears of sorrow? The Paradox—"When we view a sorrowful situation and experience what feels like joy—are we actually expressing sorrow? And when we are in a joyful situation and experience sorrow, are we actually expressing joy?" The answer is…neither. What we are actually feeling is the influence of oxytocin; the neurotransmitter that has to do with human connections (bonding). In Chapter 4, we noted that a connecting thought about a shared connection with another triggers love; elevating our oxytocin level and making us feel as one. When we view actors in movies or TV shows, or read about a character in a book or magazine, they portray what we're thinking and we share similar thoughts. It doesn't matter that the actor or character really isn't experiencing elevated oxytocin levels, although they may; we assume that they are if their acting is convincing enough—mediocre actors are rarely convincing enough. So, the next time you are in a quandary about whether you are feeling sad in a happy situation or are feeling happy in a sad one, just enjoy the oxytocin high for as long as you can.

Sorrow and positive emotional energy—A bait and switch?

Sorrow doesn't in itself emanate positive emotional energy, but when the disconnection that causes it is identified and quelled by the relator style it allows us to reconnect, become of one mind, bond with another and express love, which emits strong positive emotional energy. In summary, the task-oriented emotions of anger or fear emanate negative emotional energy and the people-oriented emotion of joy emanates positive emotional energy. Sorrow indirectly emanates positive emotional energy through reconnection and love. This energy goes beyond the inner-world definition of personality, although it communicates strong emotional states to the outer-world as well as to our inner-world.

Surviving our emotional energies

Since personality is all about physical and social survival, emotional energy should be too, or else why would it exist. Let's look at each symbiotic emotion/style and see how it plays out. Our intense *negative* emotional energy creates a wall between others and us; it pushes them away. If anger, the intense negative energy would tell those confronting us to watch out, back off, that we are not someone they want to mess with. If fear, the intense negative energy would instantly broadcast the danger to others who may not have sensed it. Our intense *positive* emotional energy negates any wall that might come between us; it pulls others towards us. If joy, the intense energy, along with a natural smile, would tell someone that, we recognize him or her as an important connection. If a positive connection, it invites immediate interaction and if a negative connection, it gives us time to get away before they realize it. If sorrow, followed by reconnection and love, the intense energy would tell another that we are one with him or her and are looking out for his or her interests. This may not be exactly why we have emotional energy and needs further research.

In conclusion, it's your personality, your survival, so finesse it as best you can to lead the most fulfilling life possible!

Handy References

Synopsis – *A Combined Table-of-Contents/Index:* Read it in its entirety to get the gist of every chapter at a glace or skim it for the pages where there are topics of interest to you.

Appendix A – *Precise Personality Analysis:* This handy reference provides you with a comprehensive method for determining your true personality pattern. Included is a *"One-Second* Personality Analysis" that will allow you to instantly determine the strongest rational style and primary emotion of others.

Appendix B – *Symbiotic Personality Patterns:* This handy reference provides you with a complete description of the symbiotic personality *pattern* you determined in Appendix A.

Appendix C – *De-Stressing Yourself:* This handy reference provides you with an uncomplicated understanding of stress and distress and a means for identifying your major stressors and how to deal with them.

Appendix D – *The Relationship Game:* This handy reference provides you with the materials and procedures to reconnect with those that you disconnected from long ago.

Glossary/Index: This provides you with a handy reference for defining terms used in this book and where you can quickly locate information about them.

Synopsis of Chapters

Non-fiction books (like the one you're reading) are not usually read from cover to cover, but in part depending on what the reader is interested in. To help you find the information you seek this book is browser-friendly. Each chapter has a theme containing sections (listed in the table of contents), with each section containing a flow of related topics that have a bolded phrase at the beginning.

This synopsis allows you to follow these topics more succinctly and to get the gist of what is in each chapter and topic. You can browse this synopsis to find the information you desire, and once fond, turn to the page indicated on the right for the details. Many of the bolded phrases are adaptations of well-known sayings[1]—enjoy!

Chapter-1: Nature's Gifts

Nature and Nurture

The Human Brain: Personality

Chapter-2: Symbiotic Personality

Human Personality

Symbiotic Personality

Nurturing Our Free Will—Personality *Finesse*

Chapter-3: Memory, The Other Half of Personality

Nurturing Our Personality

Types of Memory

It takes up to two years to create long term memory from mid-term memory.

Once mid-term memory becomes long-term memory, it's weaned from the hippocampus.

Human evolution is moving away from emotional alerts from physical threats and towards emotional alerts from repetitious experiences with those close to them.

The mammalian brain has instinctive memory for physical survival.

We all acquire memories (knowledge)—apply that knowledge to survive (intelligence)—and some of that knowledge is a fact (wisdom).

Chapter-4: Sorrow and its Symbiotic Relator Style

Sorrow and the Relator Style

Sorrow alerts us to disconnection from our connections—for physical survival —the relator style reconnects for social survival.

Strong relators have more sorrow and memories than do weak relators—but that doesn't mean that weak relators are devoid of these memories.

Strong relators have a hair-trigger on their sorrow alert—it senses nonexistent, erroneous disconnection—it can be embarrassing.

Disconnection herald by *mild* sorrow is typically erroneous—caused by indifference.

We don't need to trigger sorrow to *think* with relator memories and feel love.

Love is difficult to define in the *outer-world,* but not so in our *inner-world.*

Sorrow is causes by *decreased* oxytocin brain levels—feelings of love are caused by *increased* brain levels—they're just *variations* from normal brain levels.

Love is triggered by an *unconscious* shared thought about a common connection triggering higher oxytocin levels in the brain.

We share many loving thoughts with our family and pets.

Inner-World of the Relator Style—Maintaining Our Connections

Chapter-5: Anger and its Symbiotic Director Style

Anger and the Director Style

Inner-World of the Director Style—Getting Resolution

Outer-World's View of the Director Style

Chapter-6: Fear and its Symbiotic Analyzer Style

Fear and the Analyzer Style

Inner-World of the Analyzer Style—Proceeding Unerringly

Outer-World's View of the Analyzer Style

Chapter-7: Joy and its Symbiotic Socializer Style

Joy and the Socializer Style

Every connection alert produces a smile that quickly changes for negative connections.

Nature intended joy to alert us to connections that are threats to be avoided.

Joy can be strong even in very weak socializers—it can trigger other emotions.

If we made a list of our important connections, we'd be constantly editing it.

Strong joy alerts us to important connections —mild joy alerts us to *possibly* important connections.

Mild joy can also alert us to negative connections—if we don't heed it we may be sorry.

When alone our brain's dopamine levels decrease—when in a crowd they increase.

Laughter—a smile extension—caused by surprise—but surprise can mean many things.

Negative connections distract us from the socializer style, replacing it with our strongest style/emotion.

Weak socializers feel uncomfortable or embarrassed using their outgoing socializer style.

Extreme joy alerts us to extremely important connections, strong joy to important connections, and mild joy to possible connections.

Rationalized erroneous joy causes mania in socializers—to there's and other's dismay.

Our connections are our lifeline to the outer-world—for our physical and social survival.

Inner-World of the Socializer Style— Addressing Our Connections

The one thing that makes all humans attractive is a contagious smiles—others have a natural tendency to mimic our smile and we theirs.

A natural *smile of the eyes* makes our day—unlike a forced *smile of the mouth*.

Chapter-8: Extreme Symbiotic Cycles

Extreme Symbiotic Cycles

Extreme symbiotic cycles override naturally healthy symbiotic cycles with intense, uncontrollable emotion.

Extreme Symbiotic Cycles of *Terror*

Extreme Symbiotic Cycles of *Rage*

Extreme Symbiotic Cycles of *Despair*

Extreme Symbiotic Cycles of *Ecstasy*

Chapter-9: Outer-World's View of *Style Attributes*

Chapter-10: **Natural** *Compatibility With The Outer-World*

Genetic Compatibility

Genetic Compatibility Chart

Self-Incompatibility

Although moderate, the Director/Relator and Analyzer/Socializer patterns produce the greatest self-irritation—because they're opposite.

Chapter-11: Who's in Charge Here

Who's in Charge Here?

Reacting Appropriately

Chapter-12: The **Inner-World's** *Symbiotic Brain*

Location of the Symbiotic Styles

Cell Biology 101

The neuron is the building block of memory connected to other neurons across synapses to dendrites—these cells fire and excite and inhibit each other in a pattern we call memory.

Dendrite receptors are scattered throughout the brain—they react to peptides, monoamines, and hormones (called modulators) that help to excite or inhibit neuron firing.

Processing of the Symbiotic Brain

The amygdala has many more inhibitory than excitatory receptors—so does the left brain.

The "Orbito-Frontal Cortex"—located behind the eyes—is responsible for deciding on urges —if excitatory, we decide—if inhibitory, we don't decide.

The "Anterior Cingulate Cortex"—in the middle layers of the PFC—holds on to memories the PFC decides with—if excitatory, it connects and holds on—if inhibitory, it doesn't.

The "Dorso-Lateral PFC"—in the outer layers of the PFC—makes rational decisions and acts on them—if excitatory, we react—if inhibitory, we don't react.

All of a style's outer-world's motivations and attributes can be accounted for with one simple inner-world survival purpose.

The left brain's inner-world structure creates an outer-world analyzer style that "unerringly proceeds" with "fear of loss," "differences" and "necessities" motivations.

The right brain's inner-world structure creates an outer-world socializer style that "addresses our connections" with "desire for gain/pleasure," "similarities" and "possibilities" motivations.

The right brain's inner-world structure creates an outer-world director style that "gets resolution" with "decisive," "self-directed" and "self-concerned" motivations.

The left brain's inner-world structure creates an outer-world relator style that "maintains our connections" with "indecisive," "others-concerned" and "others-directed" motivations.

Chapter-13: Finessing the Inner-World's Memories

Personality *Imbalance*

Finessing *Memories*

My Personality Evolution

Chapter-14: Finessing Strong Emotions & Weak Styles
…Short-Term Solutions

Finessing Strong Emotions…Short-term

Finessing a Weak Relator Style

Finessing a Weak Director Style

Finessing a Weak Analyzer Style

Finessing a Weak Socializer Style

Chapter-15: Your *Personality Evolution*
…Long-Term Solutions

Your Personality Evolution

Completing a *Strong Director's* Evolution

Chapter-16: Beyond *Personality*

Lacking Personality—*Non-thinking*

Automatic Personality, *Instinctive Thinking*

Have to do with physical survival—are triggered in millisecond—the emotional brain's timeframe.

Positive & Negative Emotional Energy

REFERENCES:

Gregory Titelman, *America's Popular Sayings, 2nd edition,* (Random House Reference, 2000)

Appendix A
Precise Personality Analysis

Precise Personality Analysis
The "*One-Second* Personality Analysis"
The *Basis* of our Style Strengths

Precise Personality Analysis

You probably already have a realistic understanding of what your inner-world personality pattern is, but use this appendix to precisely determine it. To get started, choose the *one* emotion below that you feel you express the ☒Most daily, especially when distressed. Also choose the *one or more* emotions that you express the ☒Least daily (rarely use). Those left blank are used some of the time as needed. When done, you should have *only* one ☒Most checked off above and one or more ☒Least; if you can't decide which Most you are among two, think of the emotion you express when "stressed out" and choose that one.

☐Most	☐Least	**Fear** (or *cautious* in its milder form)
☐Most	☐Least	**Anger** (or *assertiveness* in its milder form)
☐Most	☐Least	**Sorrow** (or *concern* in its milder form)
☐Most	☐Least	**Joy** (or *cheerfulness* in its milder form)

Your *emotional* inner-world is comprised of the four *primary* emotions of fear, anger, joy and sorrow, which allowed us to evolve to our present state by fulfilling their *physical* survival purposes. The physical survival purpose of *fear* is "to alert us to danger;" the physical survival purpose of *anger* is "to alert us to confrontation;" the physical survival purpose of joy is "to alert us to our connections;" and, the physical survival purpose of sorrow is "to alert us to disconnection." With this in mind, lets move on to your *rational nature.*

Your *rational* inner-world is comprised of four rational *styles* of reacting to daily situations, and like the physical survival emotions, each rational style has a *social* survival purpose as noted below. To help determine your rational nature, choose *only one* of the following styles that you feel you use the ☒Most daily, especially when distressed and choose the *one or more* styles that you use the ☒Least daily. You can determine this by selecting the *style purpose* that you use the Most or Least throughout the day; you use those left blank as needed.

☐Most ☐Least   *Analyzer Style*   – **"to unerringly proceed"**
                                   – the *perfectionist* style

☐Most ☐Least   *Director Style*   – **"to get resolution"**
                                   – the *get-it-done* style

☐Most ☐Least   *Relator Style*   – **"to maintain our connections"**
                                   – the *caring/nurturing* style

☐Most ☐Least   *Socializer Style* – **"to *address* our connections"**
                                   – the *fun loving* style

You should have only one ☒Most checked off above and one or more ☒Least; if you can't decide which ☒Most you are among two, think of the purpose used when you are "stressed out." Actually, you may have two rational styles that you use most of the time, but you use *only one* of them when you are distressed; cross off only that one above as ☒Most.

You have probably noticed, or know because of this book that there is a one-to-one relationship between the four primary emotions of your emotional nature and the four rational styles of your rational nature. Fear pairs off with the analyzer style, anger pairs off with the director style, sorrow pairs off with the relator style and joy pairs off with the socializer style. Thus, if you chose ☒Most for anger and ☒Most for the director style above, you've proofed them as your strongest emotion and style. This paired off "proofing" also applies to your weak emotions and rational styles. If you chose ☒Least for sorrow and ☒Least for the relator style, you've proofed them to be a weak emotion and style of yours. If your Most and Least choices *all* pair up and proof out, you truly know the strong and weak aspects of your genetic nature. If your Most and Least choices did not all pair up, you might want to rethink them or continue on in this appendix to improve your understanding of your genetic nature from an outer-world view.

As discussed in Chapter 9, each rational style has many *outer-world* motivation, sensory, and attitude attributes that are what most of us refer to when discussing someone's "personality." Examples of *attitude* attributes are accurate, methodical, etc., for the analyzer style; aggressive, demanding, etc., for the director style; compassionate, sympathetic, etc., for the relator style; and, expressive, talkative, etc., for the socializer style. You can also use the four *sensory* attributes (how we think) and the 12 *motivation* attributes (three per rational style) to precisely determine your personality pattern.

Since each rational style has three unique *outwardly observed* **Motivation Attributes,** we can use them to proof the strong and weak styles identified above. Listed below are the six sets of opposing motivations. To do your proof, first check off the motivations that you use the ☒Most daily (especially when distressed). Second, choose the motivations that you express the ☒Least daily; these are your weak motivations that are rarely used. Those left over are your moderate motivations.

☐Most ☐Least   **Pain/Loss** – "I always avoid pain or loss"
☐Most ☐Least   **Pleasure/Gain** – "I usually seek pleasure or gain"

☐Most ☐Least   **Necessities** – "I do what I'm *obligated* to do"
☐Most ☐Least   **Possibilities** – "I do what seems new and exciting"

☐Most ☐Least   **Differences** – "I typically *distrust* the actions of others"
☐Most ☐Least   **Similarities** – "I typically *trust* the actions of others"

☐Most ☐Least   **Self-directed** – "I *reject* the beliefs of others"
☐Most ☐Least   **Others-directed** – "I *embrace* the beliefs of others"

☐Most ☐Least   **Self-concerned** – "my needs are crucial"
☐Most ☐Least   **Others-concerned** – "others, needs are crucial"

☐Most ☐Least   **Decisive** – "I get results"
☐Most ☐Least   **Indecisive** – "I leave decision-making to others"

The rational style you are strongest in should have its three motivations checked off as ☒Most above. To determine this, compare your ☒Most responses above with the following table. If the three ☒Most motivations match your strongest style then you have proofed that style strength; if they did not proof out you may need to rethink your responses.

Analyzer	Socializer	Director	Relator
Pain/Loss	Pleasure/Gain	Self-Directed	Others-Directed
"I avoid pain/loss"	"I seek pleasure/gain"	"I reject other's beliefs"	"I embrace other's beliefs"
Necessities	Possibilities	Self-Concerned	Others-Concerned
"I do what I'm *obligated* to do"	"I do what's gratifying"	"my needs are crucial"	"other's needs are crucial"
Differences	Similarity	Decisive	Indecisive
"I *distrust* other's actions"	"I *trust* other's actions"	"I get quick results"	"I leave decision-making to others"

If you are weak in one or more styles, you should have their motivation attributes checked off as ☒Weak above. To determine this, compare your ☒Least responses above with the following table and match them to those styles; they should all match up. If the ☒Least motivations match your weak styles then you have proofed that weak style strength; if they did not proof out you may need to rethink your responses. Those left blank are your moderate motivations and will match your moderate styles indicated above.

Once your findings above are accurate, summarize your style strengths below. As noted in Appendix B, there are strong style patterns and moderate style patterns. *Strong* patterns have one strongest style and three moderate to weak styles. *Moderate* patterns have two moderately strong styles (but only one *strongest* style) and two moderate to weak styles (i.e., either two moderate styles, two weak styles, or one moderate and one weak style).

If you have a **STRONG** rational, style pattern (one strong style) check it off below—if known, check off your weakest style. If your pattern is not strong, skip the table below, and go to the next one for a moderate pattern.

Analyzer style:	☐Strongest	☐Moderate	☐Weak	☐Weakest
Director style:	☐Strongest	☐Moderate	☐Weak	☐Weakest
Relator style:	☐Strongest	☐Moderate	☐Weak	☐Weakest
Socializer style:	☐Strongest	☐Moderate	☐Weak	☐Weakest

If you feel that you have a **MODERATE** rational style pattern (two moderately strong styles with one being strongest), summarize your overall findings below. If known, also indicate your strongest and weakest style.

Analyzer style: □Strongest □Strong   □Moderate   □Weak □Weakest

Director style: □Strongest □Strong   □Moderate   □Weak □Weakest

Relator style: □Strongest □Strong   □Moderate   □Weak □Weakest

Socializer style: □Strongest □Strong   □Moderate   □Weak □Weakest

Now that you know your precise style pattern, refer to Appendix B for a summary of its outer-world attributes, categorized into 4 *strong* patterns and 12 *moderate* patterns.

If you want to know the rational style patterns of others, give them a copy of pages A-1 through A-3 to complete. Once known, you can refer to Chapter-10 to determine your natural compatibility with each other. Another method of determining the personality patterns of others is to do a "*One-Second* Personality Analysis."

The *One-Second* Personality Analysis

We all do a *One-Second* Personality Analysis every time we meet someone new—some of us are just more aware of it. There's nothing magical about it; it's part of our survival mechanism. When a stranger walks up to us, we are not sure of their intent and automatically revert to our strongest emotion to alert us because it is the most excitatory of our emotions. We express subtle emotion and not strong anger, fear, joy or sorrow unless the person is an obvious threat. Since we all have this reaction, we can use it to determine the strongest style of any person we may meet as long as they do not know or expect us at that moment.

It is helpful to know the strongest style of someone we just met since we'll probably have to interact with them. For example, consider going into a store and meeting a rude clerk with a strong director style. Using the *one-second* analysis, we can instantly determine that he or she is a strong director and dismiss the rudeness as the store's inability to hire people-oriented clerks. This is better than trying to figure out what we did to offend that rude clerk.

The *one-second* analysis is helpful when meeting new clients or customers with whom we want successful relations. By instantly knowing their strongest styles/emotions we can better understand and interact with them. We know that if they are decisive, easily hindered by us and not interested in small talk that they are strong directors. We know that if they are cautious and want to unerringly proceed that they are strong analyzers. We know that if they are concerned with staying connected and not offending us that they are strong relators. You know that if they want to talk a lot and have a short attention span that they are strong socializers. In essence, by first knowing a person's strongest style you can then better understand them and be able to predict how they will interact with us.

The *one-second* analysis allows us to detect a person's strongest style through the instant perception of warmth or coolness emanating from them, the instant we meet them. This warmth or lack of it naturally gives them away; they have no control over emanating it and we have no control over recognizing it. The warmth comes from subtle emanation of positive emotional energy, and the coolness comes from subtle emanation of negative emotional energy—refer to Chapter 16 for emotional energy.

The *one-second* analysis works when we make a conscious effort to be aware of it. There are two "warm" people-oriented feelings (relator and socializer) and two "cool" task-oriented feelings (analyzer and director). Sometimes, there is a striking "coldness" when a very strong director or analyzer is severely distressed upon meeting them, emanating strong negative emotional energy.

When we first meet someone who does *not* know us, *we* feel one of the following:

- ❖ a *concerned warmth* from a strong **relator**
- ❖ a *cheerful warmth* from a strong **socializer**
- ❖ a *cautious coolness* from a strong **analyzer**
- ❖ a *dismissive coolness* from a strong **director**

The "concerned warmth" of people-oriented relators makes us feel relaxed. We know that they would never offend us and that we would never want to offend them. They make us feel at peace with ourselves for that fraction of a second; afterward, they tend to avoid anything that might cause disconnection. To test your own automatic reactions in perceiving concerned warmth from a relator, think of the relators you know and how they made you feel the instant you *first* met them.

The "cheerful warmth" of people-oriented socializers draws us to them, making us excited in their presence. They have an engaging smile and typically move toward us (bend forward or move closer); a few seconds later they speak in an excited, expressive and excessive manner. Think of the socializers you know, then how they made you feel and how they physically acted the instant you *first* met them.

The "cautious coolness" of task-oriented analyzers makes them shy away from anyone new. They need to *physically* retreat (turn aside or bend away or move back a few inches from us) to regroup and see where they stand with us. After they are comfortable with us, they are cordial and listen intently to what we have to say. Think of the analyzers you know and how they made you feel and then how they physically acted the instant you *first* met them.

The "dismissive coolness" of task-oriented directors comes from the director style's result-oriented purpose to move on to the next task, giving us the feeling that they're done with us as they turn away from or ignore us, appearing to be mentally far away. In general, when directors are expecting us, they will be friendlier after the first second, but if they are not expecting us and see no need to prolong the relationship, they will rudely ignore us or depart. Think of the directors you know, then how they made you feel and how they physically acted the instant you *first* met them.

The reaction we get when we meet new people has nothing to do with *our* strongest style; we would get that same reaction from them no matter what our strongest style. That's the wonderful thing about the *one-second* analysis: we automatically know why we feel the way we do when meeting new people. We know that there isn't anything wrong with us or the other person since we're both just reacting "naturally." For example, think of a director that you met recently that made you "feel like dirt." Didn't it make you feel as if you did something wrong or didn't it make you angry and want to get even? The fact is, you didn't offend the director, and he or she was not trying to offend you. The director was just reacting instinctively, and so were you. People are just people. They aren't perfect, and they react instinctively without thinking. Knowing how and why they react will help you to better understand them and yourself so that you can get the most out of a relationship and not automatically dislike or be hurt or embarrassed by someone new.

So the next time you sense the concerned or cheerful warmth from someone—enjoy it. And the next time you feel a retreating coolness from analyzers understand that they just need to feel more comfortable with you, which should only take a minute or two. And the next time you meet directors who makes you feel like dirt, don't throw the dirt back in their face; ignore their reaction and get on with your relationship if there is to be any.

The *One-Second* **Personality Analysis** is easy to do; you should practice it daily to become proficient at it. Apply the *one-second* analysis in the following manner:

1. Walk up to someone and introduce yourself; the meeting should be one-on-one.
2. The person must *not* know or recognize you or be expecting you, although he or she may know of you.
3. You must meet the person by surprise; just walk up and say hello.
4. Maintain eye contact for one or two seconds after you meet.
5. Determine the person's concerned (relator) warmth or cheerful (socializer) warmth, or the cautious (analyzer) coolness or dismissive (director) coolness.

It's very simple! If they're not warm, they're cool. First, determine their warmth or lack of it, and then determine what kind of warmth or coolness it is. THAT'S ALL THERE IS TO IT!

After you apply the *one-second* analysis, you automatically know a person's strongest rational style and all that accompanies it. Unfortunately, you may not always believe your results, especially when the person analyzed switches to another style soon after you correctly analyze them. You must not let this switch in styles negate your initial analysis. Stick with your initial findings and the person will eventually prove you correct.

Note! You cannot always use the *one-second* analysis under ideal conditions. Sometimes you have no control over the situation. Others may meet you when you aren't prepared to meet them; you can't of course meet people you already know. But, with continued practice of the *one-second* analysis, you will quickly attain an accuracy of 90 percent.

As you consciously perfect the analysis, you won't have to meet the person to determine their strongest style, you can determine it in passing or even over the phone. For example, as you drive through a tollbooth you have momentary contact with the person collecting your toll, which is long enough to accurately tell their strongest style—my family and I do this for fun on car trips and we usually agree.

We also guess the strongest style of servers in restaurants, which tells us the kind of service to expect and how to best interact with them. For example, we know that if the server is a strong socializer that he or she naturally doesn't listen, so we make sure that we precisely order and that he or she correctly records it. This cuts down on incorrect orders and the negative experiences that they create, which can ruin a good meal. There is no end to what you can do to make life better when you know who you're dealing with and what you want your relationship to be, especially when it cautions you to avoid the relationship.

In conclusion, the "*One-Second* Personality Analysis" is a simple, useful tool for determining someone's strongest rational style. It allows you to establish a more fulfilling relationship right from the start because you know what to expect. You can consciously perfect your one-second analysis by using it every time you walk into a store, eat in a restaurant or meet someone new—identify at least six new people a day. Eventually, you will *unconsciously* detect their strongest style and automatically deal with them in the most productive manner.

Appendix B
Symbiotic Personality *Patterns*

Strong and Moderate Patterns
The Four *Strong* Patterns
The 12 *Moderate* Patterns

Strong and Moderate Patterns

The genetic components of your natural style pattern that you precisely determined using Appendix-A or inferred from Chapter 2 through Chapter 9 are contained herein. These outer-world descriptions help us to understand why we act similarly, even though our inner-world's rational and emotional memories are unique.

There can be an indefinite number of Patterns, depending on your definition, but 16 suffice. Every Pattern consists of four rational styles (analyzer, director, relator and socializer), which can be strong, moderate or weak—the style's daily usage defines its strength:

Strong rational styles—*we use it much of the time* throughout the day

Moderate rational styles— *we use it as needed* throughout the day

Weak rational styles— *we rarely use it* throughout the day

We can have either a "Strong Pattern" or a "Moderate Pattern." Strong patterns limit us and moderate patterns give us flexibility:

Strong Patterns use their *one* strongest style most of the time, their weak styles very rarely and their moderate styles as needed—there are four strong patterns.

Moderate Patterns use their *two* moderately strong styles most of the time (except when distressed, when only the strongest style is used) and use their moderate to weak styles as needed—there are 12 moderate patterns.

B-1

The Four *Strong* Patterns

Strong ANALYZER Pattern:

☺ This pattern's *task-oriented* **Purpose** is:
"to unerringly proceed"

☺ This pattern's *Symbiotic* **Emotion** is:
Fear (whose purpose is: *"to alert us to danger"*)

☺ The **Sensory Attributes** of this pattern is either:
- Visual-words: *think in visualized words about things*
- Kinesthetic: *think in tactile sensations about things*

☺ The *outer-world* **Motivations** of this pattern are:
- Loss/pain: "I avoid loss or pain"
- Necessities: "I do what I am obligated to do"
- Differences: "I *distrust* most situations"

☺ The *outer-world* **Attitudes** of this pattern are:
Cautious, conventional, diligent, disciplined, introspective, logical, methodical, meticulous, modest, negative, preparative, reserved, respectful, self-conscious, self-controlled, shy, tactful, tedious, thrifty, touchy.

Strong RELATOR Pattern:

☺ This pattern's *people-oriented* **Purpose** is:
"to maintain our connections"

☺ This pattern's *Symbiotic* **Emotion** is:
Sorrow (whose purpose is: *"to alert us to disconnection"*)

☺ The **Sensory Attribute** of this pattern is:
Auditory: *think in the sounds of words about people*

☺ The *outer-world* **Motivations** of this pattern are:
- Others-directed: "I embrace other's beliefs"
- Others-concerned: "others needs are crucial"
- Indecisive: "I leave decision-making to others"

☺ The *outer-world* **Attitudes** of this pattern are:
Agreeable, amiable, compassionate, considerate, empathetic, gentle, humble, kind, lenient, loyal, obliging, patient, protective, sensitive, submissive, sympathetic, tolerant, trusting, worrisome.

Strong DIRECTOR Pattern:

☺ This pattern's *task-oriented* **Purpose** is:
"to attain resolution"

☺ This pattern's **Symbiotic Emotion** is:
Anger (whose purpose is: *"to alert us to confrontation"*)

☺ The **Sensory Attribute** of this pattern is:
Visual-action: *think in action pictures about things*

☺ The *outer-world* **Motivations** of this pattern are:
- Self-directed: "I reject other's beliefs"
- Self-concerned: "my needs are crucial"
- Decisive: "I make decisions to get results"

☺ The *outer-world* **Attitudes** of this pattern are:
Adventurous, aggressive, arrogant, assertive, competitive, compulsive, concise, controlling, critical, demanding, distant, dominance, faultfinding, independent, persistent, pioneering, temperamental, tenacious.

Strong SOCIALIZER Pattern:

☺ This pattern's *people-oriented* **Purpose** is:
"to address our connections"

☺ This pattern's **Symbiotic Emotion** is:
Joy (whose purpose is *"to alert us to our connections"*)

☺ The **Sensory Attribute** of this pattern is:
Visual-action: *think in action pictures about people*

☺ The *outer-world* **Motivations** of this pattern are:
- Gain/pleasure: "I seek out gain/pleasure"
- Possibilities: "I do what seems gratifying"
- Similarities: "I trust most situations"

☺ The *outer-world* **Attitudes** of this pattern are:
Boisterous, capricious, carefree, careless, charming, creative, enthusiastic, ex-aggerative, exciting, expressive, fickle, generous, impulsive, inspiring, inquisi-tive, persuasive, playful, positive, talkative, and teasing.

NOTE: In the "Twelve Moderate Patterns" descriptions on the following pages, the "bullets" refer to the style: **A** = Analyzer, **D** = Director, **R** = Relator and **S** = Socializer in the "moderate" style descriptions to contrast the attributes of the two unique strongest styles.

The Twelve *Moderate* Patterns

Analyzer/Director (**A/D**) Pattern:
Director/Analyzer (**D/A**) Pattern:

☺ Pages 138/139 discuss these two *somewhat self-conflicting patterns.*

☺ These *highly task-oriented* patterns have two **Purposes:**
    A   *"to unerringly proceed"*
    D   *"to attain resolution"*

☺ These patterns' **Symbiotic Emotions** are:
    A   *Fear* (whose purpose is *"to alert us to danger"*)
    D   *Anger* (whose purpose is *"to alert us to confrontation"*)

☺ The **Sensory Attributes** of these patterns are:
    A   Visual-words: *think in visualized words about things*
    A   Kinesthetic: *think in tactile sensations about things*
    D   Visual-action: *think in action pictures about things*

☺ The *outer-world* **Motivations** of these patterns are:
    A   Loss/pain: "I avoid loss or pain"
    A   Necessities: "I do what I am obligated to do"
    A   Differences: "I *distrust* most situations"

    D   Self-directed: "I reject other's beliefs"
    D   Self-concerned: "my needs are crucial"
    D   Decisive: "I make decisions to get results"

☺ The *outer-world* **Attitudes** of these patterns are:
    A   Cautious, conventional, diligent, disciplined, introspective, logical, methodical, meticulous, modest, negative, preparative, reserved, respectful, self-conscious, self-controlled, shy, tactful, tedious, thrifty, touchy.

    D   Adventurous, aggressive, arrogant, assertive, competitive, compulsive, concise, controlling, critical, demanding, distant, dominance, faultfinding, independent, persistent, pioneering, temperamental, tenacious.

Analyzer/Relator (**A/R**) Pattern:

Relator/Analyzer (**R/A**) Pattern:

☺ These mixed *task-oriented* and *people-oriented* patterns have two **Purposes:**

    A *"to unerringly proceed"*

    R *"to maintain our connections"*

☺ These patterns' **Symbiotic Emotions** are:

    A *Fear* (whose purpose is *"to alert us to danger"*)

    R *Sorrow* (whose purpose is *"to alert us to disconnection"*)

☺ The **Sensory Attributes** of these patterns are:

    A Visual-words: *think in visualized words about things*

    A Kinesthetic: *think in tactile sensations about things*

    R Auditory: *think in the sounds of words about people*

☺ The *outer-world* **Motivations** of these patterns are:

    A Loss/pain: "I avoid loss or pain"

    A Necessities: "I do what I am obligated to do"

    A Differences: "I *distrust* most situations"

    R Others-directed: "I embrace other's beliefs"

    R Others-concerned: "others needs are crucial"

    R Indecisive: "I leave decision-making to others"

☺ The *outer-world* **Attitudes** of these patterns are:

    A Cautious, conventional, diligent, disciplined, introspective, logical, methodical, meticulous, modest, negative, preparative, reserved, respectful, self-conscious, self-controlled, shy, tactful, tedious, thrifty, touchy.

    R Agreeable, amiable, compassionate, considerate, empathetic, gentle, humble, kind, lenient, loyal, obliging, patient, protective, sensitive, submissive, sympathetic, tolerant, trusting, worrisome

Analyzer/Socializer (**A/S**) Pattern:
Socializer/Analyzer (**S/A**) Pattern:

☹ Pages 136/137 discuss these two *highly self-conflicting patterns*.

☺ These *task-oriented* and *people-oriented* patterns have two **Purposes:**
    A *"to unerringly proceed"*
    S *"to address our connections"*

☺ These patterns' **Symbiotic Emotions** are:
    A *Fear* (whose purpose is *"to alert us to danger"*)
    S *Joy* (whose purpose is *"to alert us to our connections"*)

☺ The **Sensory Attributes** of these patterns are:
    A Visual-words: *think in visualized words about things*
    A Kinesthetic: *think in tactile sensations about things*
    S Visual-action: *think in action pictures about people*

☹ The *conflicting* **Motivations** of these patterns are:
    A Loss/pain: "I avoid loss or pain"
    S Gain/pleasure: "I seek out gain/pleasure"

    A Necessities: "I do what I am obligated to do"
    S Possibilities: "I do what seems gratifying"

    A Differences: "I *distrust* most situations"
    S Similarities: "I *trust* most situations"

☺ The *conflicting* **Attitudes** of these patterns are:
    A Cautious, conventional, diligent, disciplined, introspective, logical, methodical, meticulous, modest, negative, preparative, reserved, respectful, self-conscious, self-controlled, shy, tactful, tedious, thrifty, touchy.

    S Boisterous, capricious, carefree, careless, charming, creative, enthusiastic, exaggerative, exciting, expressive, fickle, generous, impulsive, inspiring, inquisitive, persuasive, playful, positive, talkative, teasing.

Director/Relator (**D/R**) Pattern:
Relator/Director (**R/D**) Pattern:

☹ Pages 134/135 discuss these two *highly self-conflicting patterns.*

☺ These *task-oriented* and *people-oriented* patterns have two **Purposes:**
  D *"to attain resolution"*
  R *"to maintain our connections"*

☺ These patterns' **Symbiotic Emotions** are:
  D **Anger** (whose purpose is *"to alert us to confrontation"*)
  R **Sorrow** (whose purpose is *"to alert us to disconnection"*)

☺ The **Sensory Attributes** of these patterns are:
  D Visual-action: *think in action pictures about things*
  R Auditory: *think in the sounds of words about people*

☹ The *conflicting* **Motivations** of these patterns are:
  D Self-directed: "I reject other's beliefs"
  R Others-directed: "I embrace other's beliefs"

  D Self-concerned: "my needs are crucial"
  R Others-concerned: "others needs are crucial"

  D Decisive: "I make decisions to get results"
  R Indecisive: "I leave decision-making to others"

☺ The *conflicting* **Attitudes** of these patterns are:
  D Adventurous, aggressive, arrogant, assertive, competitive, compulsive, concise, controlling, critical, demanding, distant, dominance, faultfinding, independent, persistent, pioneering, temperamental, tenacious.

  R Agreeable, amiable, compassionate, considerate, empathetic, gentle, humble, kind, lenient, loyal, obliging, patient, protective, sensitive, submissive, sympathetic, tolerant, trusting, worrisome.

Director/Socializer (**D/S**) Pattern:
Socializer/Director (**S/D**) Pattern:

☺ These *result-oriented and people-oriented* patterns have two **Purposes:**
  D *"to attain resolution"*
  S *"to address our connections"*

☺ These patterns' ***Symbiotic* Emotions** are:
  D ***Anger*** (whose purpose is *"to alert us to confrontation"*)
  S ***Joy*** (whose purpose is *"to alert us to our connections"*)

☺ The **Sensory Attributes** of these patterns are:
  D Visual-action: *think in action pictures about things*
  S Visual-action: *think in action pictures about people*

☺ The **Motivations** of these patterns are:
  D Self-directed: "I reject other's beliefs"
  D Self-concerned: "my needs are crucial"
  D Decisive: "I make decisions to get results"

  S Gain/pleasure: "I seek out gain/pleasure"
  S Possibilities: "I do what seems gratifying"
  S Similarities: "I trust most situations"

☺ The **Attitudes** of these patterns are:
  D Adventurous, aggressive, arrogant, assertive, competitive, compulsive, concise, controlling, critical, demanding, distant, dominance, faultfinding, independent, persistent, pioneering, temperamental, tenacious.

  S Boisterous, capricious, carefree, careless, charming, creative, enthusiastic, exaggerative, exciting, expressive, fickle, generous, impulsive, inspiring, inquisitive, persuasive, playful, positive, talkative, teasing.

Relator/Socializer (**R/S**) Pattern:
Socializer/Relator (**S/R**) Pattern:

☺ Pages 137/138 discuss these two *somewhat self-conflicting patterns.*

☺ These highly *people-oriented* patterns have two **Purposes:**

   R *"to maintain our connections"*
   S *"to address our connections"*

☺ These patterns' **Symbiotic Emotions** are:

   R **Sorrow** (whose purpose is *"To alert us to disconnection"*)
   S **Joy** (whose purpose is *"to alert us to our connections"*)

☺ The **Sensory Attributes** of these patterns are:

   R Auditory: *think in the sounds of words about people*
   S Visual-action: *think in action pictures about people*

☺ The **Motivations** of these patterns are:

   R Others-directed: "I embrace other's beliefs"
   R Others-concerned: "others needs are crucial"
   R Indecisive: "I leave decision-making to others"

   S Gain/pleasure: "I seek out gain/pleasure"
   S Possibilities: "I do what seems gratifying"
   S Similarities: "I trust most situations"

☺ The **Attitudes** of these patterns are:

   R Agreeable, amiable, compassionate, considerate, empathetic, gentle, humble, kind, lenient, loyal, obliging, patient, protective, sensitive, submissive, sympathetic, tolerant, trusting, worrisome.

   S Boisterous, capricious, carefree, careless, charming, creative, enthusiastic, exaggerative, exciting, expressive, fickle, generous, impulsive, inspiring, inquisitive, persuasive, playful, positive, talkative, teasing.

Appendix C
De-Stressing Ourselves

Stress…Nature-Nurture Integration
Tree Types of Stress
Our "Stress Bucket" and "Stress-O-Meter"
Identifying Our Mental Stressors
Identifying Our Chemical Stressors
Identifying Our Physical Stressors

Stress…Nature-Nurture Integration

How's your cortisol doing? Stress (distress) and cortisol are virtually synonymous and cortisol can be found coursing through our veins in every organ in the body. It has been shown[1] that stress, whether real or imagined, increases the level of cortisol in the body, which results in a reduced immune system response to disease by reducing the number, activity and life of lymphocytes, which fight disease.

Technically, here's how it seems to work. Sensory information and memories trigger emotions and rational reactions that cause the hypothalamus to send a signal to the adrenal cortex that triggers the CYP17 gene to produce an enzyme that converts cholesterol to cortisol. Cortisol then switches on the TCF gene, which produces a protein that suppresses interleukin-2 (a chemical that makes white blood cells ever-vigilant for germs), thus reducing the lymphocytes and making us more susceptible to disease. There's short-term cortisol stress (momentary increases in cortisol) caused by natural primary emotional reactions. There's long-term cortisol stress (cortisol build-up over time) leading to an unhealthy state of distress, which we need to control—but how?

One would assume that if we reduce our cortisol buildup we could reduce our stress and avoid distress. We might also assume that if we reduce our cholesterol we could reduce the amount available to make cortisol. Unfortunately, cholesterol is plentiful and available to the genome responsible for manufacturing cortisol—the *body* is in control.

Sensory information that triggers memories that cause emotional reactions affects the level of cortisol in the body. Since we can't trigger emotions without learned emotional memories stress is learned—the *mind* is in control.

In reality, the entire stress/distress cortisol syndrome is a coordinated effort by the entire body and mind to deal with life and has no central control. Thus, to reduce stress that can build up to distress, the best thing to do is avoid the kind of things that create distress, which we can classify into three types of stress.

Three Types of Stress

When we encounter the normal amount of daily stress, our reactions involve our total natural personality: learned plus genetic, emotional plus rational. If excessively stressed, called "distress," we become a "prisoner of our strongest style and emotion." This makes us act inappropriately in most situations and causes pain and suffering for everyone around us. The bottom line is "if we don't reduce our stress we won't be able to finesse our personality to get the most out of life."

Normal stress gives us the drive to do what we don't want to do, for example, the stress of meeting deadlines with our decisive director style. Distress just gets in the way of what we want out of life, for example, when we have a regretful angry outburst that upset our loved ones. Most stresses are minor and subside immediately or within a reasonable period. For example, remember the last time you bumped your "funny bone," causing intense physical stress that quickly faded away, or the last time somebody cut you off, causing mental stress that quickly faded away. Examples of long lasting daily stress are: virus infections, setbacks at work and financial problems. There are also very profound stresses, for example, the loss of a family member through relocation, disability or death.

Stress is simple to understand, yet vast and complicated when we try to get a handle on it. Actually, stress and distress are simple to understand since 95 percent of it involves three principles:

❖ There are three types of stress: *mental, chemical* and *physical.*

❖ Stress is cumulative, becoming distress when excessive.

❖ Stress is genetic—distress is learned.

Mental stress is anything emotionally or rationally conceived that adversely affects our health and well being. *Chemical* stress comes from the foods we eat and drink and the contaminated air we breathe. *Physical* stress comes from invading organisms, physical injury or anything that affects the body that is neither mental nor chemical in nature. The three stress categories are broad and each can have many subcategories, but they are adequate to identify *your* stress, allowing you to reduce it for a calmer, more fulfilled, better finessed life with those you love.

Our "Stress Bucket" and "Stress-O-Meter"

There are many books on stress and distress and how to deal with them; this appendix cannot replace that wealth of experience and information. This appendix can, however, make you aware of the stressors in *your* life; that conscious awareness can help you reduce them.

The most important aspect of stress is that it's cumulative; we accumulate stress (and thus cortisol) throughout the day. Naturally accumulated mental, chemical and physical stresses appear and disappear momentarily, making us more or less distressed from moment to moment to deal with life as nature intended. We can think of stress as accumulating in a "Stress Bucket"—we fill this stress bucket with mental, chemical and physical stress throughout the day, week or year, even throughout our lives. Most of our stressors are natural, coming and going as needed, but some are chronic, such as a chronic disease, permanent physical injury or strong negative emotional memories—these keep the stress bucket mostly full. When the stress bucket *overflows,* we become distressed and are susceptible to mental and physical illnesses. We can never empty our stress bucket, but we can keep it from overflowing by identifying and reducing our stressors.

For example, if we have allergies we must avoid the foods or environments we're allergic to. If we are distressed because we have little money and many bills to pay, we need to have a brighter outlook, assume all will be well and think of ways to generate that money instead of being distressed over not having it. If distressed from lack of sleep, we should take a nap or get a few long nights of uninterrupted sleep—this seems too simple, but it works!

We should try to reduce our stress as much as possible, to keep our stress bucket from overflowing. We can alleviate certain types of mental, chemical and physical stress within a matter of minutes or hours; some stresses require days or weeks to alleviate. Some stressors, such as rehabilitation from a severe accident or illness, may require months to alleviate. And some stressors such as the loss of a family member take years to alleviate.

Prolonged distress shows up in the use of our strongest style, followed by a physical or mental breakdown. We all, however, have though, a built-in "Stress-O-Meter" that alerts us to pending distress, we just need to determine what it is. For example, before I gained control over my stressors I had a four-step Stress-O-Meter: 1) When my stress bucket was full, I excessively used my strong director style. 2) As my stress bucket started to overflow, my sinuses stuffed up along with the excessive use of my director style. 3) As my stress bucket overflowed, my jaw joint (TMJ) became painful along with the stuffy sinuses and excessive use of my director style. 4) If my stress bucket were gushing, I would get eczema along with TMJ pain, stuffy sinuses and the excessive use of my director. My natural Stress-O-Meter helped me to realize that I needed to back off, appraise the situation, and identify and reduce my stressors.

We all have our own Stress-O-Meter; we just have to figure out what it is. For example, I have a friend who first shows excessive use of her strongest socializer style, then experiences eczema, then stuffy sinuses and finally colitis. Another friend shows only excessive use of her analyzer style when becoming distressed and then shows a twitch in her right eyelid when her stress bucket is gushing. Another friend shows excessive use of his director style at first and then a red patch on his forehead when distressed. We are all different and our family and friends can probably help us determine our unique Stress-O-Meter.

Once aware of our distress through excessive use of our strongest style or physical manifestations, we can identify our mental, physical, and chemical stressors and then alleviate them. This will cause our stress bucket to stop overflowing and allow us to take control of our personality and our physical and mental health.

Since we all have a certain level of cortisol in our system, some more than others, we go through life with a partially full stress bucket and increase or decrease our bucket's level throughout the day, overflowing it at times and causing distress. The stress filling our bucket is sometimes obvious, but it can be insidious. Unlike obvious stress, such as financial disaster, insidious stress can creep up on us and take control without our realizing it. These insidious "little stresses" include: being cut off on the ride to work; the rude wait-person at lunch; that slight pain in our lower back; the tuna fish sandwich that we're sensitive to; the boss wanting to see us, but we don't know why; and the countless other little everyday stresses that fill up our stress bucket and cause it to overflow.

But, as long as we know that, our stress bucket is continuously filling and emptying throughout the day with large and small stresses we can monitor that stress accumulation with our Stress-O-Meter and do something about it before it becomes distress.

Listed on the following page are examples of the three types of stress. The list is by no means exhaustive, but it does identify our daily stressors. At the end of each physical, mental and chemical stress section there is a place to list *your* prioritized physical, mental and chemical stresses. Knowing your most common stresses in each category is very important since they mostly fill your stress bucket daily. Thus, when your stress bucket overflows, you can identify and reduce the stresses affecting you, resulting in a happier and healthier life.

Identifying Our *Mental* Stressors

Mental stress is any stress created by a rational thought or emotional out-burst; the most common mental stresses are:

Pecking order: Having others ordered us about is the most stressful thing in our lives as one study[1] conclusively shows. Thus, the more people we have above us (parents, bosses, etc.) having a say in what we do the more dis-tressed we will have, especially if we are strong directors or if we are using our director style. We could work for ourselves, but then our customers would be our bosses. The only way to get around this is to stay connected (avoid disconnection) with our bosses. This will reduce the implication that they are not happy with our work; and when they are, they will construc-tively tell us so that we can respond in an appropriate manner. Refer to Ap-pendix D and Chapter 4 to better understand this concept.

Financial: This is the most common type of mental stress, especially for analyzers. Although it is usually short-term stress, lasting days to months it can be devastating if we have many financial obligations and few financial resources. Lack of financial wherewithal cuts to the very core of our being by denying us the life-style we covet. If we are having problems paying our bills or living the kind of life we desire, we are probably experiencing this type of mental stress. Think about a time in your life when you experienced financial distress, how devastating it seemed at the time and how much it distressed you, even though it was eventually resolved. If you can balance your assets with your liabilities, as discussed in Chapter 6, you can get around this type of distress.

Personal Loss: This is a devastating type of long-term mental stress: It re-fers to the loss of a loved one through death, divorce or abandonment. When it occurs, we go through numerous stages of loss, usually over a 2-year period, before this stress subsides. If we experience this loss at a very young age, through the loss of one or both parents, we can be scarred *emo-tionally* for life, living our lives with an overflowing stress bucket. Personal loss may also include possessions, such as the loss of savings/investments, a car, a home, etc. If you have experienced this kind of loss, think about it and how much it distresses you; should it happen again, try to avoid think-ing about its consequences and say to yourself "that's life; no guarantees!"

Obligations: This kind of stress drives us to complete tasks we promise or are paid to complete, but find it difficult to complete. We experience this stress all day long, from minor obligations, such as promising to pick up something at the market, to completing a complicated time-consuming project for our boss or client. Reflect upon your daily obligations, the stress they cause and what you might realistically do to better schedule yourself to resolve them and avoid stressing yourself.

Family: There is always natural conflict between the many personality patterns within a family (see Chapter 10 on compatibility) that we can't avoid. For example, it's difficult for parents not to be authoritative and discipline their children when required. It's difficult for children not to be jealous of each other and vie for their parent's attention. It's difficult for parents to deal with the constant noise, bickering, mess, loss of sleep and lack of personal time when rearing children. This is all part of being in a family, and it *is* stressful. If we recognize these stresses as they occur and put them in perspective, we can lessen their stress and improve our family life. If you have a family, you are well aware of these stresses, but you might want to think about the ones that stress you the most and try to get past them through understanding and compromise. It also helps to use "The Relationship Game" in Appendix-D.

Male–Female: This is one of the oldest types of stress. Today it is fueled by the many publications we read, TV shows we view, and friends we have with unsatisfying relationships with the opposite sex. Whether male or female we all want the same things out of life. We all want love and we all want to be respected for ourselves and what we accomplish, nothing more and nothing less. But we don't always get what we want, which causes us to blame it on the opposite sex. If we are having relationship problems, we are probably experiencing this type of stress—as we mature it tends to lessen. Think about your relations with the opposite sex. If they distress you, you need a more realistic perspective on how to positively interact with the opposite sex a better self-image would help.

Self-Image: This type of stress occurs when we don't love and respect ourselves. If you feel such stress, seek out those who can help you feel better about yourself and avoid those who don't. Many believe that if we know that our parents love us that we will have a good self-image and that if we think they don't, we won't. This is not easy to think about, for many of us feel that they do love us—well maybe. The fact is your parents always did and always will love you, whether connected or disconnected!

Excitement: This refers to the good stress we feel when things go very well for us and we are "on top of the world." We are very emotional and excited at such times and "don't know what to do with ourselves." This hidden stress overflows our stress bucket making us only use our strongest style, which may negate the joys we are experiencing. For example, if our strongest style is director we may become arrogant, alienating those around us, thus destroying our excitement. It is important to realize that when we are in a highly excited state of mind that it is stressful and can backfire on us. Think of the last time you were very happy and excited, didn't it cause you to excessively use your strongest style?

Unfulfilled Strongest Style: We experience this stress when we have not fulfilled the purpose of our strongest style. Analyzers feel a strong need to unerringly proceed on a task, but haven't. Directors feel a strong need to attain a nagging result, but can't. Relators feel a strong need to maintain relationships, but the other person avoids reconnection. Socializers feel a strong need to interact with others, but nobody is available. Think about it for a moment; think about when you felt uneasy about things in general and how much better you felt after fulfilling the purpose of your strongest style.

Overly used Strongest Style and Symbiotic Emotion: We experience this stress when we excessively use our strongest style to attain its purpose, knowing that it is inappropriate much of the time. Unfortunately, the stress caused by the need to use our strongest style less causes more distress and the need to use it more. This is compounded by the excessive expression of our strongest emotion and thus, its symbiotic style, creating a series of symbiotic cycles that is hard to break. Think of the last time you were distressed from overusing your strongest style and emotion: Didn't that knowledge distress you even more?

Job or School: We feel this stress when we are unsuccessful in our chosen profession or if we dislike the work we do or the environment in which we do it. The same applies to education stress in students whose job it is to learn. We also experience this type of stress when our work is unfulfilling; if so, we should change jobs if it is the only solution, although, change is stressful.

Life Change Units: If we have too many changes in our lives over a twelve-month period, it creates distress. This is especially true with strong analyzers and relators, who are stressed by even minor changes. The chart on the right is an updated version of a Life Change Units Test (developed over a half-century ago by Dr. Holmes). Test yourself; if you test high—over 250 life change units in the past year—you are definitely distressed by excessive life change units. Some strong analyzers or relators are excessively stressed when their total is over 150.

Life Change Units

(circle the units that apply to you in the past *12 months*)

Death of your spouse or child	100
Divorce	73
Marital separation	65
Death of close family member	63
Jail term	63
Personal injury or illness	50
Marriage	50
Fired at work	47
Marital reconciliation	45
Retirement	45
Change in health of family member	44
Pregnancy	40
Sex difficulties	39
Gain of new family member	39
Business readjustment	39
Change in financial state (+ or –)	38
Death of a close friend	37
Change to different line of work	36
More or less arguments with spouse	35
Break up of a long-standing relationship	34
Mortgage or loans over $100,000	31
Foreclosure of mortgage or loan	30
Change in responsibilities at work	29
Son or daughter leaving home	29
Troubles with in-laws	29
Outstanding personal achievement	28
Spouse begins or stops work	26
You begin or end school	26
Change in living conditions	25
Revisions of personal habits	24
Trouble with your boss	23
Change in work or working conditions	20
Change in residence	20
Change in schools	20
Change in recreation	19
Change in church	19
Change in social activities	18
Mortgage or loan less than $100,000	17
Change in sleeping habits	16
Change in number of family get-togethers	15
Change in eating habits	15
Vacation (13 *per* vacation)	____
Christmas (holiday season)	12
Minor violations of the law (11 *per* ticket)	____

Total of All Life Change Units for Year	

Guilt: If we have strong guilt we experience guilt stress much of the time—this is common in us strong relators and analyzers. We have little control over our false feelings of doing something wrong, especially if we are distressed, which exacerbates the guilt. The only defense is to realize that our guilt is excessively strong and try to ignore it as much as possible. Reducing the total stress in our stress bucket always helps. Do you think that you are an excessively guilty person? Ask those who work and live with you, it's usually obvious to them if you are.

Mental Disease: If we suffer from a mental dysfunction that is stressing our lives we are probably not able to identify and alleviate this stress. This falls out of the "normal" use of our personalities into the abnormal use and requires professional help.

The above mental stresses provides a reference for prioritizing (1, 2, 3, 4) *your* two to four most powerful mental stresses. You must know your strongest mental stresses to reduce your overall stress, keep your cortisol level down, and keep your stress bucket from overflowing. Once identified, you must create the memories (see Chapter 15) that will consciously, then unconsciously, reduce these stressors.

Priority of *mental* stresses that plague you—list from most stressful (1) to less stressful (4):

1) _____

2) _____

3) _____

4) _____

Identifying Our Chemical Stressors

Chemical stress affects "sensitized" (allergic) people most, but even non-allergic people can be sensitive to certain foods, chemicals or inhalants and should evaluate the possible chemical stressors below. If you suspect that you may be sensitive to certain foods, read about "The Allergy Addiction Syndrome"[2], which severely affects about 25 percent of the population and has some effect on the other 75 percent.

Inhalants Allergy: This occurs when we are allergic to the usual dogs, cats, pollen, ragweed, mold and mildew, dust and other natural substances we may inhale into our sinuses and lungs. It's easy to determine whether our environment affects us since the "allergy seasons" severely affect us. For example, in the northeastern United States the inhalant allergy season is typically from mid-May to mid-July, when the tree and grass pollen proliferates. Your area of the country will have its own allergy season. The allergy symptoms are a runny nose, itchy eyes, clogged sinuses, etc. It is difficult if not impossible to avoid the stress of the allergy season, but by keeping our stress buckets from overflowing by reducing our *other* stresses, we can usually reduce the cortisol and thus increase the lymphocytes in our system to better deal with the allergens.

Toxic Inhalants: This occurs in people who are allergic to the natural inhalants noted above. The toxic substances are household cleaning agents, nail polish, glue and any product with a heavy chemical vapor. The reaction to inhaling these substances may be an overall weakness, nausea, euphoria, asthma, eczema or other more severe reactions, such as anaphylactic shock. We must avoid these inhalants once detected or when we know that someone will use them, for example, when someone is about to apply nail polish.

Food Sensitivity: This is probably the most severe type of chemical stress for sensitized (allergic) people, but it also affects non-allergic people. If we have inhalant allergies, we usually have food allergies. Foods are graded as to their allergy potential: very high allergy potential (VHAP), moderately high allergy potential (MHAP) and very low allergy potential (VLAP). Typical VHAP foods are chicken eggs, most fish (especially canned fish) and shellfish, corn (and corn oil, syrup and other corn products), wheat (and wheat products), and deep-fried junk foods. Peanut butter is a VHAP food that causes shock or even death in some people. Typical MHAP foods are alcohol, chocolate, caffeine (in coffee, black tea, soft drinks, etc.), milk (and milk products), sugar, pork (and pork products), green beans, green peas, potatoes, soybeans (and soybean products), tomatoes, orange juice and strawberries. This is not an exhaustive listing, but accounts for most of the very high and moderately high allergy potential foods commonly consumed.

Yeast Infestation: This is as debilitating as an infectious disease and is potent enough to affect every organ in our bodies. Yeast lives in our stomach and intestinal walls and in other openings in our bodies. It lives on carbo-hydrates and thrives on sugar-foods; its by-products are toxic. When the yeast dies, it goes through a "yeast die-off cycle." It embeds itself in the walls of our stomach and intestines, and in dying, gives off potent chemicals that are absorbed into our bloodstream and affect most of our organs, especially the endocrine glands, responsible for our protection and healing. If you numerous physical problems take a test[3] to determine whether yeast may be your main problem—at one time it was mine. The reference also contains a four-stage Yeast Elimination Diet to remove the yeast and the severe distress it causes.

Substance Abuse: This refers to the chemical stress caused by using, or withdrawing from, drugs such as weight-loss drugs, "uppers" or "downers," tobacco, alcohol and other more potent controlled drugs. You are chemi-cally stressing your body if you use such drugs, for example, you will coun-teract the useful of alcohol to help reduce the mental stress of a busy day, but more than four drinks per day can cause more distress than it reduces.

Priority of *chemical* stresses that plague you—list from most stressful (1) to less stressful (4):

1) _____

2) _____

3) _____

4) _____

Identifying Our *Physical* Stressors

Physical stress stems from many sources and includes all stresses not classified as mental or chemical. Examples of physical stress are listed below.
Check off suspicious stresses and prioritize your daily physical stresses at
the end of this section.

Chronic Diseases: We usually know if we have these problems and if we
have them, we are trying to keep them under control. But sometimes we
don't know that we have them, and they can be stressing us, especially later
in life. It is best to have a complete medical check-up if you think that you
may have any of these kinds of problems.

- ☐ Head/neck problems: migraine and other headaches, head and neck
  muscle pain, T.M.J. pain or dysfunction, etc.
- ☐ Neural diseases: epilepsy, seizures, numbness/ tingling, etc.
- ☐ Eye problems: pain, pressure, light sensitivity, etc.
- ☐ Ear problems: pain, noise, dizziness, nausea, balance, loss of hearing,
  etc.
- ☐ Nose/sinus problems: obstruction, stuffiness, runny nose, etc.
- ☐ Throat problems: sore throat, swallowing difficulties, persistent cough-
  ing, etc.
- ☐ Breathing problems: asthma, tuberculosis, wheezing, shortness of
  breath, coughing up blood, etc.
- ☐ Back/shoulder/extremities problems: aching muscles, cramps or weak-
  ness in arms or legs, stiffness, etc.
- ☐ Bone problems: arthritis, joint swelling or back pain, etc.
- ☐ Heart problems: coronary heart disease, high blood pressure, chest pain,
  angina, heart murmur, palpitations, etc.
- ☐ Urinary problems: urgent, painful or frequent urination, blood in urine,
  kidney infection or stones, bladder infection, etc.
- ☐ Stomach and intestine problems: ulcers, pain, heartburn, nau-
  nea/vomiting, constipation, diarrhea, gall bladder disease, intestinal dis
  ease, etc.
- ☐ Endocrine problems: lack of ability to heal or fight off infection,, etc.;
- ☐ Liver problems: sclerosis, hepatitis A/B, etc.
- ☐ Pancreatic problems such as diabetes, loss of energy, etc.
- ☐ Blood problems: hemophilia, anemia, clots, stroke, etc.
- ☐ Skin problems: eczema, itchy, oily, or dry skin, etc.

- ☐ Dehydration caused by insufficient water and potassium intake
- ☐ Other problems: cancer, HIV+ and others

Acute Diseases: Even the healthiest of bodies can be taken over and distressed for days by infectious diseases. When stressed by a cold or infection, staying home can take care of it, making it pass quickly; Echinacea helps. If instead, we mask the symptoms with drugs and conduct our daily routines, the stress is still there and it will probably increase due to a depressed immune system from excessive cortisol. If a cold or infection is starting to attack us, we should realize it from our "usual" sub-clinical symptoms (such as "an uneasiness," increased or decreased diet, lack of energy, etc.). Early recognition can alert us to take steps to keep the infection from spreading, and thus, reduce the long-term stress that could last days, weeks or longer.

Acute/Chronic Pain: This has many causes and most are listed above. Humans adapt to almost anything over time; we have daily pains that we take for granted, but they still stress us! The pains may be from old injuries and may not be great enough to overflow our stress bucket, but enough to keep it mostly full. Taking an accounting of every part of our body can identify this suppressed pain—doing something about it is also helpful.

Oral Dysfunction: This may come from oral problems such as T.M.J. dysfunction, poor occlusion, and dental disease (root canals, gum disease and caries). These types of stress may be ever present and unknown to us, until they cause pain. Even in the sub-clinical stage, they can be causing us stress, and we may never realize it. It is best to have a thorough oral exam by a dentist if you suspect a problem; routine cleanings are highly recommended.

Lack of Sleep: THIS IS A BIGGIE! Sleep is an important aspect of daily health and well-being because it affects the two parts of metabolism: catabolism (breaking the body down during the day) and anabolism (building the body up when sleeping at night). In the deep phases of sleep, we manufacture the hormones, etc., required to operate our bodies; if we don't get enough deep sleep, we may be deficient in them. If we receive adequate, restful sleep, our anabolism will build up our bodies, allowing us to meet the physical challenges of a new day.

Injuries: When we experience a minor injury it reduces normal function of the injured area, which may distress us for days or weeks. If we have a serious accident that causes constant pain or dysfunction, it can distress us our entire lives. We should take inventory of our injuries and when they act up realize that they are causing us stress and do something about it.

Excessive Body Fat: If we are highly overweight or obese (more than 20 percent over the "healthy" weight for our sex, height and frame), we are stressing our bodies in many ways. We stress our muscles, joints, heart and every cell in our body and can lead to diabetes and its repercussions. If we are obese, we should shed our fat if we want to reduce this stress.

Lack of Exercise: Our bodies require some form of exercise to stay healthy and help reduce many types of physical stress. A daily or weekly strength exercise schedule can help keep our structural muscles strong, keeping our spine strong and healthy. It is also important to do aerobics at last three days a week to help keep our heart within its "target range." A moderate exercise program helps reduce the physical stresses listed above. A strenuous daily program is not necessarily better; if we lay off it for a while we will experience *withdrawal stress* from the drop in endorphins.

Lack of Nutrition: Proper nutrition is essential if we are to reduce physical stress. Stress caused by lack of proper nutrition is usually a "hidden" stress. The body cannot respond to its daily rigors if we fill it up with junk. It's true, we can abuse our bodies with poor nutrition and we will adapt, but by our mid-thirties our body starts telling us "I'm not going to take this any more, and you'd better take better care of me or else I'm not going to work for you any more." There are many philosophies of *good nutrition*, but most people not out for the buck usually agree that the food pyramid gives healthy advice. If you have special nutritional requirements, you should follow them. Also, what we like to eat may not be very good for us, stressing us out, as noted in the section on chemical stress.

Dehydration: Dehydration can cause us to feel weak with constant headaches due to a lack of fluid intake and an improper potassium/sodium ratio. We all get too much sodium (<2,400 milligrams is healthy) and need >4,000 milligrams of potassium every day along with 64-80 ounces (8-10 glasses) of fluids (water, juices, tea, coffee, etc.) per day. Sixteen ounces of orange juice/day will give 20-25 percent of fluids plus 900 mg of potassium.

Radiation Exposure: Most of us think that electromagnetic energy has no effect on us because we do not live near high-voltage lines; this is not true! An electric clock two to three feet from our head at night gives us more electromagnetic radiation than living near a high voltage tower—replace it with a battery operated clock. Exposure to the sun can cause overheating of the body and radiation poisoning of the skin—avoid excessive exposure. We also hear a lot about Radon radiation in our homes and places of business. If we suspect this is a problem, we should use a Radon detection system to measure it, and then reduce the Radon if it is excessive. Radiation stress is not typically a problem, but if it is, it may be a big one, and you must reduce it.

Priority of *physical* stresses that plague you—list from most stressful (1) to less stressful (4):

1) _____

2) _____

3) _____

4) _____

Now that you know the main mental, chemical and physical stressors that cause you to lose control of your personality, do something about them! The control you get back will make your life more fulfilling than you ever thought possible, and you will live that more fulfilling life longer.

Use the following procedure to reduce your distress through your awareness:

1. Be aware that you are distressed.
2. Reflect on your most potent mental stressors, and decide whether they are making you distressed; if so, talk yourself out of them.
3. Reflect on your most potent chemical stressors, and decide whether they are making you distressed; if so, remove them from your life.
4. Reflect on your most potent physical stressors, and decide whether they are making you distressed; if so, deal with them.

The above procedure makes you aware of your stressors and gives you the choice to reduce them or not. Using "Mind-Set" (see Chapter 14) can also help reduce your cumulative mental stressors, reducing the possibility of distress, but the best way is to eliminate the stress through a healthier life or by resetting your memories as discussed in Chapter 15.

REFERENCES:

1. Matt Ridley, *GENOME, The autobiography of a species in 23 chapters*, (Perennial, 2000), Chapter 10
2. Robert Fortman, Ph.D., *How To Control Your Allergies*, (Larchmont Books)
3. John Parks Trowbridge, M.D., and Morton Walker, D.P.M., *The Yeast Syndrome,* (Bantam Books)

Appendix D
The Relationship Game

The Relationship Game
Short Version

The Relationship Game

The Relationship Game is a realistic way to reconnect with someone that we have been disconnection from for years, no matter who disconnected from whom. It is also a realistic way to reconnect with someone that we have been disconnected from for days. Once reconnected, the relationship game provides a wonderful opportunity to acknowledge others and share their love. However, all of this comes at a price—it is emotionally frightening to play this game the first time—but once played you'll wish you'd played it all of your life. Please read this entire appendix before scheduling a game.

Game Definitions:

Rules Keeper: The player in charge of the game to make sure that everyone abides by the rules. The rules keeper changes each time you play the game, giving every player a turn at it, especially the very young.

Speaking Player: the player bringing forth an issue or acknowledgement.

Listening Player: the player receiving the issue or acknowledgement.

Issues: something that you did that invalidated another player or that another player did that invalidated you.

Issues Worksheet: where you write down the issues, you have with up to three players. Make many copies of page D-8.

Feelings for Issues: how you felt when another player invalidated and disconnected from you—on the right side of the *Issues Worksheet*.

D 1

Acknowledgements: of something that another person does that you admire him or her for or something that brings you great joy when you think about it (i.e., makes you feel love for them).

Acknowledgement Worksheet: where you write down the acknowledgements, you have for up to three players. Make many copies of page D-9.

Feelings **for Acknowledgements:** how you feel when you think about what you are acknowledging another player for—on the right side of the *Acknowledgements Worksheet.*

Request Sheet: used *by* one player to make a request *of* another player. The request is usually something one player wants another player to do, or not to do, between this and the next scheduled game. Make many copies of page D-10, cut them in half and have them available.

Objects of the Game:

- To allow a speaking player to tell a listening player how he or she feels without interruption or rationalization on the part of the listening player.
- To reconnect with those you have disconnected from, due to an issue that you have with them (they did something to upset you).
- To reconnect with those who have disconnected from you, due to an issue that they have with you (you did something to upset them).
- To acknowledge others for what they do well or just for the wonderful person that they are.

The Players (three to six total players is ideal):

- *All* family members if played at home.
- *All* immediate coworkers if played at work.
- Just those involved if played among friends.

How Often Played:

- Play the game weekly for the first two to four consecutive weeks.
- After that, play the game monthly, for example, the first Sunday of the month if at home or the first Friday of the month if at work (people are happier and more open when going into the weekend).
- If not played monthly or on a particular schedule, play as you feel the need—which will be obvious because it will nag at you.

Game Environment:

- Play in any place where *all* players feel emotionally safe and comfortable; all must positively agree and desire to play in that location—this may not be easy.
- If at home, play in the living room or family room—kitchen?
- If at work, play in a conference or break room where all feel comfortable, hopefully without any interruptions (turn off all phones/beepers).
- If done among friends, do it at a mutually convenient, emotionally comfortable location.

The Arrangement of Players:

- Sit on chairs, all at the same eye level, in a tight circle.
- All players should be physically comfortable.

Game Rules—very important!

The Rules Keeper reads the five rules below to all first time players and gets each player to agree to follow the rules:

1. ONLY the speaking player may speak; others should pay attention to what the speaker says and not talk in the backgound.
2. As a speaking player, maintain eye contact with, and speak only to, the listening player.
3. As a speaking player, do not hedge or downplay your issue; just make direct, succinct statements.
4. As a listening player, do not speak or divert attention way from the speaking player, just focus on what he or she is saying.
5. As a listening player, do not use self-righteous justification to distract yourself from listening—you can't listen if you're rationalizing.

Preparing for Play:

1. In private (not in a circle), complete an *Issues Workshheet* and an *Acknowledgements Worksheet* **on every other player** by writing the player's name on the top of the sheet; also write your name on a sheet. If you have, no issues with a player enter "no issues," including yourself if you have no integrity issues with yourself. It is important though, to fill in at least one acknowledgement for each player and for yourself.
2. If you have many issues with another player, just list two or three important issues; you can resolve minor issues at subsequent games.

3. When writing issues, make sure that you mention how you *felt* when the disconnection occurred—it is better to use your own words, but if not sure, there are example feeling on the worksheet.
4. Make sure that you mention how you *feel* when writing an acknowledgment about another player—again, it is better to use your own words, but if not sure, there are example feeling words on the worksheet.
5. When all have completed the preparation, comfortably sit in a circle.
6. At the beginning of play, the Rules Keeper asks each player whether he or she feels comfortable with playing today. If not comfortable, determine why and resolve it before playing—do whatever works.

During the Play:

-   The Rules Keeper (going clockwise around the circle) asks the first person (the speaking player) to state one issue that he or she has with another player.
-   As a speaking player you must succinctly describe the place and time of a specific issue or succinctly describes the most recent reoccurring issue, noting the feelings evoked in you when it occurred.
-   As a listening player, you must appreciate how the speaking player felt and never use rationalization to negate those feelings—you can't because those feeling exist whether you like it or not. This is not about the listening player, it's about the speaking player's need to "get it out and get past it."
-   When the speaking player has delivered his or her one issue, the listening player simply says, "I understand," or "OK" or "I apologize" or whatever feels comfortable—the listening player does NOT belittle the importance of the issue—there are no small issues!
-   When done with the first speaking player and issue, the Rules Keeper asks the next player around the circle to deliver an issue; this is continued until every player has delivered *one* issue to *one* player.
-   Go around the circle again with each player bringing forth an issue with another player (or the same one as the first time). Go around the circle again and again until all issues, along with their accompanying feelings are brought forth. Don't forget the issues you have with yourself and how it makes you feel.
-   REMEMBER: NO hedging, NO rationalization and NO interruptions of any kind when someone is bringing forth an issue.

- The Rules Keeper keeps the game moving along by interrupting the players when they circumvent the rules and to get them back on track.

Requests:

- You ("BY") use the *Request Sheet* to make a request "OF" another player, which they can either accept or reject.
- The request is to do or not do something between now and the next game, typically anything that would help avoid a reoccurring issue.
- Write down your request and give it to the Rules Keeper to keep in a request file (envelope, etc.). If needed, a copy is given to the person accepting the request.
- The next time the game is played, the Rules Keeper first reads the requests and asks the player accepting the request if it has been fulfilled. If not, a second request can be made and rejected or accepted until the next game. A player may make the same request twice—if not fulfilled by then it never will be.

Ending the Game:

- Take a short break before the acknowledgement part of the game and look over your planned acknowledgements.
- Reseat yourself comfortably in the circle in the same chairs as before. Before restarting, make sure that you have one acknowledgement for each player, including one for yourself.
- Start with the first person clockwise in the circle bringing forth their acknowledgement for *one* listening player; any player will do.
- The speaking player joyfully expresses the acknowledgement.
- The acknowledged listening player gives a simple "thank you" to the speaking player for their kind acknowledgements and never qualifies, belittles or embellishes on the acknowledgement, which would invalidate the speaking player—only the speaking player's opinion counts.
- When done with the first speaking player, move around the circle in a clockwise rotation until each player has given an acknowledgement to *one* other player.
- Continue around the circle again and again until every player has acknowledged every other player with the acknowledged player graciously accepting the acknowledgement.
- Go around the circle once more and have each player acknowledge him or herself for something they are proud of.

- When done the Rules Keeper declares the game over, congratulates all for their issues and acknowledgements.
- Complete the game with something pleasant, for example, lunch at work or some treat at home or with friends.

The WINNERS:

All players are winners! They resolved their issues, reconnected, acknowledged others, and others have acknowledged them.

Short Version

Once reconnected it is important to be aware of future *spontaneous* disconnection, especially reoccurring emotional issues that are difficult to resolve. When disconnected, it produces sorrow in us, in another, or in both. When *both* feel the sorrow, it's easy to reconnect. When *we* feel the sorrow and avoid rationalization, we can allow ourselves to reconnect, if the other person is aware of the disconnection. When the other person feels the sorrow and we don't, it is more difficult to reconnect (typically because we have some other emotion in place blocking the sorrow), but we still must try to be aware of the need to feel sorrow and to try to reconnect.

If you are automatically aware (you feel sorrow) or if the person makes you aware, you can reconnect immediately by apologizing for the invalidation, etc., and by acknowledging them. For example, if they give their opinion on a situation and you immediately invalidate it, you can apologize for the outburst and discuss the merits of their opinion. And once you validated their opinion, you may find a combined opinion that is more appropriate than the separate opinions.

If another invalidates you, you can reconnect immediately by making them aware of their invalidation and how it made you feel. For example, if you gave your opinion on a situation and it was immediately invalidated, you can: stop, look the invalidating person in the eye and say something like "My opinion may not be perfect, but it has some merit and I feel *demeaned* by your put down. And once said the other person has the choice to immediately apologize, bring out its value and reconnect or can choose not to do so, requiring playing The Relationship Game in the near future to settle this issue.

See page D-8 for the "Issues Sheet"

See page D-9 for the "Acknowledgement Sheet"

See page D-10 for the "Request Sheets"

ISSUES that you have with: (name) _____		Examples of *Feelings*
1) _____ _____ _____ _____ _____ _____ _____	*My Feelings* ⇨ _____ _____ _____ _____ _____	abandoned, angry, annoyed, cheated, confused, controlled, criticized, cut off, deceived, depressed, desperate, devastated, disgusted,
2) _____ _____ _____ _____ _____ _____ _____	*My Feelings* ⇨ _____ _____ _____ _____ _____	distrustful, dominated, embarrassed, frightened, frustrated, hateful, hopeless, humiliated, hurt, ignored, insulated, irritated, let down, manipulated,
3) _____ _____ _____ _____ _____ _____ _____	*My Feelings* ⇨ _____ _____ _____ _____ _____	misunderstood, nauseated, offended, overwhelmed, perplexed, pressured, put down, rejected, sickened, suspicious, tormented, unheard, up tight, used, etc.

ACKNOWLEDGEMENTS...for: (name) _____	Examples of *Feelings*
1) _____ _____ _____ _____ _____ _____ _____ _____ *My Feelings* ⇨ _____ _____ _____ _____ _____	accepted, appreciated, amused, calm, confident, cared for, delighted, elated, encouraged, excited, fulfilled, grateful, happy, heard,
2) _____ _____ _____ _____ _____ _____ _____ _____ *My Feelings* ⇨ _____ _____ _____ _____	honored, hopeful, inspired, invigorated, liberated, loved, optimistic, playful, reassured, recognized, refreshed, relaxed, relieved,
3) _____ _____ _____ _____ _____ _____ _____ _____ *My Feelings* ⇨ _____ _____ _____ _____	respected, safe, satisfied, supported, thrilled, understood, valued, vindicated, wanted, worthy, etc.

Request

OF: ____________________

BY: ____________________

____

____

____

____

____

Request

OF: ____________________

BY: ____________________

____

____

____

____

____

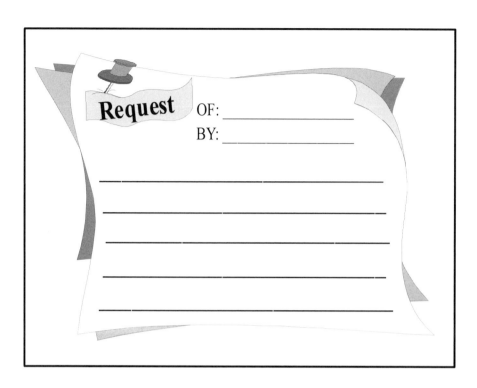

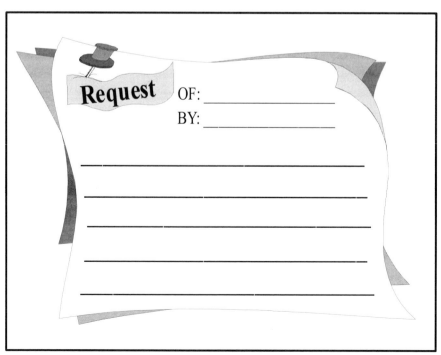

Glossary-Index
Why have two when one will do.

Cheerful warmth – emitted by the socializer style in the *one-second* analysis A-6/7

Concerned warmth – emitted by the relator style in the *one-second* analysis A-6/7

Compassion – Deep awareness of the suffering of another coupled with the wish to relieve it. .... A-3, B-2 to B-9

Compatibility & Incompatibility:
- Compatibility – when we don't naturally irritate each other too much CHAP-10
- Compatibility Chart – reference table for who we are naturally compatible with 130-133
- Incompatibility – when we naturally irritate each other 127-133
- Self-incompatibility – when we are naturally conflicted 133-139

Connections – memories connecting our inner-world and outer-world ... 5-7, CHAP-4, CHAP-7

Cortisol – a protein in the blood that that increases with stress; it depresses the immune system making us susceptible to disease .... APP-C

Crucial style usage – when an emotion must trigger its symbiotic style, even if it is weak 189, 206

Decisiveness – making new decisions with the conscious brain and acting upon them............. .... 66-68, 116-126, 158-160,

Dendrites – the part of a neuron that is excited by other connected neurons that have fired 153-155, 229

Director – a person strongest in the director style CHAP-5

Director style – a rational style symbiotic with the anger emotion CHAP-5

Director style's *social* survival purpose – "to get resolution" ..... 14, CHAP-5, C HAP-10, APP-B

Disconnection – when our relationship with others (or ourselves) is lost 6, 13, 15, 18-21, CHAP-4
- Ongoing disconnection – involves long-standing unresolved issues difficult to resolve 51-52
- Spontaneous disconnection – involves issues that can be resolved within seconds 51-52, D-6

Dismissive coolness – emitted by the director style in the One-Second Analysis A-6/7

Distraction – socializer style attribute that causes a short attention span 67, 98-99

Distress – excessive amounts of accumulated stress – see "Stress and Distress"

Dorsolateral PFC – located in the outer layers of the PFC – makes rational decisions and acts on them 156-159

Emotional brain – the 190 million year old survival brain - see "Amygdala"

Emotional chemicals – the hormones, monoamines and peptides that make us *feel* our emotions 12, 17, 34, 43, 57, 77,145

Emotional energy (negative) – debilitating energy emanated when anger or fear is expressed 145, 230-232, A-6

    Extreme Symbiotic Cycle of Despair – sorrow that cannot be identified and quelled by the relator style

    Extreme Symbiotic Cycle of Ecstasy – joy that cannot be identified and quelled by the socializer style

    Extreme Symbiotic Cycle of Hatred – anger that cannot be identified and quelled by the director style

    Extreme Symbiotic Cycle of Terror – fear that cannot be identified and quelled by the analyzer style

Four primary emotions – anger, fear, joy and sorrow – the only emotions that cannot be faked and that have a universal facial expression – see individual emotions

Four rational styles – analyzer, director, relator and socializer – an evolutionary outgrowth of the four primary emotions – see individual styles

Free will – see "*Pure* free will"

Reaction (rational) – our response to the outer-world based on our inner-world's interpretation of it

Reconnection – see "Connection"

Relationship Game – a game to reconnect disconnected people

Relator – a person strongest in the relator style

Relator style – a rational style symbiotic with the sorrow emotion

Relator style's *social* survival purpose – "to maintain our connections"

Repetition – that which helps everyone to eventually attain perfection in a task

Righteous justifications – thinking about why we are right instead of acting appropriately – see "Rationalization"

Self – the sum total of us

Self-invalidation – when we express our strongest emotions for absurd reasons

Sensory attributes – see "Outer-world" – Sensory attributes

Shying-away coolness – emitted by the analyzer style in the *one-second* analysis

Socializer – a person strongest in the socializer style

Socializer style – a rational style symbiotic with the joy emotion

Socializer style's *social* survival purpose – "to address our connections"

Sorrow emotion – a primary emotion symbiotic with the relator style

Sorrow's *physical* survival purpose – "to alert us to disconnection"

Sorting out an emotion – rationally identifying what triggered a primary emotion to quell it

Sponge – the first animal (see "Animal")

Stress and Distress

- Chemical stress – comes from the foods we eat and the air we breathe
- Mental stress – anything emotionally or rationally conceived that adversely affects our health and well being
- Physical stress – from invading organisms, physical injury or anything that is neither mental nor chemical stress
- Stress Bucket – an imaginary bucket that accumulates and spills off accumulated stress, overflowing when distressed
- Stress-O-Meter – a built in awareness of our distress

NOTES

NOTES